JOSÉ LIMÓN

A STUDIES IN DANCE HISTORY BOOK

JOSÉ LIMÓN
AN UNFINISHED MEMOIR

Edited by Lynn Garafola

Introduction by Deborah Jowitt

Foreword by Carla Maxwell

Afterword by Norton Owen

WESLEYAN UNIVERSITY PRESS
PUBLISHED BY UNIVERSITY PRESS OF NEW ENGLAND
HANOVER AND LONDON

Wesleyan University Press

Published by University Press of New England, Hanover, NH 03755

© José Limón Dance Foundation

Printed in the United States of America   5 4 3 2 1

CIP data appear at the end of the book

The photographs in the insert following page 42 are courtesy of Charles H. Woodford; those following page 106 are courtesy of the José Limón Dance Foundation.

Contents

Illustrations follow pages 42 and 106.

I was privileged to work with José Limón for the last seven years of his life. Considering that I have now been with the Limón Dance Company for nearly thirty-five years, that's not a very long time. Yet those seven years were enough to establish José as my artistic father and to endow me with a sense of belief in myself and in the wonderful work he created and left to us.

José was a private and formal person. We "youngsters" in the company did not know very much about his personal life. What we did know was that he was a charismatic visionary, a brilliant choreographer and electric performer, a man with a great appetite for life and work, who loved the dance and fought vigorously to have it recognized as an important and vital art form. He was single-minded and relentless in his pursuits. Although movement and dance seemed to pour effortlessly out of him, he claimed to struggle endlessly over every step. At many rehearsals he would tell us that he had been up all night battling "the demons" so that he would be ready for the next day's work.

To me, José was a warrior. He was not only fighting his choreographic "demons" and battling for respect for the modern dance, but he seemed to be wrestling with his own personal demons as well. He carried on the battle through his dances. He often told us, "You will know me by doing my dances." An avid reader, a wonderful cook, carpenter, gentleman farmer, musician, painter, and writer, José gave the impression of being the perfect renaissance man.

José's work has always been lifegiving because it is so full of hope and harmony, even in his most extreme tragedies. He was letting us know that we have a choice, that we do not have to act out our darker sides. I believe that this power and life-giving force in his work is what has enabled his company to continue these many years.

Reading this autobiography, I realized it was the first time I had ever heard about José's childhood—the smells and colors and rhythms of Mexico, the violence and terror of war and personal loss, the feelings of exclusion and isolation in a new country. One can sense here the seeds of all his choreographic explorations. It was his gift and his genius to be able to transcend those experiences and make them into universal statements of hope for all of us.

I treasure these pages, and even if the story they tell is incomplete, I am grateful for the light they shed on one of our great American artists.

—Carla Maxwell
Artistic Director
Limón Dance Company

Introduction

DEBORAH JOWITT

"There is no other male dancer within even comparing distance," wrote John Martin in *The New York Times* of 10 April 1949. José Limón was six feet tall, but looked taller. His large head had a lot to do with it: cheekbones that belonged on a Mayan bas-relief and dark, deep-set eyes that seemed always fixed on something beyond the dance or deep within himself. His hands, fingers spread, looked huge; his arms molded the air around him. Critics pulled out adjectives like "leonine," or compared him to a bull, an eagle. (Dorothy Bird, who performed with him briefly during the 1940s, put it more pragmatically: he was "so solid, like a tremendous wooden fence I could climb.")[1] I most often picture him as Othello in his 1949 masterpiece *The Moor's Pavane*: his arms, drawing back, turn the flamenco dancer's curving port de bras into the priming of a bow; for a moment he suspends, then thrusts himself into motion. He had a way of averting his gaze, swinging his torso, as if Iago's poisoned messages were the picadors' banderillas and he a bull at bay. No one has matched him in this role, although the piece has been performed all over the world, and Rudolf Nureyev numbered among its interpreters.

As Limón's unfinished memoir chronicles, the charismatic dancer-choreographer, a dominant figure in American modern dance for at least twenty-six years, had no idea of becoming a performer until he was twenty. Not long after he arrived in New York in late 1928 or early 1929—having ridden a motorcycle across the country to join the other aspiring painters like himself who thronged the city—he attended a recital by the German Harald Kreutzberg, the man he refers to as his artistic father. Years later, writing of the cataclysmic effect of that performance, he said he'd never realized before that "a man could, with dignity and a towering majesty, dance."[2] Seeing Limón dance, watching him at work, one could believe that he forged his own image, both on and off the stage, around those qualities: dignity and towering majesty.

The unfathomable gaze was part of his personal style too. No matter how eagerly he greeted people, wrote Eleanor King—who danced with him in the 1930s in the company directed by Doris Humphrey and Charles Weidman—those eyes "seemed focused at the same time on some far distant planet."[3] His way of speaking contributed to the majestic persona he cultivated (though he certainly liked a good time and was reputed to have a taste for racy jokes). He had been seven years old when his family moved from Mexico to the United States; teased by schoolmates in

Texas for his pitiful English, he resolved to speak the language better than the natives. As an adult, he espoused faultless articulation and a showy vocabulary. In rehearsals for his great *Missa Brevis* in 1958, he would order dancers to pass through the "interstices" formed by colleagues standing a couple of feet apart, or, charmingly, ask the men to "permeate" a crowd of women. Teaching a class, he might leave students frozen in mid-plié while he ardently discoursed on a Eugene O'Neill play he had seen. King remembers that, exhausted and winded after strenuous rehearsals for the Little Group (a company formed within the ranks of Humphrey-Weidman in the early 1930s), he still found breath to rummage through his mental store of Shakespeare and gasp, "I am dying, Egypt, dying."[4]

As a performer and a choreographer, he had gravitas. Comedy, even levity, didn't suit him, although he occasionally gave it a whirl. He admits in these pages that when he first began to choreograph, he was "over-serious and often pretentious beyond my experience and ability." The dances of others that he most admired were dark—like Martha Graham's solo, *Immediate Tragedy* (1936), spawned by the civil war in Spain—or blazing with moral fervor and an optimistic vision of humankind—like *New Dance* (1935) by his adored mentor Doris Humphrey. He was impressed by the powerful ensemble patterns of Léonide Massine's "symphonic" ballets. Among his gods were Michelangelo, El Greco, Shakespeare (the tragedies, of course). You could see shadowed in his dancing the brooding Hamlet; El Greco's luminous, distorted figures set against turbulent skies; Michelangelo's massive curves—like those of the Sistine Chapel sibyls crammed into their architecturally defined caverns.

He seemed to share with the sixteenth- and seventeenth-century artists and writers referred to as mannerist the vision of a world troubled by a loss of equilibrium and harmony. In *The Moor's Pavane*, every freighted "dialogue"—between Othello and Iago, Iago and Emilia, Emilia and Desdemona, Desdemona and Othello—tugs at the structure of the court dance that binds the characters together. Each dissonant encounter seems to make it more difficult for the four to return to their symmetrical patterns, and the final tragic tableau skews their opening cluster—the characters now collapsed or straining away from the design's unstable center. The world seen through the eyes of the crazed protagonist of *The Emperor Jones* (1956) swirls around him, adrift in time and space. In *The Traitor* (1954), which cast Limón as Judas Iscariot, the tableau of the Last Supper keeps shifting. Holding a white cloth in such a way as to give the illusion of a tabletop, the disciples form the familiar grouping, but they also rush to turn the "table," offering it from different perspectives. When they slant it toward the audience, the Christ figure, now at the far end and lifted from beneath, becomes unnaturally high and unstable, as if he might accidentally slide head first into the coming peril.

The art historian Wylie Sypher wrote that mannerism in painting was "expressive in a taut, uneasy way, as if the figures had the resistance of a coiled spring. Yet they appear passive, suffering mutely from internal and unintelligible strain."[5] Limón's heroes, like the irresolute Hamlet, had something of this quality. Their bodies are so besieged by alternatives that they have to fight their way into forthright action; the dancing—weighted, slow, pressured—curves back upon itself, straining against the high pitch of emotion. In *The Traitor*, when Limón entered to betray his master, he looked deformed by guilt and self-loathing—arms hanging, head thrust forward, body pitching ahead at an angle the dragging feet could scarcely brace.

* * *

The second birth Limón refers to—his emergence as a performer—roughly coincided with the birth of what John Martin referred to as "The Modern Dance." Martin, America's first full-time dance critic, had been appointed to *The New York Times* in 1927, the year Isadora Duncan died. (Limón, like many Americans, was enthralled by her posthumously published autobiography *My Life*, with its exalted tone and romantic vision of art.) 1928 marked the departure, both actual and ideological, of Doris Humphrey, Pauline Lawrence (later Limón), and Charles Weidman from Denishawn. Over the next few years, Denishawn and its exotic repertory faded away, undermined by financial losses and the breakup of the marriage and partnership of its leaders Ruth St. Denis and Ted Shawn. 1929, the year a very raw Limón began to dance with the Humphrey-Weidman company—only weeks after he showed up to enroll in classes at the 9 East Fifty-Ninth Street studio—was also the year that Martha Graham founded her all-female Group and began to create powerfully austere works that allied her with modernism. Charismatic German exponents of *Ausdrucktanz* toured America: Kreutzberg and Tilly Losch in 1928, Kreutzberg and Yvonne Georgi in 1929 and 1930; Mary Wigman made the first of several tours in 1931.

As Limón wrestled with his recalcitrant body, modern dance struggled to define itself. The stock market crash of 1929 and the ensuing Depression stirred the social consciences of dancers whose manifestos proclaimed their dedication to speaking with the voice of the times. For several years, their works straddled the old and the new. Martha Graham continued to perform delicacies like "Tanagra" from her *Three Gnossiennes*, even as she was creating sterner works. Limón made his rough-and-ready debut in Weidman's Denishawn-style *Rhythmic Patterns of Java* in 1929, but the featured premiere on the company's two programs (March 31 and April 7) was Humphrey's atavistic study of conflict *Life of the Bee*, in which an intruding queen (played by Humphrey) successfully challenged a newborn resident queen for leadership of the hive. In later versions, it was the in-house ruler who won the fight and led the swarm in the final flight offstage to a new destiny, but, in 1929, Humphrey's recent aesthetic battle with another entrenched monarch, Ruth St. Denis, and her new status as a dance radical may have colored her concept of the drama.

During this period, Graham, guided by her musical director and lover Louis Horst, stopped choreographing to the works of nineteenth-century greats that Duncan favored—such as Brahms, Schubert, and Scriabin—and the salon composers who created the kind of *à la orientale* pieces that had served Denishawn well. Humphrey went further, setting her *Water Study* (1928) to the breath-filled silence of women; their bodies captured the cresting and breaking of waves within larger spatial patterns that also traced the trajectories of water. For the early performances of *Life of the Bee*, Pauline Lawrence stood backstage humming on a tissue-paper-wrapped comb.

Limón writes of Humphrey the dancer as a lover might. She is "a goddess, a nymph, a caryatid"; her body evokes Botticelli's "Primavera." She is "music and poetry, Ariel, Artemis, and Echo, a creature enamored of the air." But what really inflamed him was the way she articulated great ideas and human drives through formal designs. She had no truck with ballet (which he, like all the radical modern dancers, saw as sterile, academic, and effete); her movements derived their shapes from human gesture, and their vital rhythms from human breath—the dual forces of inhalation and exhalation. While he was making himself into a performer fit to serve her, she was exploring how a large group of dancers could become not just a symphonic structure, as in Ruth St. Denis's music visualizations, but the embodiment of a society in which individuals may inspire the group or combat it, may merge with it yet retain their individuality. He experienced Humphrey's compositional genius from the inside, notably in her masterpiece (choreographed with contributions from Weidman) the *New Dance* trilogy (1935–1936)— which painted a flawed, competitive society in the satiric *Theatre Piece*, a dictator-driven one in *With My Red Fires*, and a Utopian vision of democracy in *New Dance*.

To be a modern dancer then was to decry systems and codification—although, ironically, choreographers devised training techniques that would hone dancers to perform their individually designed styles. It was held necessary to express the American experience in dance, just as American painters were seeking to debunk the notion that Europe was the mecca, the source of all currents in art. The word "race" was used frequently to refer to the national heritage and social milieu a choreographer should express. Especially in the years prior to the founding of the major American ballet companies, the notion of "serious ballet" was all but a contradiction in terms. The modern choreographers' high-minded program notes, articles, and statements to the press were meant to separate the new dance from the old, with its aristocratic roots, centuries of tradition, and (to them) confectionary stories. "There must be implicit some attitude toward the meaning of existence," announced Doris Humphrey in a 1932 article entitled "What Shall We Dance About?" and went on to affirm the necessity of building a style on one's own body and sensibilities: "In general, no man can dance convincingly like any other man whose experience lies outside his own."[6]

Beginning to choreograph in 1931, while still in the Humphrey-Weidman company, Limón could not but be influenced by the vision shared by its founders. However, the times, as well as a close personal relationship with Charles Weidman that lasted about ten years, dictated a checkered apprenticeship that he might not, with hindsight, have chosen.

Modern dance had not reached a broad audience, yet it was, in a sense, "hot." Although most so-called "concert dancers" could give only a single performance or two (usually on Sundays, when Broadway theaters were dark and available), the most important of the choreographers were solicited to provide movement for serious dramas and dances for musical comedies. Weidman's *Ringside* and Humphrey's *The Shakers* and *Water Study* were featured in the Shuberts' revue *Americana*. Shortly after Limón became a Humphrey-Weidman dancer, he and some of his cohorts spent most of 1930 in Norman Bel Geddes's production of *Lysistrata*, choreographed by Humphrey and Weidman. Especially during the Depression years, such jobs were a godsend for hungry dancers.

Humphrey disliked, and for the most part avoided, the constraints and hassles of musical comedy choreography, but Weidman thrived on commercial work—his gift for humor and the telling gesture, as well as his compositional expertise, earned him jobs on a number of shows. Limón went with him, juggling his own early experiments in choreography and performances in the Humphrey-Weidman company, with appearing for over a year in *As Thousands Cheer* (1933)—thus missing the landmark first summer (1934) of the school and festival at Bennington College, where the rivalrous moderns assembled to teach and perform. He also danced in operas in Cleveland and for George Balanchine in *Keep Off the Grass* (1940) and *Rosalinda* (1942).

He may have done more Broadway-style work than he let on. The *Upton Nooz* of 14 May 1943 credits him with having been "dance director" of *I'd Rather Be Right* as well as of *Roberta* (to which it's known he contributed one number) and a performer in *Flying Colors*. (The information was intended to add weight to a laudatory review of Private Limón's dancing in one of the army shows he was involved with—performing "Begin the Beguine" "in a wine colored wool gabardine outfit that stunned.")[7] Like Isadora Duncan, consolidating in her autobiography the image of herself as an intellectual and spiritual artist, Limón writes that most of his early work in commercial theater had been degrading, ending his acknowledgment of *As Thousands Cheer*'s polish by defining it as "a very plush, high-class whorehouse"; his return to the Humphrey-Weidman fold was "a redemptive experience" after what he came to consider a fall from grace. He never quite forgave Weidman for liking his show-biz ventures and not sticking exclusively to concert work. But there is no reason to suppose that Limón didn't occasionally enjoy himself in those "whorehouses." Assuredly, he learned from them. One number he composed for an army revue, Austin Rigg's *Fun for The Birds* (1943), might have been a prototypical Limón dance, in which the hero (Limón) broods at the cusp of dilemma. Called "What Does a Soldier Dream of?" (with mood music composed by the choreographer), his dance apparently expressed the thoughts of a new recruit facing the changes in his way of life. A publicity shot of another number from the show features Limón in full uniform, including helmet, leaping lustily in front of a seated male chorus, hoisting rifles.

A burning issue during the years Limón matured in dance was the status of the male dancer. From the inception of Denishawn in 1915, Ted Shawn had proselytized on the subject of dance as a virile activity, suitable for "real men." He wrote a book, *Gods Who Dance*, whose not-so-hidden agenda was to dignify male dancing by offering examples, such as Shiva's cosmic dance, from Asian cultures. When he toured, articles in newspapers across the country printed his proclamations, and sometimes weighed the degree of his onstage masculinity against that of Anna Pavlova's hunky partner Mikhail Mordkin, as if these two stood out alone against a sea of epicenity. During the 1930s, Shawn's Men Dancers (mainly physical education majors he had met while teaching at Springfield College) aroused "Who would have believed it" reviews about men who danced and still managed to look like men. (Years later, Edward Villella and Jacques d'Amboise were still campaigning to convince the public that a male ballet dancer was a species of super athlete—just as tough and bruised as a football player.)

Weidman too felt the burden, devising exercises with men in mind, conducting special classes for Humphrey-Weidman's male dancers, most of whom, like Limón, had started late. In its choreography, the Humphrey-Weidman company showed men and women as equals, and often in unison, but not as identical. Limón saw the differences as a matter of physical structure: "The male anatomy...was muscularly more powerful than that of the female; it could jump higher, but its leg extensions, because of a narrower pelvis, were more limited. The quality of its movement could be heavy, massive, and monumental, in contrast to the softness and delicacy of the female. The sexual differences must be observed and emphasized, as in the art of singing, with its separation of male from female voices." He ignored, seemingly, the amazonian strength of many female modern dancers and couldn't foresee the flexibility men would later attain with the help of early starts and good training. During the years he built a career, male dancing had to be distinguished from the female in order to give it credibility as a profession. In an article titled "The Virile Dance," Limón took a swipe at ballet, degraded at birth, he said, by its association with the "highborn sycophants and courtiers" surrounding Louis XIV and later guilty of a "feminization of technique."[8]

Limón found a key to his own performing in the images of the bullfight; to him, this was a dance—profound, formal, and elegant. Mindful of his artistic "mother," Isadora Duncan and his mentor Doris Humphrey, Limón understood that taking his place in the family of American modern dance involved investigating his Mexican-ness. He too needed to speak with the voice of his birthplace, of his "race." The corrida, compounded of spectacle and controlled violence, was part of Mexico's ambiguous heritage from Spain. However, Limón magnified the role of torero beyond any bloody local contest with a bull: he was performing "an ancient ritual drama that would cleanse and purge us, its spectators."

Judging from photographs of Limón in his early choreographies, such as the 1939 *Danzas Mexicanas*, and from a film of his 1942 solo *Chaconne*, he began to develop his image well before forming his own company at the end of 1945, after his discharge from the army. The deep, weighted lunges; the slow drawing up to a narrow stance that evoked the flamenco dancer as well as the bullfighter; the mixture of elegance and brute force are all visible.

A stroke of fortune contributed to the fuller definition of his identity as both performer and choreographer. Doris Humphrey's painful arthritic hip forced her retirement from the stage in 1944. Her partnership with Weidman had become increasingly shaky over the war years, as Weidman's love affair with Broadway peaked. In 1946, she became the artistic director of the newly founded José Limón Company. He was in awe of her gifts. In his extravagantly laudatory prose: "I have repeatedly over the decades, tried to achieve the compelling dramatic power of Doris's abstractions and failed. I have found myself imitating or plagiarizing her. I lack her artistic stature. I am highly talented. Doris was a genius." For the next dozen years, she provided Limón with encouragement and guidance, and contributed dances to his company's repertory.

The artistic relationship was unique in its intensity. For many years, Louis Horst gave Martha Graham suggestions and feedback, but I can think of no mature choreographer beside Limón who accepted the advice of another choreographer as part of the working process, and none but Humphrey who could position herself so deeply inside another's sensibility.

One of the two pieces Humphrey choreographed for the company's debut program at Bennington College expanded on the persona he had chosen for himself. *Lament for Ignacio Sánchez Mejías* took its title and text from Federico García Lorca's elegy for a bullfighter. Actress Meg Mundy as Witness and Mourner, and former Humphrey-Weidman colleague Letitia Ide representing a Guardian of Destiny, recited passages from the poem. In this lean, constricted trio, the bullfighter becomes also the prey. The fate figure pursues and challenges him; he, brought to his knees, leans and twists under her onslaught. A red cloth swirls as Ignacio's cape, and, covering him as he scrabbles along the floor, stands for the blood that pours from his wounds. The penultimate, elegiac lines fit to perfection the dark side of Limón the dancer: "I sing for a later time, of your profile and your grace/ The celebrated ripeness of your skill/ Your appetite for death and the taste of his mouth/ And the sadness lying beneath your joy."9

*   *   *

The company and repertory that Limón built with Humphrey's help had a different look, a different focus from that of the Humphrey-Weidman company, with its passionate abstractions and the choric sweep of its ensemble works. In the 1940s, choreographers in both modern dance and ballet were interested in revealing human relationships, in finding new ways to tell stories. Martha Graham turned from her earlier, formal group dances toward setting individual characters in nonlinear narratives such as her masterwork *Appalachian Spring* (1944). Antony Tudor brought his bittersweet *Lilac Garden* and *Dark Elegies* to Ballet Theatre from London and choreographed his great study of repression and redemption *Pillar of Fire* (1942). The very young Jerome Robbins created not only *Interplay* and his sassy sailor ballet *Fancy Free*, but the Freudian triangle *Facsimile* (1946). In 1948, Agnes de Mille made a ballet about the ax murderer Lizzie Borden (*Fall River Legend*). Spurred on, perhaps, by an interest in myth and psychology that was shared by artists in all fields, choreographers probed the human psyche. Passionate drives and inner dilemmas became a subject for dance: how one felt, more than what one did, shaped choreography.

Humphrey understood how to elevate drama above literal storytelling. In her tender *Day on Earth* (1947) for the fledgling company, Limón, as a kind of Everyman, performed themes derived from plowing and planting. The stages in the unfolding of his life—the departure of a young love, the coming of a mate, the loss of a child—are reflected in how he does that "work," how its rhythms falter, its gestures rage. In his own choreography, Limón began to refine a vision of a small world, often centering around a man in crisis: Othello, Macbeth, Judas Iscariot, Adam, Julian the Apostate, O'Neill's Emperor Jones. In its glory days, that world was peopled most notably by Ide, Pauline Koner, Lucas Hoving, Ruth Currier, Betty Jones, Lavina Nielsen. A shifting cadre of six men appeared during the 1950s. Koner—small, dark, and vivid—with a career as a solo performer behind her, was a striking contrast to the fresh, golden-haired Jones, and the fragile lyricist Currier.

Hoving, fair, with long slender limbs, portrayed in many dances Limón's antagonist or alter ego: Iago to his Othello in *The Moor's Pavane*, Christ to his Judas in *The Traitor*. In the 1952 *The Visitation*, Hoving played the angel of the Annunciation to Koner's Virgin Mary and Limón's St. Joseph. For the most part, his presence sparked conflict. In *Dialogues* (1951), Limón cast him as Córtez come to destroy Montezuma, then as the doomed Hapsburg Emperor Maximilian at the mercy of Juárez. In Limón's fine trio *La Malinche* (1949), Hoving was again Córtez, Koner the Indian mistress who betrayed him, while the choreographer assumed the role of the archetypal "Indio." In *The Emperor Jones*, Hoving played all the corrupt white men inhabiting the demented protagonist's dreamworld.

Limón's dignity was never Apollonian; in an insightful 1955 article for *The Saturday Review*, Norma Stahl linked him with the Brontës' rough romantic heroes, Heathcliff and Rochester. "His style," she wrote, "always with the suggestion of something Spanish, combines the elegance of some kingly being with a primitive crouching strength."[10] In some way, Hoving's golden, if corruptible, elegance freed Limón to explore more fully that darker, weightier aspect of himself: the peasant or slave who doesn't at first understand his oppression, the fatally flawed hero brought down. Yet, as Ann Vachon has suggested,[11] all three roles in *La Malinche* may embody aspects of the choreographer himself: the daring and driven Spanish conquistador, the disenfranchised Indio, and the Indian woman, torn between love for Córtez and love for her people, who would reconcile the opposing forces if she could. (Mexico shaped Limón as a man and an artist, yet most of his choreography on Mexican themes turned on conflict and revealed a powerful ambivalence.)

Limón didn't loosen his ties with Humphrey until 1958, the last year of her life. He was turning fifty. The piece that began the next phase of his career, *Missa Brevis*, both affirmed his stature as one of the great figures of American modern dance, and recalled the Humphrey-Weidman skill at handling masses. Availing himself of members of the Juilliard Dance Theater (a paraprofessional company Humphrey founded and directed), he embarked on a large-scale ensemble piece. Limón's religious upbringing and crises of faith had been reflected in several previous dances—as tormented as *The Traitor*, as celebratory as the beautiful *There is a Time* (1956). "I try to be an atheist," he once said, "but it's very hard."[12] To Zoltán Kodály's "Missa Brevis in Tempore Belli," he laid out an ecstatic architecture that framed the more private meditations, building cathedrals and tolling bells out of dancing bodies. He cast himself as an outsider, moved by the faith of the group, expressing his private struggles within their transfiguring ceremonies.

The Moor's Pavane had pared down and compressed Shakespeare's plot; such succinctness did not characterize Limón's later dances. Many of them tended to be longer and more effusive—in part because Limón no longer had a firm editor at his side, but, more importantly, because he was experiencing an almost exultant outpouring of invention and feeling. His 1964 *A Choreographic Offering* for an expanded company draped Bach's "A Musical Offering" with garlands of dancing. The themes were Doris Humphrey's, the choreography his tribute to her. It was as if he couldn't praise her enough, and the excess of beauty seemed not only forgivable but necessary.

The Winged (1966) reflected his unquenchably exalted vision (the program note: "Wings seen and unseen bear us aloft"), but it also revealed his delight in eighteen splendid young dancers, including his particular protegé, Louis Falco. In every avian analogy that inspired him, he celebrated their prowess and ardency. "One more solo," you imagine him telling himself, or "How wonderful my two tall guys, Fritz (Ludin) and Clyde (Morgan), would look beating against one another in mid-air!"

By 1970, when he made *The Unsung*, a powerful suite of solos in silence for eight men in his company, cancer had forced his retirement from the stage. He poured into these pieces—each named after a celebrated Indian chief—everything he knew about male dancing. And, following the death of his wife, Pauline Lawrence, in July 1971, he created *Dances for Isadora (Five Evocations of Isadora Duncan)*, honoring at once the female principle, the woman he called his spiritual mother, and the cherished women dancers then in his company (Ann Vachon, Carla Maxwell, Jennifer Scanlon, Laura Glenn, and Libby Nye).

José Limón choreographed over ninety dances. His reputation rests on a surprisingly modest number of them—arguably a baker's dozen; of those, most date from between 1946 and 1958. A few of the works he created in Mexico were never seen in the United States. (Limón's visits to Mexico in the 1950s were highly acclaimed; it is interesting that, given collaborators like painter Miguel Covarrubias and composer Carlos Chávez and—in the 1951 *Los cuatros soles*—sixty dancers and eighty musicians to work with, he chose to continue choreographing in unaffluent circumstances in his adopted country.) A handful of masterpieces have had extraordinary durability (Limón himself continued to dance *The Moor's Pavane* with increasing profundity until late in his life). His dances have been seen all over the world on the company's tours (including four sponsored by the State Department during the 1950s and 1960s); preserved as mainstays of the Limón company's repertory; revived for students at such institutions as State University of New York at Purchase, New York University's Tisch School of the Arts, and Juilliard (where both Limón and Humphrey taught). Ballet companies such as American Ballet Theatre, the Joffrey Ballet, the Paris Opéra, and the Royal Danish Ballet have staged them.

José Limón was only sixty-four when he died. It is our loss that he never finished this autobiography; as it is, his descriptive insights into dances that we will never see and into the world that shaped them are invaluable. When he began to write, both he and his wife were seriously ill. His works, once seen as expressive of the contemporary spirit, had become classics; to some, even old-fashioned. He didn't understand or sympathize with the postmodern revolution in dance that began in the 1960s with Judson Dance Theater, embracing, as it did, chaos, mess, and ordinary bodies doing ordinary things. It's small wonder that, in these pages, he views his past in a golden light and the people in it as heroes. To them, to him, choreography was a mission that could exalt our view of humankind. He would have been surprised and heartened, I think, to know that his company prospers, that it has outlived him by twenty-six years and that his works remain among the glories of American modern dance.

LYNN GARAFOLA

The following manuscript, now in the José Limón Papers at the Dance Collection, The New York Public Library for the Performing Arts, was commissioned by William de la Torre Bueno, the farsighted editor of Wesleyan University Press who published its first dance books. It was written in the late 1960s, mostly at the farm near Stockton, New Jersey, that Pauline Lawrence Limón had bought in the 1940s with savings from her husband's G.I. earnings and where she lived during her final illness. According to Charles D. Tomlinson, who designed costumes for the company and helped Limón take care of his wife, working on the manuscript helped Limón come to terms with her illness and with the realization of his own mortality. After her death, Limón continued writing, but not on a regular basis, and when he died, in 1972, the manuscript was still unfinished. It was inherited by Tomlinson and was among the fifty boxes of papers donated by him to the Dance Collection.

The manuscript, which consists of 281 pages, covers the first half of Limón's life. Written in pencil on the wide-ruled legal paper all too familiar to an earlier generation of college students, the text is about as close to Limón's voice as one can get. The writing is fluent, with remarkably few words crossed out, as though the story had simply poured out of him. The sentences are full of rhythm. Limón loves reiteration, the piling up of phrases, words, and parallel structures to create the waves of prose that sweep the reader forward on a powerful tide. He has a penchant for Latinate sentences, with their long periods and chains of subordinate clauses. At times, especially toward the beginning, when he is speaking about his childhood—that is, of events experienced in Spanish—the pulse of his mother tongue can be felt, along with the echo of foreign phrases.

For all its excellent qualities, the manuscript is still a first draft. In preparing it for publication, I have treated it not as a historical curiosity, but as a living work, editing it as I would the manuscript of a writer with whom I was in daily contact. Thus, I have occasionally changed the order of sentences and paragraphs, cut redundant or irrelevant passages, smoothed out awkward wordings, broken up sentences to clarify meaning, and toned down the ring of rhetoric that seemed closer to Spanish than to English. I have also corrected titles and names, regularized spelling and punctuation, and added a few dates for the sake of intelligibility. My goal throughout has been to make this memoir as true to the author's voice as possible. In many instances I have followed the rephasings suggested by Charles Humphrey Woodford, Doris Humphrey's son, who, at Limón's request, edited the opening pages of the first two chapters and attached the pink flags that are still on the manuscript today.

In the more than thirty years that have transpired since the manuscript was written, memories of all too many of the works and figures alluded to in its pages have dimmed. For this reason, endnotes containing brief biographies and information about premieres have been added. In addition to identifying the dancers and choreographers mentioned by Limón, I felt it essential to do the same for the composers he cites, since many of them, including Vivian Fine, A. Lehman Engel, Wallingford Riegger, and Norman Lloyd, comprised a group as influential in the development of American modern dance as Les Six was in the defining of ballet modernism in Europe of the 1920s.

I am indebted to colleagues far and near whose efforts have brought this project to completion. First and foremost, I wish to express my gratitude to Charles A. Tomlinson, who donated the original manuscript to the Dance Collection, thus ensuring that it would become part of Limón's enduring legacy; Ann Vachon, who transcribed it and very generously sent me a disk with her transcription; and Malcolm McCormick, who submitted a copy of the typescript to Wesleyan University Press. I owe special thanks to Norton Owen of the José Limón Dance Foundation for granting Wesleyan University Press permission to publish the manuscript and to Madeleine Nichols, curator of the Dance Collection, for waiving the New York Public Library's customary publication fee. In the case of Norton Owen, I am also grateful for his close reading of the edited memoir and chronology: the book that follows is infinitely better because of his suggestions. I am indebted to Charles H. Woodford for allowing several rare photographs from his collection to be reproduced without charge. Finally, I am grateful to Deborah Jowitt for her thoughtful introduction, Melinda Copel for the excellent bibliography, and Jody Sperling for her assistance in preparing the notes. Suzanna Tamminen, my editor at Wesleyan University Press, Sally Banes, president of the Society of Dance History Scholars, and the members of the Studies in Dance History editorial board supported the project from the first. Without their collective efforts this Joycean portrait of an artist in the making would never have come to fruition.

—Lynn Garafola

AN UNFINISHED MEMOIR

Early in the year nineteen hundred and twenty-nine[1] I was born at 9 East Fifty-Ninth Street, New York City. My parents were Isadora Duncan and Harald Kreutzberg. They were not present at my birth. I doubt that they ever saw one other or were aware of their responsibility for my being. Presiding at my emergence into the world were my foster parents, Doris Humphrey and Charles Weidman. It was at their dance studio and in their classes that I was born. I had existed previously in human form for twenty years. But that existence was only a period of gestation, albeit a long one, longer than that of an elephant. My grandparents were equally illustrious. They were Ruth St. Denis and Ted Shawn. All this constitutes an imposing pedigree and, with the exception of Harald Kreutzberg, a very American one. Duncan was born in San Francisco, St. Denis in Somerville, New Jersey, Shawn in Denver, Colorado, Humphrey in Oak Park, a suburb of Chicago, and Weidman in Lincoln, Nebraska. *Muy americano. Muy yanqui.*

The curious thing about this birth is its posthumous aspect. My "mother," a lady of considerable and conspicuous gallantry, an incurable romantic as well as one of the formidable artistic figures in Western history, had, in the process of riding off to her latest and, as it proved, her final amorous adventure (with, of all people, a garage mechanic), had her neck broken when her trailing scarf became entangled in the spokes of the rear wheels of the automobile. Her valedictory was consonant with her courageous and indomitable spirit, "*Adieu, mes amis, je vais à la gloire.*" And there, indeed, she remains to this day. Her tragic demise took place in the fall of 1927, and since I claim to be her child and to have been born in the winter of 1929, one can only conclude that all this is one of those miracles of which only artists and philosophers are capable. Spiritually, they are fecund and procreative long after their earthly remains have returned to the native dust.

The long road to the studio on Fifty-Ninth Street had begun in another street, the Calle Rosales, the street of the roses, in the city of Culiacán, capital of the state of Sinaloa, Mexico. My carnal father, Florencio Limón, was a musician, pedagogue, conductor, and director of the State Academy of Music. He played the clarinet and cello. To this day I cannot hear the sound of either instrument without being reminded of him. My mother, in terms biological, was Francisca Traslaviña. Don Florencio was then a tall, rather handsome, and distinguished man, a widower of French and Spanish descent. Doña Francisca, a girl of sixteen when they met, came from a good bourgeois family. Her deceased father had been a schoolteacher, and her mother, Doña Flavia, was, as I recall, a rather imposing matron. The Traslaviñas had, like most Mexicans, a dash of Indian blood, which was not too apparent and which they did their best to forget. It was not considered quite nice, in those times, in respectable provincial society, to be tainted with the blood of the wild tribes of the mountains or deserts, the peons enslaved in the gigantic haciendas, or *las plebes*, the degraded and poverty-stricken rabble of the cities. No. The *gente decente* of the late Porfirian dictatorship[2] modeled themselves after the landed aristocracy, which in turn looked to the even more exalted and prestigious nobility of the capital, which, in its turn, looked to Madrid, Paris, and Rome for its reason for being.

At some fiesta or other, my father had joined the orchestra to substitute for the cellist, absent for some reason or other. My mother was to tell us that she was present and that someone came to her with the message that *el señor don Florencio* would be honored and delighted to have the spray of orange blossoms she was wearing in her hair. Speechless with embarrassment, she surrendered it and spent the rest of the evening, as she waltzed by in the arms of a partner, surreptitiously glancing at her flowers jauntily fastened to the top of the cello. She remembered how prettily they vibrated with the action of the bow on the strings.

So the widower of thirty-five began courting the girl of sixteen. There was a wedding in April 1907, and punctually on January 12, 1908, I was delivered, using, fortissimo, all the power of a husky pair of lungs and kicking like a roped steer. My aunt Lupe would relate that I was *un fenómeno, un monstruo de energía*.

The young Francisca was further to give birth to Dora, Jesús, Estrella, who died at three months of age, the twins Juan José and Gilberto, who died almost immediately after birth, a Gilberto once again, who died at three months, and across the northern frontier, in the United States, to Florentino, Rosalva, Guadalupe, another pair of twins, one stillborn and one who survives to this day as Roberto, and finally Pedro. After Pedro the doctors advised my parents that further production would be dangerous, if not fatal, to the mother. Nevertheless, in due time she became once more pregnant (such is the *voluntad de Dios*), and as the pregnancy advanced, she became subject to acute suffering, and finally after an agonized crisis, she departed this valley of tears at the age of thirty-four, leaving an inconsolable widower, a large brood of infants, and a brutally embittered firstborn.

At eighteen years of age one is vulnerable to an appalling degree. There are no weapons for defense, no experience, no wisdom, no cynicism.

Death was no stranger to me. He came early. Little Estrella I had seen in the grip of the intestinal malady that killed her when she was only three months old. She was a beautiful little girl, and I remember that she accepted suffering gently, with a sweet patience, and that laid out in her long baptismal dress, surrounded by flowers in a sky blue baby coffin, she was a lovely and breathtaking apparition. Candles were burning at the four corners of the coffin. The incomprehensible solemnity of the scene has never left me.

Death visited us soon again. He wore a different guise. The scene, the choreography, devised by this master of theater for the death of an infant had a poignant delicacy. For the death of a young man he prescribed pure melodrama, a *Danse Macabre* performed in a nightmare. My mother's older brother, Uncle Manuel, received a bullet in the head shortly after the opening of the battle of Cananea.[3] It happened in the dining room of our house. It was early morning, and the family, which at the time included my visiting grandmother,[4] my aunt Lupe, and my uncle Manuel, was at breakfast. Gunfire interrupted the meal. At first it was thought to be the sound of firecrackers. In Mexico the saints like their festivals to be full of music, processions, and fireworks. We were disabused of this idea when bullets began to shatter the windowpanes and whistle into the room. Pandemonium. My father shouted a command. Everyone hit the floor, except my gallant young uncle. He had to see what was going on and looked out the window. My father and grandmother shouted at him not to be a fool, to take cover. He laughed, I remember, and then he was hit. He fell back, and a pool of blood grew around him. My frantic grandmother crouched over him, trying to revive him. My father crawled to the bedrooms, dragging out mattresses and quilts that he threw over us for protection. Our house was on the rising slope of a hill, caught between attacking revolutionary forces and their objective, a fort held by Federals at the summit. Bullets continued to whistle through the house. At three o'clock there was a truce, and the Red Cross picked up my half-dead uncle and took him to a hospital where he subsequently died. The battle was resumed and lasted for three days and nights. It was fought with all the feral tenacity of internecine wars. I remember being awakened periodically during the night by the sound of machine guns and artillery. During a lull in the fighting we were moved to a neighbor's cellar. We lived on water, soda crackers, and chipped beef out of tins. I have long ago reconciled myself to drinking water and eating a cracker, but the sight of chipped beef brings me close to nausea. Cowering under mattresses, with the incessant sound of rifles and cannon, I first encountered fear, fear raised to the pitch of pure animal terror. I trembled uncontrollably. The bright bloody pool, congealed like a crimson halo around the head of my prostrate uncle, had a horrid and irresistible fascination. My mother, pale and ravaged with fever, covered with overcoats, shawls, and blankets, would cry out in delirium.

After three days the Federals capitulated. A white flag was raised over the ramparts of the fort. The noise ceased. The vanquished Federals marched down to surrender and were made prisoners; a number were court-martialed and fell before firing squads. Normalcy returned. The dead on the streets and in the shattered houses were removed and buried.

Dead horses were towed away, and we children returned to our world, with new toys and games. A rich harvest of empty cartridges of all calibers awaited us. We were avid collectors, and traded and bartered our newfound treasures, so many of this size for so many of that. (So early in our infancy do we become entrepreneurs and traders that market values and rates of exchange seem to be part of our chromosomal equipment.) Bang, bang. "I'm a *maderista*, and you're a *porfirista*." Bang, bang. "I'm a *revolucionario*, and you're a *federal*. And you're dead." "No, you are. I fired first." "Yes, but you didn't hit me." "I did too." "No, no." "Sí, sí."[5]

All this was in my fifth year, in 1913, when, far away, across deserts, mountains, and oceans, in a legendary place called *Europa* and all unknown to me, Isadora Duncan, Anna Pavlova, Vaslav Nijinsky, and many other magical beings were creating an enchantment that was to engulf and possess me one day. But just now, during my tempestuous and precarious gestation, the dance, my future destiny, consisted of the *jarabe*, the Mexican national dance, that ubiquitous, traditional expression of all that is passionately patriotic in the *alma mexicana*, and the Spanish *jotas* and *fandangos*, those reminders that Mexico would have been impossible without Spain and its culture, language, religion, and dominance of three centuries. In the distance, remote and mysterious, were the echoing drums of the Indian dances.

Our world fell apart. Chaos reigned over northwestern Mexico, as indeed over the rest of the Republic. The Limón family had moved to the northern *mineral*—or mining town—of Cananea, where my father held the post of director of the Academia de Música for the state of Sonora. His duties were to direct the training of instrumentalists for municipal bands and orchestras and to conduct these at public concerts in the kiosk in the Plaza Central. He was also conductor of the orchestra at the local theater. I would on occasion accompany him to rehearsals and performances. The theater served all purposes. For a provincial copper mining center there was a surprising amount of theatrical activity. There were concerts, dramas, *zarzuelas*, and the miraculous *cinematógrafo*. There were music-hall nights, and on these I remember glittering Spanish dancers, costumed in sequined iridescence, with high combs and crimson roses nestling in sumptuous black coiffures. The electrifying pound of castanets, the magnetic intricacy of the steps and figurations, the verve of the *taconeado*, the flurries and cascades of ruffled petticoats, all these moved me to a pitch of excitement that I could neither understand nor explain. The Iberian genius for containing volcanic fires under glacial formality would not become known to me until much later. My origins were punctuated by the pluck of guitars and the sound of the *cante jondo*.

One unforgettable night a beautiful girl, a fairy, a butterfly, appeared. She was suspended in midair by an unseen wire. In each hand she held a wand from which hung incredibly long draperies of the sheerest gauze or chiffon that were somehow attached to her body as well. Waltzing, she waved the wands and created magical patterns and undulations, while colored lights played upon her. This magical vision of movement and light made an unforgettable impression on me.

A great favorite, after the Spanish *bailarinas*, was the ballroom dance couple. Handsome and distinguished, they performed in formal evening attire, he in tails, she in a high fashion gown with an aigrette on her coiffure. Their tango always brought down the house. Also on the bill were cancan dancers, cakewalk dancers, and Oriental dancers.

There was one dance that terrified, repelled, and fascinated me. This dance represented another facet of the Iberian inheritance and was regarded with the curious ambivalence with which a Mexican regards things Spanish. Spain means the conqueror Córtez, the destroyer and despoiler of ancient native cultures, a man wanton, cruel, and insatiable. Spain represents three centuries of subjection, the enslavement and oppression of indigenous populations, merciless and unscrupulous maltreatment, and exploitation.

But Spain is also the mother country. She gave us *nuestro Señor Jesucristo* and his crucifix, and his *Santa Madre, nuestra Señora la santísima Virgen María*, and Don Hernán Córtez, gallant and honorable Christian knight, bringer of enlightenment to benighted, idolatrous heathen; compassionate missionaries who consoled, healed, educated; and great viceroys, men of vision and humanism, whose architects gave New Spain one of the richest architectural heritages in the world.

The dance I found so fascinating was the bullfight. No sarabande, chaconne, or passacaglia surpasses the *corrida de toros* in its grave formality, solemnity, sober elegance, grace, and ritual. Even in provincial northern Mexico this most Spanish of dances was performed as it would be in Madrid, Seville, or Lima. All ritual must open in procession, with a formal introduction of each component. The entrance of the *toreros*, the *picadores*, and finally the *matadores* in order is an electrifying spectacle. Costumed in great splendor and breathtaking colors, the bullfighters evoke an age that knew how to enhance the appearance of a man. Gallant and heroic, the bullfighter was a being consecrated and set apart, performing an ancient ritual drama that would cleanse and purge us, its spectators, a man with symbolic powers, graces, and prerogatives. Moving with measured gait and sacerdotal majesty, he was a dancer in a cruel and dangerous ritual. I did not know, as I watched spellbound, that I was watching an art whose gesture and movement would influence me profoundly when I became a dancer. In composing dances, I would look back to this formative experience for guidance and inspiration.

But our world, our Hispanic world, was falling apart. My father, the exact antithesis of the warrior, was appalled and disgusted by the era's violence and lawlessness. The Academia, like many other institutions, disintegrated and disappeared. My father, with a family to support, accepted the post of director of military bands to several of the revolutionary *caudillos* of the north. He served by turns Alvaro Obregón and Plutarco Elías Calles, who later were elevated to the presidency of the republic.

This necessitated leaving the family to accompany the generals on their campaigns. What he saw and experienced convinced him that he would have to emigrate to the United States. There was some understandable procrastination. He moved us from one northern city to another. We lived for a time in Hermosillo, then in the frontier city of Nogales, and here Death came, saw, and conquered once again. Again I was a witness. My baby brother Gilberto became very ill on the train that took us from Hermosillo north to Nogales. He cried pitifully during the long slow ride. The track had been destroyed and badly repaired. Bridges had been burned or blown up. The makeshift replacements were an ordeal to cross. The train was crowded beyond belief. People stood in the aisles. All social distinctions and barriers were forgotten. The very poor always travel inelegantly. On the aisles of the passenger coach families stood, crouched, squatted, or lay with what pathetic possessions they could carry—blankets, cooking pots, frying pans, old pieces of furniture, the inevitable cage housing a noisy parrot. Coupled to the passenger coaches were numerous freight cars replete with displaced humanity. Our caravan included the inevitable regiment of soldiers, who carried, besides their own ragged selves, their children and a total arsenal of weaponry and ammunition—rifles, carbines, machine guns, and an astonishing number of cartridge belts crisscrossed over their chests. These last lent an unexpected aura of chic to the soldiers, who comported themselves rather jauntily. Of course, in true Mexican revolutionary style, the overflow rode the roofs of the freight cars.

There was no doctor on the train. I could see my mother becoming desperate. Various ladies tried to be helpful, prescribing warm mint tea or ointment to be rubbed on the baby's chest. Nothing helped. At the far end of the coach someone played an accordion, sad, melancholy *canciones*. It was sunset. The sun set in pure fresh gore. My mother's face, the crying of my baby brother, my frightened sister Dora and little brother Jesús, the lost, lost train, the brutal landscape of central Sonora, harsh and arid—how the memory of this scene lies in ambush to assault and torment me when I least expect it! How I abhor the sound of an accordion!

After an eternity the exhausted train limped into Nogales. My worried father collected his spent wife and offspring and took us to a boarding house. Here, a few days later, my brother Gilberto literally suffocated to death in his mother's arms, while I stood by in helpless panic.

The counterpoint to this fugue was the execution by firing squad of a man. There was a procession, the doomed man waving away a bandage from his eyes, asking for a cigarette; my mother frantically lighting candles before the crucifix, kneeling and imploring heaven for some miraculous intercession; then, the sound of the volley and the violent desolation of a woman weeping.

There are the bright memories of Mexico. For these I am grateful. My first memory of all is of sitting naked in a tub or basin of water in a charming spot, most likely the patio of our house in Culiacán where I was born. I was splashing water on myself and on a laughing young woman, my mother. It was golden in the sunlight and green and cool in the shade. There were beautiful odors. I adored my mother, and she was very happy. I had a toy guitar.

My grandmother Flavia would have me to her house to visit her. We would have breakfast together in her patio. The place was full of wonders. There were flowers everywhere—roses, carnations, bougainvillea, tuberoses, lilies, and flowers I have never seen since. She loved to water and tend them herself. There were cages with canaries, cardinals, lovely little parrots, and other birds, and they sang in the brilliant sunlight. She would visit each cage, address each occupant in baby-talk Spanish, wish it good morning, inquire about its health and disposition, and feed it its own special breakfast. Our breakfast would consist of all manner of fruits of the tropics, oranges and bananas, mangoes and pineapples, and some delectable small fishes "sautéed to a crisp golden brown," as the cookbooks say, eggs, lovely tortillas, hot frothy chocolate, and delicious sweet rolls. In the hot afternoons, after the siesta, which my grandmother took in a bed with a net canopy to keep out the ever active and famished mosquitoes, we would stroll to the plaza and the market places, and sometimes she would buy me a toy whistle or a sweet. On our return she would read to me. Fairy tales, the Arabian Nights, strange and sometimes frightening things from the Old Testament, or about the Babe in the manger in Bethlehem, or Judas. There was no end to the fascination. Doña Flavia dressed severely, in black taffeta, with white showing only at the throat and wrists. She was my early encounter with Latin formality, austerity, and protocol, which in the conduct of human relationships take precedence over love, tenderness, intimacy, anger, hatred, and passion.

My schooling began in Culiacán. The first schoolroom was a place of confrontation with the harsh realities of this world. There was the despair of being abandoned by my parents to the cold impersonality of a stranger who wielded a terrible authority. My contemporaries were no comfort. They were also strangers and seemed intent on their own problems. I wallowed in self-pity. Our teacher was a rather stylish young woman in a white blouse and long black skirt. She was sharp and shrill of voice and short on patience. To her, stupidity was an intolerable sin, and since she was surrounded by it, since all of us miserable, cowed, first graders seemed to be gifted with it, she suffered from an acute sense of outrage that she took no pains to conceal. The alphabet was the first battle. Then came numbers and the most elementary arithmetic. G-A-T-O spells cat. Two plus two equals four. She wrote letters, words, and numbers on the blackboard. She erased, wrote again, made oral interrogations and inquisitions that ended with unspeakable embarrassment on our part and bitter sarcasm on hers. One day we were given pens and ink pots to learn to write our names. It was a disastrous move. More ink ended up on our fingers, noses, desks, trousers, and shirt fronts than on the page. She had reached the limit of her patience. She exploded violently. She began with the occupant of the first bench in my row, seizing the hapless little boy by an unruly mop of hair and giving him three or four vigorous shakes. She proceeded up the aisle, her fury mounting. I was last in the row. I saw what was in store for me. I have never since known such panic. I was paralyzed. This virago, this madwoman, finally got to me, and I was subjected to the most rude, the most shocking violence I can remember. I had a lot of hair. She made good use of it. Her name was Señorita Angélica.

There were other schools. In Hermosillo, at the Colegio Sonora, the teacher of the second and third grades was Señorita Bórquez, a mature, dignified lady, who was more *correcta*. She was a good disciplinarian, but used no violence; she made our studies interesting and sometimes a pleasure, since she would make them seem like games. She smiled, she cajoled, she teased, and we learned.

In Nogales, the fourth grade teacher, Señorita Bracamonte, was a lady of culture and charm. Her voice was low and musical. She made our studies interesting. She would discuss Córtez and Montezuma as human beings, not as monoliths or legends. Arithmetic, history, biology, geography, botany, and composition became fascinating. She introduced me to Marie Antoinette and told me sad and terrible things about her life. On one occasion, she waited until the recess period to deliver a severe but well-deserved reprimand; I will be forever grateful that she spoke to me in private. One Saturday I had occasion to visit her home. A maid admitted me to the patio. This was the first time I had ever seen a teacher, one of the remote, the august, in her private domicile. Señorita Bracamonte was sitting on a bench in a dressing gown, her long auburn hair, still damp, hanging down her back over a large bath towel. I stopped in confusion and embarrassment. Her gray eyes twinkled with amusement. She put on a mock solemnity. "Advance, *señor don José*. Señorita Bracamonte does not bite her pupils." We both laughed and had a very pleasant talk.

I am happy that this is one of the last memories I have of Mexico. I was about to become, with my family, an exile in a strange country. I was seven years old. I had seen and felt many things that seven-year-olds should be spared. Much of this had been incomprehensible and would not be understood until much later. But I had learned that living was a precarious and unpredictable business and that to cope with living one had to have *valor*—courage. And I was soon to learn that for the rest of my life I was to be a translator and conciliator. It would be my task to translate, perpetually, within myself the tongue of Castile into that of the Anglo-Saxons, to reconcile many disparate and contradictory cultural habits and ways of living, and to resolve hostilities within and around me.

This began even before we crossed the northern frontier, that formidable and awesome barrier, which, like all boundaries, separated and isolated us both physically and spiritually. Beyond this line was the *norteamericano*, the *yanqui*, the *gringo*. He was powerful. He spoke *inglés*, which was a language totally incomprehensible to those who spoke the *lengua castellana* or *español*. He had, in the middle of the last century, unjustly invaded our *patria* and inflicted a humiliating defeat on a weaker nation and imposed a peace of galling ignominy. His merciless avarice had deprived Mexico of the vast territories that became Texas, New Mexico, Arizona, California, Utah, Nevada, and heaven knows what else. He was likely to intervene at any moment in the Mexican revolution. *La intervención* hung over our heads like a Damoclean sword. Fear. Dread. To a seven-year-old they are palpable, sickening realities. It was a maid or a cook, I forget which, who twitted me about our imminent migration. She informed me gleefully that the *gringos* were very fond of cutting off the testicles of little Mexican boys and frying and eating them as a delicacy. Armed with this knowledge I came to the United States.

I had encountered English earlier. In a kitchen in Mexico I had seen a wooden box used to hold firewood. It had obviously been a container for canned stuff. In large letters along its sides read the admonition "Keep in a cool, dry place." Reading English in the Spanish manner, phonetically, is something to make Chaucer and Shakespeare roll over in their graves. I had no idea what these words meant at all. All I knew was that they were mysterious and intriguing. The only English I knew I had learned from my half-sister Julia, who had preceded us to the U.S. to a convent boarding school and on her return had taught me that "yes" meant "sí" and that "no," oddly enough, meant "no."

My first, and most ignominious, because it was public, encounter with the new language was during the reading period at the Convent of the Holy Shepherd in Tucson, Arizona. A circle of little boys and girls stood around the desk occupied by Sister Cornelia. Most were blond and blue-eyed. Or so they seemed to me, one of the few dark-haired ones. These I later discovered were either Mexican like myself or strangely enough, dark-haired *americanos*. We held our books in our right hand. Each was to read a sentence. My turn came at last. I had by now learned to read in Spanish. The sentence, forever engraved in my memory, was "Would you like to ride in a boat?" I had no idea what it meant, but I knew I had to read it, and I did. It brought down the house. There were shrieks and howls of laughter and rolling in the aisles. With all the unsparing cruelty of children my classmates gave vent to their delight. I turned crimson with mortification. Tears of rage and humiliation blinded me. I was alone. I was surrounded by a horde of *salvages* and *bárbaros*.

Sister Cornelia sternly called the class to order. But it was too late. The terrible knowledge had transfixed me. I was an alien. An exile. The wound inflicted that day would take many years to heal. But when wounds do not kill they form a cicatrix, which is good tough tissue. That day I resolved a number of things. One was that I would learn this impossible language, whose capricious and illogical pronunciation hadn't the remotest relation to the way it was written, better than any of those who had jeered at me.

* * *

What makes an *hombre honrado y formal*? What virtues, excellencies, and capacities?

Señor don Florencio Limón, a man I little knew and less understood, my father, my enemy, a figure of fear, awe, contempt, hatred, and ultimately and too late, reverence and love, first posed these questions during the first two decades of my being. Not in so many words, perhaps. Not explicitly. No. He did it quite simply by example. By the way he lived his daily life. By his behavior in big and small things. By his language, voice, and intonation. By his manner and style. And by his dignity.

In Mexico he had been somebody, a man of education, accomplishment, and status. Across the border in Arizona he became one of many refugees fleeing the chaos to the south. True, he was more fortunate than most. First of all, there was his profession. As a good musician he found himself in a better position to make his way than, say, the poor, ignorant, unskilled peon. Then, too, he was obviously a man of education, a gentleman. He became conductor of the band and orchestra maintained in Tucson by the Southern Pacific Railroad. It was his task to conduct Sunday concerts in the bandstand in the park—the march from *Aida*, the overture to *Rigoletto*, light opera, *The Merry Widow*, Strauss waltzes, and, of course, Souza. When the Great War came, the draft put an end to all this, and my father had to move from place to place and take jobs with orchestras in Winkelman, Globe, and Miami, all in Arizona, and finally, after these wanderings, in Los Angeles, California.

Even then this city was the metropolis of the Southwest. To us who had known only small cities, Los Angeles was awesome in the extreme. It was to become our permanent home. The Limóns took root there. To this day my father's progeny, with the exception of myself and Roberto, live and flourish in the City of the Angels.

As the family grew, the struggle to feed, clothe, and house us became ever more brutal. We were poor. There were Mexicans we knew who, affluent to begin with, had managed to escape across the border with their wealth more or less intact. They were lucky. But for my father the struggle was incessant and often bitter.

Not once, living as we did in what one day would be referred to as the Mexican ghetto, did I see my father ever falter in his manners and his dignity. His clothes, worn and often threadbare, were always decent and in order. Those were the days of stiffly starched shirts with detachable collars. His were always immaculate. From the old days had been salvaged his gold collar buttons, stick, and cuff links, as well as the gold watch and the gold chain he wore across his vest. He had a decent felt hat for winter and a straw one for summer. His shoes were carefully shined. He was a handsome, distinguished presence.

His domestic life was equally impressive. In his shirt sleeves, which were held up by a pair of garters, he would sit at a desk, when we had one, or at the dining room table, or even the kitchen table, copying orchestral parts in a fine, careful hand. Or he would sit in the living room, a music stand in front of him, practicing the clarinet or the cello. Or he would preside at family meals, ladling out soup, filling our plates. Or he would read a book or newspaper, with a child on his lap, another leaning on his knee, and two or three others amusing themselves with a toy on the floor—a contented parent, a man of sanguine, serene temperament. But woe to those who tried his patience beyond its limits. Punishment, swift and appalling, would be visited on the miscreant. This happened only rarely. Perhaps for this reason my father's anger was all the more to be dreaded. All of us, brothers and sisters alike, could be provoking as only a large, healthy brood can be. We knew, with a sure atavistic knowledge, that with our mother we could get away with murder, that we could count on her loving tenderness to make her indulgent and even permissive. Not so with my father.

The intolerable outrage of my father's belt slashing across my posterior early made him my enemy. Even as I howled with pain and rage I cursed him and his justice, and his tyranny and power over me, and I lusted for revenge, for escape. I believe he sensed this, for gradually the relationship between us turned into an undeclared war. With me he became stricter than with the rest of us, more formal and demanding. I, in turn, would retreat from him, until eventually we grew to be like strangers. With time, the antagonism became more pronounced. My mother would seek to conciliate between us without success.

Early, an enigma, a terror, a menace had made its appearance. Unbeautiful, evil, ineffably shameful, heralded by leering, lecherous older boys in school wash rooms, sex had come to poison and to haunt. The first devastating knowledge: you were born, you breathe and walk the earth because your father did certain things with your mother in bed at night. What things? He doesn't know! Crude, terrible diagrams scrawled on whitewashed walls to instruct, prove, and appall. I could not look my parents in the face for a long time after this. And with an utter lack of logic and consistency, I gradually absolved my mother of sinfulness and made my father the sole culprit.

Dolor. Both languages use this word, as they use "union," "civil," "terrible," "irresistible," "adorable," and countless others, spelled exactly alike, or with only the final letter or syllable divergent. It has often amused me to leaf through the pages of an English-Spanish dictionary and find columns of words that are spelled exactly alike.

Adolescence. Time of dolor or pain. By now I knew that my mother was slowly dying, with one pregnancy after another, one child after another, and that the man who was slowly but surely killing her was my father. I worshipped her. To me she was beautiful, kind, and tender, always loving and understanding. She did not deserve to be killed like this.

I was eighteen years old, tall like my father and dark like my mother. I had spent the final hours at my mother's death bed, heard the death rattle become the long, drawn-out sibilance of finality, taken her gold wedding band and irrationally slipped it on my finger. Now, in the hospital corridor, I confronted a broken man, sobbing like a child, and in the cold April dawn took a terrible and heartless revenge. Why do you cry, I asked. You killed her. And God permitted you.

California was not all sorrow. After all, I was young. I was alive. Life was before me, a long road that seemed to lead to infinity. There was much to learn, to translate, to conciliate. There was even joy, a *rara avis* that appeared sometimes with the sun and rain and clouds, and the power of young muscles hurled against mountains and oceans. And there was school, which was salvation, and the excitement of discovery, the exploration of new territories, continents of the mind and spirit in books, in the arts, in ideas, in comrades, and in those unforgettable beings, our teachers.

By turns stern and benign, Sister Cornelia is the earliest I remember. She did not hesitate to use a ruler on the unruly or to translate for me, "I've been to London to see the queen, *la reina, muy bonita*," an act of mercy I shall treasure to my dying day. In Los Angeles, Mrs. Lillian Scott Remelin, a vivacious and charming widow, was my first encounter—at the vulnerable age of twelve—with a flower of Southern womanhood. She completely enslaved me. Her frank, unabashed coquetry, while very effective in teaching us about sentence structure, the English colonists' passion for independence, and the mysteries of poetry and arithmetic, made the rigors of her classroom a challenge to be met with all the ardor of my nature. I was inflamed, tremulous, enamored. For her I would have fought dragons and walked through fire, anything, that I might be rewarded with a flash of her limpid blue eyes that said with a frightening and delicious intimacy, "You and I know, don't we, how well you have done." Sometimes, on dismissing me for the day, she would further enchant me with a "*Buenas tardes, señor.*"

In high school Miss Myrta Herbert claimed me for her own. She was an art teacher, and I, being an art major, found myself under her advisory wing. With her began my encounter with men of art and their passion and legacy to the nations of the world. With her we lived in daily communion with the Parthenon, the frescos at Knossus, the Etruscans, Giotto, the Sistine Chapel, Chartres, Velázquez, Rembrandt, Goya, all the sublime achievements of Western art. Although she was a thoroughgoing conservative, she would encourage us to look at the impressionists, cubists, dadaists, and other artists of the avant-garde. In this way, Manet, Cézanne, Matisse, Brancusi, Picasso, and other strange and mysterious names first entered my awareness.

Miss Reta Mitchell had me in her choral singing class. Quite early, I had been classed as a basso profundo, but singing was not for me. I have never enjoyed doing it and like to hear it only in Monteverdi, Bach, Mozart, Richard Strauss, or Verdi. Miss Mitchell was a formidable pianist, and it was with her that I studied the instrument. It has been a lasting love. To this day, when I am by myself and have a rare spare moment, I like to play Chopin and the easier things in Bach's *Well Tempered Clavi-*

chord. Discovering in me an insatiable listener, Miss Mitchell would play in her living room an entire evening of Bach, Chopin, Couperin, Beethoven, and a strangely delectable musician named Debussy.

I have always been a lover. At seven I began to fall madly, obsessively in love, first with the Spanish-speaking girls, Laura, Aída, Armida, Aurora; later, in high school, with the Americans, Sarah, Gladys, and Charlotte. And I have always been a friend. Federico, Ricardo, Román, Gregorio—they were my first friends. Later, there was Archie, Edgar, and Owen. Their names evoke in me the very essence of my childhood and youth, when the fervor of passion brightened dismal years of pain. The innocent selflessness of loving a fellow being was pure rapture.

In my last year of high school I became acquainted with another set of mentors. These were three young men, aspiring artists, living the strangely fascinating lives of aesthetes, bohemians, and rebels. They were slightly older than I was and seemed very mature and worldly-wise. I would be invited to their studio for "evenings of enchantment." By candlelight, sitting on a studio couch or sprawled on the floor, I would listen wide-eyed while they read Omar Khayyám, Lord Dunsany, Oscar Wilde, Beaudelaire. Sometimes, one of the three, whose name was Don Forbes, would play, on an old, tinny upright piano, not only Debussy and Satie but also a terrifying composer called Schoenberg. Bourgeois society and its values, pretensions, and hypocrisies were not merely dissected, but dismembered and annihilated. To my alarm I found myself listening and, then, after much discomfort, beginning to agree. The human race was made up of two kinds of people, philistines and artists. The former distrusted and hated the latter, accusing him of depravity, improvidence, and worse, while secretly envying his emancipated and irresponsible ways. The artist, in turn, cordially reciprocated the philistine's contempt, and accused him of materialism, insensitiveness, ignorance, and other failings too numerous to mention. The two were irreconcilable. I must choose sides. The dilemma appalled me. All my friends, my parents, my teachers, belonged to the bourgeoisie. I had been most strictly brought up as a bourgeois. Fernando Félix, a fellow Mexican and another member of the trio, would take me aside and add his arguments and admonitions in Spanish. Fernando came from a "good family," one that owned haciendas and sugar refineries in Sonora. He had rebelled against his background and upbringing and urged me to do the same. Perkins Harnley, who came from Lincoln, Nebraska (as did Don Forbes), completed this trio intent upon converting me to art.

This conversion was destined. My mother's death, the break with my father, my loss of religious faith, my disenchantment with the University of California, Southern Branch (as UCLA was then called) were unmistakable signs that my young life was in a state of crisis.

My rebellion was also directed against an "alter ego," the inseparable companion and close friend of my high school years. His name was Owen Jones, and he had sternly issued an ultimatum. I was to choose between my disreputable artist friends (whose depraved influence had led me to read Oscar Wilde, Theodore Dreiser, and Eugene O'Neill, and to see lewd plays such as *Diamond Lil* with an infamous actress called Mae West) and good decent people, a category, of course, that included himself. Jones and I had met on our first day at Lincoln High School, and from that day on were bosom friends. Our relationship was like the playful rivalry between two young pups or cubs. We disagreed on practically every subject except our staunch devotion to each other. It was an endless contest, a Spartan, athletic trial of strength and endurance. It was a race across land, sea, and mountain, and had we had wings, we would have tried to outdistance the other in the clouds. At his instigation we performed a ritual that made us blood brothers. We pierced our veins at the wrist, pressed the bloody wounds together, and swore eternal friendship and devotion. This made a profound impression on me. As we grew older, it became clear that we were totally different in our thinking. He was to be a lawyer, marry his girl, raise a family, and live happily ever after. He looked with growing disapproval at the direction I was taking, and would lecture me on my defection from the path of rectitude and virtue. I was made to feel like a monster of depravity.

The "boys," who had now moved to New York from a Los Angeles they found increasingly backward and provincial, would write to me of the artistic paradise they were discovering. This siren song proved irresistible. One night, with no farewells to anyone except my friend Gladys, I rode the streetcar to the end of the line in the northern suburbs of the even then sprawling city, stuck out my thumb, and was picked up by a truck. It was a memorable night. Riding north toward San Francisco in the lovely cool night I took a long look at my life, who and what I was, and what I must do. I was talented. I was going to follow in the footsteps of Michelangelo and every other inspired man who had ever wielded a paint brush and made beauty for his fellow men. The sad, sweet past, so ugly and so beautiful, was henceforth to be as dead. The die was cast and the Rubicon crossed. There was no returning.

* * *

San Francisco in the early fall of 1928 seemed full of men looking for precisely the thing I was—a ship going, via the Panama Canal, to New York. The dingy employment agencies on the Embarcadero were always crowded, and quite naturally preference was given to experienced men who could produce the magic credentials certifying them as "able-bodied seamen." I saw that the romantic adventure on a tramp steamer à la Richard Halliburton[6] was a dream and that other means of transport had to be considered. In the meantime, one had to eat and find shelter. I sold newspapers at one of the busy intersections. Work began late in the afternoon, when a truck dropped bundles of *The San Francisco Chronicle* on the curb, and continued until well after midnight; after that there was a snack at a waterfront lunchroom and exhausted sleep in a cubicle of a room at a "flophouse." All this was accompanied by an inner music, audible only to my obsessed self, that transformed the city of St. Francis and everything in it into something magical and fabulous. After a week or so, I had hoarded twenty-seven dollars, and since I could not travel the high seas, I compromised with a night on a riverboat up to Sacramento. I couldn't sleep with excitement. My only previous sailing experience had been in a rowboat in a Los Angeles park lagoon. The bunk was hot and uncomfortable, so I sprawled on deck. There was a full moon. The banks of the Sacramento River were bathed in enchantment. Early at dawn we landed in Sacramento. Without pause, like a migratory bird winging its way unerringly, I sought the highway leading over the mountains to the East. How beautiful it all was. I met good, kind, generous people—truck drivers, salesmen, a young married couple, college boys on vacation. Then, one ineffable afternoon, I crossed the Hudson on the 125th Street ferry. I was home.

The rapture, the sense of liberation at having found, at last, the *magnum desideratum*, was almost more than I could bear. I walked on clouds. Life was a radiant, golden dream come true.

Among my earliest memories as a child were the pleasures of draughtsmanship. I used sticks, pencils, crayons, brushes, and fingers to draw. A stick would do for sand or dirt. Pencils, crayons, and brushes were for paper, walls, furniture, and other handy surfaces; fingers were for the air. Drawing was compulsive. At school, when the nuns discovered I was an "artist," they promptly set me to decorating blackboards, windows, and walls with all the appropriate symbolism for Christmas, Valentine's Day, St. Patrick's Day, Easter, Washington's Birthday, Thanksgiving, and Halloween. Besides the Catholic religion, it was art that bridged the chasm separating the scared Mexican child from the slowly, but inevitably acclimatizing youth and adult. My accent may have been ridiculed, but my prowess as an artist was accepted with total and gratifying admiration. This was my chief claim to the approval of my teachers and fellow students during my entire scholastic career. It was my aunt Lupe who first teased me by calling me a second Michelangelo. It was taken for granted by everyone, including myself, that I was destined for the career of a painter.

New York art schools, art galleries, and artistic fashions were largely dominated by the French. Impressionists, cubists, modernists, surrealists, and dadaists were the models for all aspiring painters. I had the greatest admiration for Manet, Renoir, Cézanne, Braque, and Picasso. They were undisputed masters. But what was discouraging was that everyone was imitating them. By some perverse irony, perhaps as a reaction to this dominance by Paris, I found myself turning to El Greco, a painter largely ignored by my teachers in California. The more I studied his work, however, the more I came to the fatal recognition—fatal, that is, to my life's ambition—that he had done all I hoped to do and done it supremely well. New York now became a cemetery, and I a lost soul in torment. I had been earning my living by running elevators, emptying garbage cans, tending furnaces, and posing for artists and art classes. Now that bottom had fallen out of my life, I spent my days loafing or going to the movies. All ambition was lost.

It was at this point that Charlotte Vaughan, a girl from Georgia studying at Columbia University with whom I was then going, informed me one Sunday morning after our usual breakfast that she had tickets for a matinee dance recital. I had no idea what she meant by this but obediently accompanied her to what was then the Gallo—now New Yorker—Theatre. The house was packed. The lights dimmed, and the curtains rose on a bare stage hung with black velour curtains. A piano struck up the stirring preamble to the Polonaise in A-flat Major of Chopin. Suddenly, onto the stage, borne on the impetus of the heroic rhapsody, bounded an ineffable creature and his partner. Instantly and irrevocably, I was transformed. I knew with shocking suddenness that until then I had not been alive or, rather, that I had yet to be born. There was joy, terror, and panic in the discovery. Just as the unborn infant cannot know the miracle of light, so I had not known that dance existed, and now I did not want to remain on this earth unless I learned to do what this man—Harald Kreutzberg—was doing.[7]

In a state bordering on panic, a fear that perhaps I was too late in my discovery of the dance, I ran to all my friends for help. One of them lent me a copy of *My Life* by Isadora Duncan. The book had just been published, and in its pages I discovered my artistic mother. My two friends from Los Angeles, Don Forbes and Perkins Harnley, had both attended school in Lincoln, Nebraska, with Charles Weidman. They recommended that I look into the school recently established by Doris Humphrey and himself, and begin my training. I showed up immediately. The young lady at the reception desk of the studio was Pauline Lawrence. Here, unbeknownst to me, was my future wife. But at that moment I wasn't looking for a wife. I wanted only to be born.

Birth, for a dancer, is like this. You put on a leotard, and trembling with embarrassment and terrible shyness, you step into the studio. Doris Humphrey, a goddess, a nymph, a caryatid, makes you do things you have never done before. You stretch; you bend and flex your legs, your arches and torso, every muscle, tendon, nerve, vein, and artery—all of you, your whole entire you. You run, jump, and turn; you fall to the floor and rise again. From the piano where sits Pauline comes Bach and Chopin, Brahms and Henry Cowell. You pant, sweat, and hurt. You learn that you are. You learn that the past—the *jarabes*, the bullfights, the painting, the Mexican in you, the fearful passage to the land of the *gringos*, the wounds, the deaths—have been only a preparation for this new life. In a state of pure bliss I lived (somewhat lame from muscles unaccustomed to the rigors of dance exercises) for the moment I would return to the studio.

Very gradually I learned that the radiant creature with the body of Botticelli's Primavera and the mass of red-gold hair flying behind her like a trail of fire as she leapt across the studio, had only recently left the company of Ruth St. Denis and Ted Shawn. There had been some disagreements and unpleasantness. What they were about I was to learn later. Just now the dressing room gossip focused on a newly found independence, a quest for new expression in dance. With her low yet commanding voice and coolly serene manner Humphrey would teach us both theory and practice. With tremendous lucidity she would explain the principles on which her technical exercises were based—breath suspension, fall and recovery, tension and relaxation, breath phrase, breath rhythm: always the breath. She moved like a gazelle. She was the wind, a wave rushing to break on a rocky shore, music and poetry, Ariel, Artemis, and Echo, a creature enamored of the air.

It was fortunate for me that her partner, Charles Weidman, was a totally different kind of artist. Humphrey was essentially a formalist. He, on the other hand, was an expressionist. In his classes all technical exercises were directed toward a kind of extended pantomime that had a puckish or comic flavor. Weidman himself was a superb mime and clown, and there was a great deal of fun and laughter in his classes. Still, I found his objectives and methods painfully difficult, contrary to my natural seriousness; always, it seemed, I felt stupid and inept. But in the long run this was fine training for me and a good balance to the "pure dance" that was the basis of Humphrey's teaching.

Dance, at this time, was in a state of ferment and excitement. A new impetus seemed to animate the art. Before this, it had been content to remain an exotic European import— ballet. This was only to be expected. During its comparatively short history, the young nation had had no time to cultivate the arts as creative expressions of its own nature and essence. As a colony of Europe, it had inherited from the mother continent its language and laws, political traditions and institutions, architecture and science. Very early, however, it had displayed an astonishing genius for mechanical invention as well as for politics and war. Europe learned from Eli Whitney, Robert Fulton, Thomas Edison, and other American inventors. American statesmen such as Thomas Jefferson and Abraham Lincoln and American military leaders such as Ulysses S. Grant and Robert E. Lee were second to none. But outside the cultural oasis of New England, artists found scant appreciation, and American luminaries, from the painters Benjamin West and James Whistler to the composer Edward MacDowell, had to become expatriates. Indeed, what possibility was there for a native art such as dance to flourish in a society bent on dominating an enormous continent, clearing it of forests, and exterminating its aboriginal populations? The latter, resolute in the defense of their homelands, offered a gallant if hopeless resistance to the paleface invader. The westward progress of empire was slow, cruel, and bloody.

But once the conquest was complete, at the end of the nineteenth century, creative energies sought and found other outlets. At the very edge of the continent, where those energies encountered the barrier of the Pacific,

Isadora Duncan was born—a dancer and a rebel that no American city, not San Francisco, not Chicago, not New York, could contain. She, too, became an expatriate. A visionary and an iconoclast, she sought nothing less than a renewal of the dance and a purging of all decadence and effeteness. She went back in order to go forward. She recalled the heroic dance of the Greek tragedies. She took off the pink tights, toe shoes, and tutus of the ballet, abandoned its stilted syllabus and coquetry, and gave the astonished world her half-nude bacchante, a celebrant of Hellenic mysteries. Her Dionysian ecstasies were danced to Wagner, Beethoven, Schubert, and Tchaikovsky. Her artistic flaws and pretensions were overshadowed by her virtues. A restless malcontent like her pioneer forebears, she forged ahead and blazed new trails for others to follow. There was a furor in the capitals of Europe, and the repercussions crossed the Atlantic and sent tremors through the artistic world here. Duncan's equally imposing contemporary, Ruth St. Denis, with her husband Ted Shawn, added to this renaissance with Denishawn, the company of which both Humphrey and Weidman had been members. Duncan's paraphrase of Whitman, "I see America dancing," may have been a vision, but planted in the fertile soil of America it took root, and by the middle of the 1920s, Martha Graham, another Denishawn alumnus, was giving dance recitals. So were Humphrey and Weidman. And there were others: Helen Tamiris,[8] Senia Gluck-Sandor and his wife Felicia Sorel,[9] Michio Ito,[10] Benjamin Zemach,[11] Elsa Findlay.[12] All were busy adding to the excitement.

The American modern dance, which was to give New York City the distinction of being the world capital of the dance, was a phenomenon rare in the long history of dance in Western societies. The ballet, born in Italy of ancient Hellenic and Latin antecedents and nurtured by robust peasant dances, acquired elegance and polish in Europe's princely courts. Catherine de Medici brought it to Paris as part of a glittering dowry. The atmosphere of Fontainebleau proved salubrious, and when the Sun King built his palace at Versailles the Italian import had become very French indeed. Other European princes, not to be outdone, built their own versions of Versailles, and French ballet masters were part of the splendor. Catherine the Great imported it to St. Petersburg, and here under the opulent and impassioned patronage of tsars and grand dukes, the art reached its zenith. It became, in the hands of the Russians, one of the wonders of the world.

But the curious fact is that in all its peregrinations, the more it moved from court to court, from nation to nation, the more ballet remained the same. It was an art not limited by the chaos of rival and conflicting nationalisms, but a genuinely European expression. Eventually, it spread to the four corners of the world. To this day its codes of movement remain sacrosanct and intact, whether in Tokyo, Johannesburg, Kansas City, or Moscow.

It took Americans, with their inherited prejudices against European hegemony, to reject, in toto, ballet's long and revered tradition. Precisely as they had once plunged into the unknown, untamed wilderness with no thought to the danger lurking around them, so now they had the temerity to abandon the security of the academic tradition and set out to discover or invent their own. It was my good fortune and privilege to observe at first hand the labors of those great revolutionary figures, Doris Humphrey and Charles Weidman. I was a pupil in their classes and a dancer in their company for ten years.

*   *   *

In my classes were a number of other young men. Three I remember, because they were in my first performance as a dancer—John Glenn, a miner's son from Pennsylvania, Charles Laskey,[13] who was from Staten Island, and Gino—or Eugene—LeSieur, a French-Canadian. They were already experienced dancers. Charles Weidman had not yet quite severed the umbilical cord that held him to Denishawn. He was preparing a dance with a Balinese flavor and needed an extra man. I was drafted. I was a beginner, but the men's contribution was relatively simple. Even so, he and the boys had to work like demons to shape me up. I was in a daze of glory. They grabbed, pulled, poked, and pushed me into the Oriental designs of the choreography. I was very strong and, like all athletes, muscle-bound and, by a dancer's standards, quite inflexible. But I was willing and eager, and worked long hours outside of rehearsals to prepare myself. So, one ineffable night, after innumerable rehearsals and a severely exacting examination of every detail of my costume by the boys, I made my debut.

It was at the Guild Theatre.[14] The program, I remember, consisted of solos and duets by the two stars, some small ensemble works, and the magnum opus of the evening, Humphrey's *Concerto in A Minor*, set to the Grieg Piano Concerto. The smaller things were typical of the Sunday night concerts of that era. They were studies, essays, and experiments for larger, more substantial works to come. I did not understand what I was looking at. All that I remember through the daze was that Miss Humphrey and Mr. Weidman were unbelievable, the girls ravishing, and the boys to be envied with a black, consuming envy. That night I tasted true terror and undreamed of exaltation, humility and triumph. I heard for the first time from the other side of the footlights the thundering applause that is the nectar and ambrosia of gods and artists.

When I wasn't attending to the elevators and the garbage cans, I would be at the studio, early, very early, working on the stubborn body. Power of muscle I had in abundance. It was suppleness that I lacked. I would stretch by the hour in a pool of sweat. Leaning over with legs outspread, I would gaze on my reflection, thinking of Narcissus and his melancholy obsession, and asking myself: "Where are you going, Pepe? What are you doing? How much of this is art and how much exhibitionism and narcissism?" The face below would reply: "This is art. Serious, even tragic art.

Remember Isadora and Kreutzberg. Besides, you are too ugly to be enamored of yourself. Art, the dance, is your only love."

One morning, still in her street clothes, Humphrey looked in. I was puffing, panting, and wringing wet. She smiled and said, "I'm glad to see you working so hard. For a while I had my doubts about you, and was thinking of telling you not to waste your time but to go back to your painting; you'd never make a dancer. Now I think you're going to be one of the world's extraordinary people."

One evening I arrived for class to find the studio in a buzz of excitement. In the men's dressing room the boys gave me the news. Tonight there would be an audition. The famous Norman Bel Geddes and his staff were sitting with Doris and Charles, and they would look at us and select twelve girls and six men to do the dancing in a production of Aristophanes's *Lysistrata*.[15] Panic. I wanted to bolt for the nearest exit, but two boys literally pushed me into the studio. I tried to hide in the back row in the corner. Doris related to me later that when Mr. Bel Geddes saw me, he said to her, "I'll take half-a-dozen like him." She explained that I was a beginner and couldn't really dance yet. But he insisted. Maybe I could carry a spear or something. I was selected.

Rehearsals began. I arrived in work clothes, having just finished wrestling with the furnace and the ash cans at the apartment building where I worked as a janitor. I was horrified when the stage manager ordered me to stand dead center in the large rehearsal hall, handed me a broom handle, and said, "You are the sentry at the gate to the Acropolis. You are leaning on your spear, asleep. The old women of Athens will surprise you, tie you up, and push you down the steps." So, grimy pants and all, I stood mortified beyond words for all the handsomely dressed actors and actresses to gape at. Mr. Bel Geddes was very kind and addressed me in a friendly manner as "José." Six weeks of revelation now began. I saw what it takes to be in the theater, the drudgery, dedication, and professionalism. Mr. Bel Geddes was an impatient man with a violent temper. He would rant and rave if things did not go exactly as he wanted them. Late one night in Philadelphia, at the Walnut Street Theatre during one of the final, murderous dress rehearsals when the director had had more than his usual quota of tantrums, Fay Bainter, the lovely star of the piece, stopped cold, walked to the edge of the platform, and in that beautiful low voice of hers said, "Mr. Bel Geddes, I will absolutely refuse to go on with this play if you do not stop this behavior." He stopped.

Lysistrata, that delectable comedy of the great master of satire, that sly challenge to women they have had neither the courage nor the good sense to accept, was, in the Bel Geddes version, a great success. The production was the brainchild of an elderly gentleman and scholar, Robert Allason Furness, of the distinguished Philadelphia family. Behind him, thanks to his money, was the Philadelphia Theatre Association, which aimed to produce theater classics. *Lysistrata* was expected to last three weeks. Instead, it ran for nine months. Audiences loved it.

After the first three weeks, Fay Bainter had to leave because of other commitments, so Violet Kemble Cooper took over the part of Kalonika. Later, in New York, Blanche Yurka stepped into the role. It was a great education for me to observe these three artists and their style and manner. They spoke the same lines, but the result was totally different. A nuance, an intonation, an inflection, a gesture took on new meaning and coloring. It was the expression of an individual. I learned a valuable lesson, which was to serve me in my own development. The artist is born to be what he will become. He can no more avoid this than he can change the color of his eyes. He can learn his craft, practice its disciplines, and magnify himself, but he will do so in terms of his innate temperament. Aristophanes's heroine was a strong, inspired creature, contending with human fallibility. In Bainter's hands she was all warmth and tender understanding; with Cooper she became a coolly unyielding Englishwoman; with Yurka she was all irony and mockery.

The nine months of the run were a time of excitement, wonder, and learning. Every night, except Sunday, and the two afternoons when there were matinees, I would stand in the wings, entranced, watching the actors onstage. Nothing escaped me, not even the most minute variation from the carefully rehearsed script. I saw the tense and nervous human being waiting to go on, then, through some subtle alchemy, I saw him—or her— metamorphosed into an artist.

During the day, of course, there were classes. We were dancers, after all, and the obligation to the dancer's instrument was ever present. You were free to do what you wanted only after you had paid the price of artistry—rigorous physicality and sweat. Classes with Doris and Charles were always an adventure. Each artist would present us, each day, with a new horizon, a new challenge. They were both in full impetus as innovators. They were cutting themselves off from their past and that of all other dancers in history. That this took audacity of a high order there is no question. They were in quest of their identity. As both explained, when they were young they had studied the traditional disciplines. Later, with Denishawn, they had danced as Hindus, Burmese, Balinese, Japanese, Chinese, Spaniards, and other exotics, but never as they were, two young Americans. Now they were determined to find an American language in the dance. What this was they didn't know, but they aimed to find out. If necessary, they would invent one. This was precisely what was happening in their studio and in other studios in New York City. The great traditional orthodoxy was being questioned, challenged, and rejected. Luthers, Calvins, and Knoxes, they were heretics preaching a new freedom. Truth and salvation lay not in academicism but with individual conscience and interpretation. This ferment, this epidemic, this revolt had to have a name. It got stuck with one that was not only unimaginative but also inaccurate—modern dance. Yet no one has been able to find a better one.

At 9 East Fifty-Ninth Street the quest consisted, besides the production of dances, of devising a new technique for training dancers. All the dogma of the ballet was either rejected out of hand or transformed or adjusted to new urgencies and concepts. The all-important barre was done away with, much as Protestant reformers did away with altars, statues, and crucifixes. The basic barre exercises were performed in the middle of the studio. Stretches were done standing or sitting on the floor. Nobody pointed his toes. The movements of the torso took on a new and crucial importance. Movements of the arms and legs began to be conceived as having their source in the torso. Movement was no longer decorative, but functional. Dance was not something "pretty" or "graceful," nor was it composed of "steps." It had to dig beneath the surface to find beauty, even if this meant it had to be "ugly." The elegant contours of ballet were twisted and distorted. There were no "poses"; instead, there were "patterns," "designs," and movements. Away with the debris of a decadent past: an austere, even stark, simplicity was in order.

To justify their revolutionary fervor and iconoclasm my teachers constantly pointed to the other arts, where an identical revolt had taken place, though much earlier. It was not only illogical but also absurd that dance should remain in the nineteenth century, when Debussy, Cézanne, Schoenberg, Ibsen, and Picasso, to name only a few, had catapulted the other arts into the twentieth. With the firebrand Isadora Duncan as their beacon, American dancers could do no less.

Doris had recently attained a choreographic peak in two much discussed and celebrated works. The first, set to the Grieg Piano Concerto,[16] had clearly shown the hand of a young master with a firm grasp and understanding of form and content. The work had brilliance and poetry. But above all it showed an originality and inventiveness never before seen in her work. Using "pure" movement, she created an atmosphere of drama and excitement that was all the more telling because it was "abstract" and "nonrepresentational." Water Study,[17] which was even more abstract, made human bodies into evocations of natural phenomena. Here, her mastery of the architecture, design, and dynamics of movement, unaided by music or decor, created a hypnotic sort of magic.

For some time Doris had talked about "pure" dance as a phenomenon to be discovered, invented, or both. The degradation of much of the dance that had moved Duncan to rebellion was due to the triviality and banality of its musical accompaniment. Doris railed at what she called the enslavement of dance not only to bad and stupid music but to any music. Her choreographic upbringing had been a conventional one, in which dance "steps" adhered quite literally to the dictates of the music. She was determined to liberate movement from this ancient tyranny. She began by eliminating musical accompaniment altogether. She was not the first dancer to do so. But she was the one to carry out this experiment on works of major proportions. Doris, being who she was, a person of tremendous resolution and determination, produced a formidable succession of works without music, including Color Harmony,[18] Water Study, and Drama of Motion.[19] This predilection for giving movement the freedom necessary to develop on its own terms was applied even to works with music. First, the work was choreographed; then she either found some preexisting music that seemed to suit the idea or invited a composer to view the piece and write a score for it.

Weidman concerned himself during this first period of independence from Denishawn with smaller forms. These were often miniatures—vignettes—and, for the most part, were humorous. He had a natural gift for satire, a capacity to distill the essence of comedy from the human condition. He had the rare genius of the clown, the ability to make the pathetic and ridiculous lovable. He could be subtle and raucous. He was master of the complete spectrum of comedy. On the other hand, he was capable of delicacy and tenderness, as in his portrait of St. Francis of Assisi, and apocalyptic passion, as in his Savonarola vignette.

The two artists would combine their talents and create works in the form of duos. Viewed from the distant shore of today, these dances are still memorable and even now shine with a luminous poignancy, like remembered music or an echo of poetry.

Doris and Charles were, each in his own way, artists of genius. They were favored by nature and circumstance, and they were rich in talent. Denishawn had been a unique and magnificent nursery, primary and secondary school, and university in one. Those formidable beings who were Ruth St. Denis and Ted Shawn had nurtured, instructed, and given them discipline, that priceless ingredient without which there is no artistry. In the theater, when the curtain goes up, you either deliver or you sink into oblivion. For dancers especially, theater is a cruel and merciless discipline, and only the very strong, very talented, and very determined survive it. Doris and Charles went on endless tours with the Denishawn company for more than a decade; they did one-night stands in every state of the Union, in every town that had a railroad stop and a theater; finally, as a climax, they took part in a fabulous tour of the Orient that lasted eighteen months and included China, Japan, Indo-China, Siam, Burma, and India. These experiences molded and tempered them, enriched and readied them for independence.

I knew Charles Weidman for a decade, Doris Humphrey for three, and my wife Pauline Lawrence for even longer—up to the present. They never ceased to speak of their Denishawn experiences. The company left an indelible mark on their lives and their art. Even their rejection of its two masters proved ultimately to be a constructive and not a negative act in their emergence and growth as artists.

151 West Eighteenth Street: The Nursery

Parent birds, obeying a primordial imperative, eject their fledglings when they begin to crowd the womblike nest that can no longer contain them. At a formal meeting of their faculty and staff, St. Denis and Shawn expelled Doris, Charles, and Pauline from Denishawn. Their crimes were heresy and insubordination: heresy against the artistic credo of Denishawn, insubordination to its hegemony. The three had become malcontents and were beginning to indulge in artistic practices of a highly questionable character. This could not be tolerated, for it did violence to all that the prestigious house of Denishawn represented.

The newly emancipated trio reveled in the exhilarating challenge of independence. They found a new home, a studio at 9 East Fifty-Ninth Street, where they tasted the first raptures of flight. They laid claim to the domain of art and proceeded to grow and flourish. But the crude realities of real estate and landlords had to be confronted. The location, ideal from many standpoints, was an exhausting drain on energies and exchequers. Endless hours of teaching had to be done, with Doris and Charles demonstrating, exhorting, pushing, and poking, and Pauline at the piano accompanying them—all this to pay what was even then a high rental, when what they most wanted to do was to dance, explore, and experiment. There was only one alternative: a cheap, roomy loft in an unfashionable manufacturing district. After much searching, Doris, who had the talent and tenacity for such things, found 151 West Eighteenth Street. A new hard maple floor was laid; the brick walls and raftered ceiling were whitewashed, and a phonograph, percussion instruments, and a memorable grand piano moved in. The former machine shop was now a temple of Terpsichore.

The neighborhood was dingy, noisy, and untidy, filled with warehouses, garages, and manufacturing establishments. Eighteenth Street was always choked with mammoth trucks, loading and unloading, and their accompanying debris. But once you climbed the inelegant staircase to the third floor you entered another world, the enchanted precincts of art. The rent was very cheap. It gave Doris and Charles the freedom they needed to devote themselves to creativity. They held the minimum of classes necessary to make a living and pay the rent for the studio and their respective domiciles. They worked harder than any beaver would think possible. There were classes and rehearsals in the mornings, afternoons, and evenings. Life outside the studio had no reality. Pauline devoted herself to

the practical side of the enterprise. She was business manager, bookkeep
building superintendent, impresario, costume designer, seamstress, a
accompanist for classes and performances—on the piano, at the acco
dion, with percussion instruments, including the tissue-covered com
used in *Life of the Bee*.[20]

Lysistrata, like all things mortal, came to an end, and I returned
doing what many young dancers did for a livelihood, posing for painte
and sculptors. This had its advantages. You could work part-time a
have most of the day for classes and rehearsals. Living became very si
ple. You lodged in a tiny room, just big enough for a narrow cot, a dress
a small table, and a chair. You paid three dollars a week rent. You ma
some hot cereal in the morning on an electric hot plate. For lunch a
dinner you had a couple of buns and some slices of bologna or liverwur
No tea. No coffee. No cigarettes. No liquor. No frills. Life was spartan.

At the studio there was always an almost unbearable excitement. Do
and Charles put me into their new works, for by now I had become mo
proficient. The two masters knew how to use their instruments, and I w
used effectively. Weidman put us all into his new ballet, *The Happy Hy,
ocrite*.[21] This delightful work had a bright and witty score by Herbe
Elwell. Max Beerbohm's charming fable, which dealt with the dissolu
George Hell, redeemed by the love of a pure maiden and transformed in
Lord George Heaven, was made to order for Weidman. He was incred
ble. Not only was his choreography for the other characters outrageous
funny, but the sheer virtuosity of his own performance as the sybarit
lecher turned, quite unintentionally, into a saint, was a high point in h
career. Here, for the first time in an extended humorous form, were all tl
innovations of the non-balletic trend in the American dance. *The Happ
Hypocrite* was superb comic theater in high style.

I was also put into his graphic vignette *Ringside*[22] opposite Charl
Laskey, an accomplished young dancer. This striking little ballet abo
pugilistic doings, ending in a fast knockout, taught me a great deal. F
the first time I was given the responsibility of a soloist. I was in no sense
finished dancer. It was Weidman's skill as a choreographer and showm
that enabled him to put me in a role where a certain crudity, heavy muscu
larity, and the look of a "pug" were in order. I fulfilled the requiremen
and *Ringside* was a success.

Weidman's trio *Steel and Stone*[23] utilized himself, Laskey, and me. Tl
score was by Henry Cowell. This was an "abstraction" having to do wit
the bones and sinews of our metropolis, and its insatiable thrust upwar
not to scrape, but to wound the firmament. Mr. Cowell, a dear sou
would come to morning rehearsals and make notes of counts and phra:
lengths. We labored nightly to learn the movements Weidman had devise
for us. I watched with fascination the process of choreographic creativit
and invention. Why this movement but that gesture? Why was the ar
here and the leg there? Why this formation, juxtaposition, balance, asyn
metry? Why this or that accent, this or that turn or jump? Why was th

slow and that fast? I saw Weidman wrestle with the problems of commu-
nication, form, and style. He had good days and bad ones. *Steel and
Stone*: even the title sounds naive and dated now, but in its day it was a
significant link with the future that is our present. What we are now is
only because of what there was then.

Doris was working on *The Dance of the Chosen*, which, when finished, was retitled *The Shakers*.[24] This had to do with the pious frenzies
practiced by that curious nineteenth-century Calvinist sect known as the
Shakers. The Shakers practiced in acute form the spiritual aberrations of
the Puritan recrudescence. Pauline philosophy, adopted and perpetrated
by the early fathers of the church, found a new impetus when transplant-
ed to the English colonies. The Shaker dictum, "My carnal life I will lay
down, because it is depraved," was the motif of the piece. Doris set the
work in a Shaker meeting. There were six men, six women, and the
Eldress. In the first edition of the piece, six of Doris's girls, dressed in
long, black Hasidic-looking coats and flat hats, took the men's parts. The
"men" and women were strictly segregated, each to one side of an imaginary and impassable barrier. The Eldress sat upstage center on a crude
bench. To the offstage chanting of a female voice (Pauline Lawrence)
accompanied by a reed organ, the kneeling congregation swayed with a
slow, devout intensity. There were sudden violent spurts, a gathering hys-
teria, and frenzy. Men traced mystical symbols in the empty air. Women
saw celestial visions. The sacred dance proceeded in lines and circles, gathering impetus. With a shocking suddenness there was an interruption. A
man's voice, charged with delirium, announced, "My carnal life I will lay
down, because it is depraved." The dance resumed its pulsating course,
the gestures and configurations now more extreme, more violent. The
Eldress (Doris), who until then had maintained a trancelike stillness,
stood up on the bench and in an eerie yet jubilant voice proclaimed, "It
hath been revealed ye shall be saved when ye are shaken free of sin."
Almost like an automaton she began, very slowly at first, then gradually
accelerating, a movement, crude and possessed, where the body in its
entirety was stretched upward with a shuddering tautness, from which it
fell forward and backward, passing through the tormented vertical in
transit. This was the movement on which the rest of the ballet was based.

Doris, like all great composers, was first and foremost a formalist. To
her the equilibrium between content and form was the basis for all composition. She did not just string movements together. She created or
selected a theme, and with the utmost logic and inventiveness would pro-
ceed to develop it. In this case she used certain basic ideas that she was
then exploring, such as the "fall," "rebound," and "suspension" of the
body's weight. From this point to the end of the work she displayed an
astonishing virtuosity of choreographic invention. The work drove
implacably to its dramatic conclusion. There was a rhythmic canon that I
have never seen equaled. The convulsive shudders and shakes, intended to
rid the body of its sinfulness, made a formidable contrapuntal architec-

ture. The components of "pure dance"—movement, rhythm, dynamic form, and style—were fused into an overwhelming dramatic experience Flawless in concept and construction, this work was a milestone in the development and progress of the American dance.

Needless to say I watched every performance. Later, Weidman and five men—Bill Bales,[25] Lee Sherman,[26] Kenneth Bostock,[27] Bill Matons,[28] and myself—replaced the girls. I believe this strengthened the work. I found performing *The Shakers* a deeply moving experience. It was a tough demanding assignment. It has influenced me in an infinite number of ways, both as a performer and as a choreographer. It helped to mold me and led me always to seek an impassioned formalism. I have repeatedly over the decades, tried to achieve the compelling dramatic power of Doris's abstractions and failed. I have found myself imitating or plagiarizing her. I lack her artistic stature. I am highly talented. Doris was a genius.

* * *

Another work that was first composed by Doris with six of her girls taking the roles of men and another six those of women was *La Valse*, which was set to Ravel.[29] An earlier work than *The Shakers*, it was enchanting and romantic, as befitted the lovely music. And just as Ravel had used the traditional waltz as a point of departure for the creation of new sounds new rhythms, and new delights, so Doris found and added a fresh aspect to the beguiling dance.

Pauline costumed the work with her usual taste and sophistication She set it in the late Directory period. The "men" wore black velvet jackets, white tights, and cravats up to their chins; the ladies, sleeveless black satin bodices and graceful gauzy skirts. The effect was severely elegant Doris was a fantastic apparition in a pink organdy gown with a long train the manipulating of which, during the complex and difficult configurations, was a miracle of dexterity.

There were many waltzes, all reflecting the music— light ones, elegant ones, languorous, romantic, and aristocratic ones, pompous and sinister ones. Charles and Doris, a dazzling couple, were the protagonists of mysterious, enigmatic drama, in which the ensemble participated as audience, conspirators, and manipulators. At the last moment, the two extricated themselves from the orgiastic chaos that threatened to engulf them recovering their aristocratic *hauteur* just as the curtain fell. Doris had trained a group of girls who were a wonder to behold. Some, of course were more gifted than others. But you had to be very good to meet her standards. I remember Eleanor King,[30] Cleo Atheneos,[31] Sylvia Manning,[32] Celia Rauch,[33] Katherine Manning,[34] Virginia Landreth,[35] Dorothy Lathrop,[36] Rose Crystal,[37] Rose Yasgour,[38] Letitia Ide,[39] and Ernestine Henoch[40]—later known as Stodelle—during this period.

Doris's *Drama of Motion*, another work done entirely without music was in sonata style, with three movements—an opening formal andante, a middle largo, and a spirited finale. Here, uninhibited by musical accompa niment, she created visual music from pure motion. All her past themes and ideas were present—fall and suspension; the breath phrase, a movement motivated by the length of a breath and having the legato quality of breathing; the kinesthetic and the muscular phrase, which, unlike the chronometric or musical phrase, were predicated on the intrinsic properties of movement. The result was a dance that stood complete and convincing on its own merits without the traditional support of music.

* * *

Her predilection for the abstract led to bold innovations in movement. She composed a solo to piano music of Schoenberg that she called *Descent Into a Dangerous Place*.[41] It was a distillation of dissonance, asymmetry, and distortion, the vision of a creature of ambiguous species, half-bird, half-insect, bent on an enigmatic errand, alert to unseen menaces and dangers. Doris's body, lithe and powerful, performed prodigies of evocative gesture. It leapt, crouched, quivered, whirled, and held itself poised in the most exquisite and precarious equilibrium on the brink of an imaginary abyss.

This solo was related to a larger work of the period, *Life of the Bee*, which derived from Maeterlinck's study. This was a grotesque insect ritual set in the hive; a nascent queen emerges, is nurtured by her subjects, develops, matures, and begins her rule. Presently, an older, strange queen appears to challenge her hegemony. A duel is fought. The challenger kills the legitimate queen and assumes command of the swarm.

This work was an example of Doris's meticulous and precise choreographic thinking. The entire pattern and sequence of the ballet was an uncanny evocation of the rigidly ordered apiarian society. The contest between the two rivals, the older one danced by her and the younger one by Cleo Atheneos, was a piece of spectacular ritualized malevolence. With this opus Doris gave the dancer's instrument an astounding new range of expressive power and added to the fund of choreographic knowledge and experience from which future dance artists, including myself, were to benefit.

Pauline's insect-like costumes, in metallic gold and silver and velvety brown and black, enhanced the highly theatrical representation. This most versatile and talented of collaborators also devised a means of creating a curiously appropriate sound accompaniment for the ballet. A comb, covered with a layer of tissue paper, was held to the lips and "played," producing a sound that was very close to the buzzing of a beehive. Everyone backstage was recruited for this task. One buzzed and hummed, sometimes "ad lib," sometimes in tempo with the insect-like movements. Thus, one learned about order and discipline, the ways and means of mastery, and the alchemy of creative transformation—how arms can be made to say "wings, transparent, powerful wings"; how a human head can be turned, inclined, poised, jerked, lowered, and lifted to convey the imperious, implacable character of an insect monarch; how a human biped can be made to represent a six-legged insect; how twelve dancers can be deployed to suggest a swarm of thousands; how the human torso can be flexed and articulated to evoke unknown and unknowable insect passions; finally, how the human hand can be transformed into a deadly sting.

There was a charming solo that Doris danced to a gigue from one of the Bach suites for clavichord. The music, in the master's most delectable vein, seemed to call for fleet, airy suspensions and leaps or twirlings in a seemingly endless tarantella. This Doris did, dressed in a short crimson tunic. Her enchanting legs, as long and slim as a boy's, appeared to lift her without effort through space. Then, she would stop and, abandoning herself to another intoxication, pivot swiftly, seemingly forever, on one foot, while the rest of her body— torso, arms, and free leg—described a dazzling sequence of spiral patterns.

Was it Benjamin Franklin, that sagacious and witty man, who, on signing the Declaration of Independence that hot July day in 1776, admonished his colleagues that they had better hang together lest they all hang separately? Equally intransigent and rebellious, the American dancers who were their descendants appeared to be moved by this same Franklinian impulse toward solidarity and union, even as they declared their independence from the traditions of Europe.

Martha Graham, Doris Humphrey, Charles Weidman, Helen Tamiris, and Agnes de Mille formed what was called the Dance Repertory Theatre. Sharing expenses, responsibilities, and programs, they hired a theater and presented a season. Two seasons, in fact.[42]

A good precedent existed in Irene Lewisohn's productions.[43] A member of a cultured, prestigious, and wealthy family, Miss Lewisohn subsidized over the years a number of works that used personnel from the dance department of the Neighborhood Playhouse, her main concern, along with distinguished soloists. These independent artists, although deeply individualistic, would work together more or less amicably under Miss Lewisohn's aegis with good results. Although I never saw them, I heard Doris, Charles, and Pauline discuss the productions of Richard Strauss's *Ein Heldenleben*,[44] where Graham and Weidman performed together brilliantly, and Schoenberg's *Die Glückliche Hand*,[45] where Doris and Charles, also with great success, interpreted the leading roles. These were the legends told by my colleagues in the dressing rooms at the studio.

In February 1931 I found myself, dizzy with excitement, involved in preparations for the second season of the Dance Repertory Theatre. We rehearsed mightily, of course. Weidman was putting the finishing touches to *The Happy Hypocrite*. The enchanting Letitia Ide was to dance opposite him as the innocent Jenny Mere. Eleanor King, a gifted actress, was to dance the role of the mysterious mask maker, who at the elegant orgy hosted by Lord George Hell and his wanton Paramour La Gambogi, played delectably by Cleo Atheneos, was to change milord's entire nature by asking him to wear the mask of a saint. There was a dwarf, who was also a cupid, danced with brilliance and wit by Sylvia Manning, one of the most talented Humphrey-Weidman dancers.

Doris had just finished *Dances of Women*, which had a score by Dane Rudhyar and presaged a new direction in her work.[46] Here I saw a different Doris. The poetic lyricism of the Grieg *Concerto in A Minor* and her duets with Weidman, and the eerie stylizations of *Life of the Bee* and *Descent into a Dangerous Place*, were giving place to the vision of a strong, heroic woman. In her newest work, the expression of emotion was no longer neoromantic, but contemporary, actual, and immediate. Here was a declaration about woman and her place in our society and in our time. The work, in what was obviously an exploratory and as yet unfamiliar idiom, was not a success, although it contained the seeds of a great flowering to come.

My role in this work was minuscule but fraught with responsibility. There was a box, placed upstage center, on which Doris stood during her first long solos. The box was an unsteady affair, and since Doris, perched precariously on top of it, had some rather active dancing to do, and since stage weights did not provide the necessary stability, I was recruited to sit inside the box and hold it steady. Over the next decade I would support Doris in a succession of works, and this was a good beginning.

My horizons extended themselves immeasurably. At the Craig, now Adelphi Theatre (where the Dance Repertory season took place), the upstairs dressing room was assigned to Charles Laskey, me, and an imposing gentleman named Louis Horst, an orchestra conductor and piano accompanist to Martha Graham and the other artists participating in the season.

Laskey, a splendidly proportioned young man, had been a weight lifter and was proud to have been named "the American Apollo" in a contest held by a journal devoted to the exaltation of muscularity. I was a fresh young athlete from the Golden West. Both of us were awed by the portly Mr. Horst, who was a man in his forties at the time. How anyone could be that ancient was beyond our comprehension. We spent hours putting on makeup and discussing ways of improving it, sometimes rubbing everything off and starting all over again. All this was deadly serious business. Mr. Horst would look up from his scores with amusement and make a wry comment or two. Presently, he would begin to change into his tux and tails. This being February, it was cold backstage at the Craig Theatre. Horst, being a sensible man, would wear a thick, one-piece woolen union suit that gave him the appearance of a huge blonde bear. We could hardly believe our eyes. On the street we, with the bravado of youth, wore a minuscule pair of underdrawers and no hat, even in a blizzard. We would lace up his corset, help him with his cuff links and studs, brush his elegant coat, admire his truly distinguished presence, and continue our own preparations.

From the wings I would watch Helen Tamiris. This superb creature, by turns Amazon, earth mother, celebrant of the Negro's joys and miseries, and devotee of Walt Whitman, was one of the most robustly alive human beings ever created. Her uncomplicated art had élan, openness, and compassion. Her dancing was an ode to life.

Agnes de Mille was a young dancer, as fresh and pink as the tropical lilies I remember on dewy mornings in my native land. I had never seen such a flawless complexion. She was no end baffling. Although surrounded by dancers who were barefoot and costumed with stark simplicity, she appeared in the full panoply of elegance. While her older colleagues were intent on discarding the past, she seemed to be holding it gently, tenderly, even protectively sometimes, in the voluminous folds of her skirts, petticoats, and tutus. The past was not dead, her dances seemed to say, only somnolent. It would awaken presently, refreshed and renewed.

My first sight of Martha Graham was from the darkened wings of the Craig Theatre. I watched her spellbound dancing a solo—a dark woman, standing on a small pedestal, dressed in blood-red, addressing the universe, arms raised to the zenith. At the end of the solo came numerous curtain calls. She passed me breathless on her way to the dressing room. Presently, the stage manager came and told me that Miss Graham would not tolerate being watched from the wings. I slunk away. For years she remained a distant planet, forbidding and forbidden.

In the merciless cold of the streets, ragged, hungry men huddled together in dumb desperation. Some lined up waiting for bread and soup and a night's lodging. Some sought refuge in the recesses of doorways and covered their misery with newspapers. These were the great horde of the unemployed, victims of a catastrophic failure of the economic machinery. The president, Herbert Hoover, appeared unable or unwilling to do much that was effective, and the sick economy grew progressively worse.

The intelligentsia rose in rebellion against the seeming callousness and indifference. Writers, poets, playwrights, painters, and dancers, in furious protest and in defense and support of the disinherited, began a new era in the history of the American arts. For most of the decade books, poems, plays, paintings, and dances were concerned with the hungry and the dispossessed. There was anger, protest, and compassion.

At the studio we knew that the malady afflicting the outside world would in time invade our sanctuary. The crude reality could not for long be excluded. Art would go on, but it would have to confront the desperation rampant in the city, in the nation, in the world.

And so, very gradually, Doris and Charles reacted, each in his own way, to the historic pressure.

With the Dance Repertory season behind us, we small fry returned to our private problems. I ran around posing for artists to earn a living. Once more, classes became paramount. And, having seen dances being composed, performed, and wildly applauded, I burned with desire to try my hand at the art of choreography.

I had started in the basement of the apartment house where I ran the elevator. I cleared a space next to the furnace. Then, late at night, after most of the tenants had been delivered to their respective floors and I had collected the garbage, emptied the ashes from the furnace and banked it for the night, and neatly lined up the ash cans on the sidewalk, I would descend to my domain, wind the tiny, tinny portable phonograph, and start. Filling the empty space with movement was not as simple as emptying it. There you are, alone, facing your adversary, emptiness. The weapons you have brought to this duel are your body, which has been disciplined to be strong, supple, and resilient, to move beyond ordinary human capacities and limitations; your total sensibility; an idea; and above all, an indomitable determination.

The attempt to fill the vast, eternal emptiness of space and time is indeed an act of arrogance and presumption. I didn't know this, and being young, I didn't know I didn't know it. All I knew was that I wanted to put movements together, to make a dance. I have no idea what went on in that dimly lit cellar. I moved. I sweated. Nothing, absolutely nothing came out of that furnace room, except for great frustration and determination.

After *Lysistrata* and Dance Repertory Theatre I was better equipped. Certainly, when inspiration and creativity failed, I could plagiarize both my teachers. But this was always the very last resort, since I knew they would disapprove.

I had my eye on some of Doris's girls. They were the ones I considered the most beautiful and the best dancers. Their names were Letitia Ide, Eleanor King, and Ernestine Henoch. We formed a small company and christened it "The Little Group," and with me as choreographer began to create and rehearse a repertory of dances. I was ambitious, aggressive, and indefatigable. With Letitia I composed a duet to an étude of Scriabin; with Eleanor another duet to a mazurka by the same composer; with Ernestine a dance with a Latin American flavor done to percussion that we called *Tango*; with all three girls a dance to Debussy's *Cortège*, a *Bacchanale* to percussion, and a dance to Medtner's *Marche Funèbre*; and a solo for myself, *Two Preludes*, to music of Reginald de Koven.[47]

This prodigious outpouring, all within a few months, was possible only because I drove the girls and myself with merciless determination. We rehearsed night and day, improvised simple costumes, and made our debut at the studio before an audience made up of our teachers, our colleagues and a few outside friends and acquaintances. It was a sensation.

I look at the creative efforts of our young students at Juilliard and remember my own first efforts thirty-five years ago. These, in retrospect, seem very simple and naive by comparison to the much more knowing and complex dances of today's young people. But those callow profusions of mine had one quality in their favor, the youth and radiance of the performers. Very few women have been as beautiful as these three colleagues of mine. Letitia Ide, Eleanor King, and Ernestine Henoch were true and natural beauties. As dancers they were far superior to me, having begun their training much earlier than I had. Of the three, Eleanor would presently emerge as a choreographer of considerable gifts. Ernestine also composed some lovely dances. Letitia alone was content to remain a performer, with no disturbing ambitions to compose. All three were superb performers.

For me performing was a species of agony. By nature I am shy, and by inheritance and family upbringing reticent and formal. In my "prenatal" period, that is, before Kreutzberg and Duncan entered my life, the very idea of exchanging my conventional male attire for a dancer's costume, painting my face, and prancing around in public would have killed me with shame. *Vergüenza*—shame in my native tongue—is a potent word for the dignified reserve that is a man's most essential attribute. I was brought up to be *un hombre formal*, and now I was dedicated to a life that, in terms of my early upbringing, was that of a *sinvergüenza*, someone lacking in shame. Bringing those strong, divergent currents—my painful self-consciousness and my irresistible urge to be a dancer—to a confluence was a torment that before every performance would become a crisis. I am certain that the reason why Doris's works were more consonant with my natural bent and ability was her essentially formal outlook and style. I was never any good in Charles's comedies.

Our little studio performances were such a success that we were asked to repeat them. Presently, we were invited to perform in all sorts of places, such as the Henry Street Playhouse, the auditorium of St. Bartholomew's Church, the Brooklyn Ethical Culture School, settlement houses in Harlem, and a summer arts center in Connecticut. We went anywhere that would have us. We even danced on the minuscule stage of the Provincetown Playhouse, cradle of Eugene O'Neill and other American playwrights. To me it was some sort of miracle that our dances elicited an enthusiastic and, at times, even noisy response. It was even more unbelievable that my solo dances, to two trashy piano pieces by Reginald de Koven, would invariably bring down the house. I have since found the explanation; nothing is so electrifying as the magical freshness and beauty of youth, especially when it has talent.

* * *

Miss Irene Weir was a lady painter, upper-class and well-connected, the niece of the Victorian painter J. Alden Weir.[48] When I knew her, she in her late sixties, the head of an *atelier* on the top floor of one of those handsome, now vanished brownstones on Central Park South. She called her establishment the New York School of Design. It was bohemian in a very well-bred, genteel way. Young ladies from good families came to paint still lifes and draw from live models. I was one of these last. Miss Weir took a maternal interest in me and decided, good high church Anglican that she was, to redeem me and bring me back to the Church, this time not the errant one of Rome, but the right one. Over tea and cookies, we would have some good-natured discussions and arguments. I believe she would have been perfectly happy to be a Catholic if it hadn't been for such nuisances as the Pope and the existence of Irish, Italian, and Polish

Catholics. Miss Weir lived in the Italian Renaissance. Florence, Ravenna, Siena, and Rome were her spiritual habitats, as they had been the physical ones of her youth. She repeatedly urged me to accompany her to services at St. Bartholomew's Church on Park Avenue. I had sworn in Los Angeles never to be caught dead inside a church again. I was a crudely positive atheist, and the idea of God revolted me. However, I liked Miss Weir, and to please her, I went.

I was prepared for the sumptuousness of the cathedral. But the expensively elegant congregation and the unctuous platitudes of the sermon I found repellent, a vicious parody of the Christian spirit, especially since only a few blocks away there was hunger, misery, and neglect. I was thinking of some pretext to escape this odious place when the organ began. It was music I had never heard before. The church was flooded by a compelling and serene majesty. I tensed, breathless, as it went from peak to peak, mounting finally to an unbearably poignant summit, from which a mighty torrent of voices proclaimed the greatness of the human spirit. This was the opening of the Passion of St. Matthew. Forgetting my mother's admonition that "Men don't cry," I wept, silently I think, all through the ineffable oratorio. I wept with rapture and anguish, with the unendurable pain that only beauty inflicts. To Miss Weir, handmaiden of art and pious, proper spinster, I will be forever grateful for this first encounter with that voice of God, Johann Sebastian Bach.

* * *

Miss Irene Lewisohn's limousine would deposit her elegant person, covered in sumptuous furs, on the littered sidewalk. Her chauffeur, loaded down with a large picnic basket, would follow her up the dingy stairs to the studio. There, in practice clothes, "warmed up" and ready to work, Doris and Charles awaited her. She would sit; the chauffeur would open the hamper, hand her a fine damask napkin, and serve her lunch, while she directed or supervised the rehearsal. The work was to be part of one of her productions, and preparations went on for weeks.

The program was given out of town, in Washington, D.C., I believe, and then at the Kaufmann Auditorium of the YM-YWHA at Ninety-Second Street and Lexington Avenue, for several performances. I sat in the back row of the balcony, in the cheapest seats available, with Eleanor King. The first work of the evening was danced to Provençal madrigals, sung by Nina Koshetz. Charles Weidman, Blanche Talmud,[49] and some of the other girls from the Neighborhood Playhouse were revealed as figures in a medieval tapestry; they became animated, danced in a way that reflected the spirit and text of the songs, and at the end returned to their tapestry. The effect was charming. Next came a work with Benjamin Zemach, assisted by an ensemble of Playhouse dancers, to Bach's Toccata and Fugue in D Minor. This was quite imposing. Zemach, an intensely dramatic figure, evoked an impassioned prophet from the scriptures.

The major item of the evening was danced to a beautiful string quartet of Ernest Bloch.[50] This was the work that Miss Lewisohn had supervised at 151 West Eighteenth Street. It was a dramatic work, and she had devised the themes. Simply stated, the plot concerned a woman, Doris Humphrey, lost in a strange and forbidding landscape represented by an arrangement of steps and platforms that gradually ascended to the rim of a yawning crater. (From the back row of the balcony, we could look down into its black depths.) A chorus of robot-like dancers, representing the protagonist's confusions, frustrations, and torments, sought to draw her into the abyss. Charles appeared, and, together, they found the courage and the unity to triumph over the darkness of the pit. The work was probably autobiographical, a Freudian account of Miss Lewisohn's own dilemma and salvation, although it certainly could apply to anyone's experience. It was a stunning and strangely moving ballet.

What does the soul look like? What is the shape of the psyche? To the Hellenes it was a beautiful young woman, whose inquisitiveness drove away Cupid—Eros. Here, in *Bloch String Quartet*, costumed in a simple clinging sheath the color of pale fire, Doris symbolized this entity that animates our existence. The strange shadowy world was the subconscious, and the other dancers were the fears and menaces that haunt the dark recesses of the spirit. Her dancing reached a pinnacle here. She moved with a tremendously evocative eloquence and power. She explored regions up to then unknown in the technique of the dance. I believe that at this point her artistry arrived at a summation of all previous achievements. She attained a mastery of expressive power by means of a nonrepresentational spectrum of movement and gesture.

There were two facets to Charles's talent. He was peerless as a comedian. His comic genius, completely spontaneous and instinctive, had a flavor, precision, and subtlety unmatched by anyone, anywhere, in his time. By comparison Chaplin seemed obvious and puerile. (I say this as a staunch admirer of Chaplin from my earliest years to the present.) As a serio-dramatic performer, Charles was also impressive. He partnered Doris over the years of their association in a series of duets that had poetic depth and formal distinction. In the *Bloch String Quartet* he was fully a match for her. Their passages together were things of rare beauty. There was a power, a simplicity, and a nobility to his gesture and demeanor that had a profound effect on my own subsequent development.

This serious side of his led to a significant trend. He was always interested in the intrinsic abilities of the male dancer, and devoted much thought and time to devising a syllabus of technical studies quite distinct from that for women. He taught classes composed entirely of men where the emphasis was distinctively masculine. The entire vocabulary of the dance came under a close scrutiny in terms of what men could or could not do. Certain things were obvious: the male anatomy, because of its basic structure, had advantages and limitations. It was muscularly more powerful than the female; it could jump higher, but its leg extensions, because of a narrower pelvis, were more limited. The quality of its movement could be heavy, massive, and monumental, in contrast to the softness and delicacy of the female. The sexual differences must be observed and emphasized, as in the art of singing, with its separation of male from female voices.

At the studio there was much concern with the weight and substance of the body. Both our teachers abandoned the traditional concept that the body had to appear free of all gravitational pull and movement devoid of all effort. The weight of the body should be recognized and exploited. Its muscular effort was beautiful and should be revealed. Elevation, soaring into the air, would in consequence have more drama, more meaning. It would become a triumph, a conquest. As the decade advanced, moreover, the sobering effect of the economic debacle would encompass the dance. Dances became more and more serious, more concerned with the human condition, which was far from happy. This, I believe, led to a technique of dance, a language really, that could deal with austerities and the dilemma that surrounded us.

* * *

Doris Humphrey, temporarily weary of effort and accomplishment, went off on a vacation to the West Indies, and returned, rested and restored, with a suitor. Captain Charles F. Woodford, an Englishman, second officer on the Furness Line cruise ship "Dominica," was a quiet reserved man. His career was the sea, but we became accustomed to his periodic visits at the studio to watch rehearsals when his ship was in port. Before we knew it, there was a wedding, and in due course Doris announced that she was with child. But many classes, rehearsals, and dances were to precede the *accouchement*.

At this time she was creating *Dionysiaques* to music of Florent Schmitt.[51] It was Doris's habit to approach each new idea with as few preconceptions as possible. She maintained that a new work must create its own distinctive spectrum and style of movement. For weeks she experimented, explored, and probed. The work was to evoke ancient Crete. It was to be a ritual of sacrifice. A chosen victim was to be honored at the rite, which would end with the act of sacrifice, an orgy, and catharsis.

It was presented at a Sunday concert at the Guild Theatre. The curtain rose to reveal a stunning vision. There was much applause. A long procession, in attitudes of arrested movement, stood before the audience—two male figures, Gene Martel[52] and myself, half-escorts, half-guards of the victim; Doris, the victim, followed by the celebrants. Slow and solemn, the procession made a wide curve around the stage to the place of sacrifice. Doris devised some stunning archaic effects for this procession. The costumes designed by Pauline, inspired by the friezes at Knossus, were among her most effective. They were painted by hand in bold horizontal stripes. I remember Pauline and volunteer helpers spreading the cloth over the entire floor of the studio after rehearsals and, armed with pots of paint and brushes, working far into the night. The entire color scheme was in blues, from vivid turquoise to deep cobalt and ultramarine. Doris was in white and gold. With her red-gold hair in a golden net, she was a breathtaking vision.

The Chosen One danced a dedicatory dance. This was one of those extraordinary passages that Doris could create for herself. With its strange, convulsive, quivering movements of arms, shoulders, and torso, the dance was an exalted frenzy, compounded of joy and terror. There were wild abandoned leaps, ending in astounding backward falls to the floor, from which the body would rebound in some incredible fashion and stand on tiptoe, in breathless attenuation, seemingly for an eternity. Turns, drunken and possessed, would end with the weight balanced on one foot, while the other would extend to the side at a high, oblique angle, and from this precarious balance the torso would fall sideways to the floor and rebound instantly, with the extended leg undisturbed.

The celebrants, witnesses of this sacred abandon, enticed the victim to greater and greater excesses. With the two sacerdotal figures lending her support, the ritual grew more convulsive, more abandoned. Never once, however, did it overflow the carefully prescribed stylistic boundaries Doris had set. The celebrants joined the ritual, which reached its climax when Doris ran up my leg to my shoulders, stood poised and trembling, then fell forward in one piece into an abyss formed by a ring of the girls, where Gene, concealed by them from the audience, would catch her before she struck the floor. A funeral orgy followed. As the two men, in slow, solemn procession, carried the inert body of the sacrificed victim over their heads, the celebrants purged themselves with Dionysian abandon. This was a formidable coda to the work. With uncanny kinesthetic insight, Doris created formal chaos, using wild dissonant movements, explosive distortions, and rigid, stamping vibrations to evoke a primeval female rite.

Weidman, meanwhile, using Sylvia Manning, Cleo Atheneos, and myself, worked on two pieces to some witty and charming music of the Italian composer Riccardo Pick-Mangiagalli. The first was *The Little Soldiers*,[53] a quick, light, bouncy piece, with overtones of humor, full of delightful invention. This I was happy to do, for I needed to counteract my natural tendency, which was over-serious and often pretentious beyond my experience and ability. The second, *Nocturne*,[54] was full of mysterious, opaque imagery, slow and sustained, of a dreamlike, almost submarine beauty. Both works proved very successful and remained in the company repertory for years.

Doris and Charles were whistling in the dark, so to speak, to keep up their spirits and courage. Things were going from bad to worse in the country. The unreal world of politics, senseless and strident, would impinge crudely on our minuscule universe. One day we learned that a certain Franklin Delano Roosevelt, of whom we had been vaguely aware as a remote figure in a place called Albany, where he was governor of New York State, had supplanted the ineffectual Mr. Hoover and was now president of the United States. So removed, so isolated, so ignorant were we when it came to anything that did not concern our obsessive preoccupation with dance!

This innocence was not to last much longer. There was widespread deprivation, hunger, misery, and protest. The wolf, raging and slavering, was at the door, making ready to lope up the stairs of many homes in America, including ours on Eighteenth Street. Most of the girls in the company came from comfortable middle-class families and were immune to the contagion of poverty. But others were not so fortunate. Those who were on their own, who had to work as salesgirls or waitresses or at odd jobs, felt the pinch, as did the young men.

It was at this point that the writer J.P. McEvoy, whose musical revue, *Americana*, was being produced by the Shuberts, persuaded the producers to engage the Humphrey-Weidman company to perform some of their concert pieces intact, as part of the show. There were many visits to the studio by McEvoy, an earnest, affable man and a humanist, and the producers, composers, and staff, many whispered conferences with Doris and Charles, and presently we were in rehearsal for a Broadway musical. It was agreed that *The Shakers, Water Study, The Little Soldiers*, and *Ringside* would fit nicely into the production. Doris chose not to appear personally. Charles would; moreover, he was to create several original production numbers for the show.

Opening night at the Shubert Theatre on Forty-Fourth Street was a sensation.[55] *Americana* had for its theme the Depression that was afflicting the land, treated with irony and compassionate humor. McEvoy had written an unusually adult show, and the miracle was that it was such a great success. The dances, especially, excited comment. For the first time the New Dance was introduced into the commercial theater, a prophetic and auspicious event that was to lead to a fecund association over the next decades. Charles, in particular, was to function successfully in the Broadway arena, presaging the later success of Hanya Holm, Helen Tamiris, Agnes de Mille, and Jerome Robbins.

Charles had been planning a production of Voltaire's *Candide*.[56] He had been literally living, sleeping, and eating with the book and had finally written a choreographic adaptation of it, a plan for work. He assembled his cast, which was to include all of Doris's girls and every man around the studio who could stand on two legs without falling over. We rehearsed for months. Charles was to dance the role of the ingenuous youth; Eleanor King would be Cunégonde and Bill Matons would play Dr. Pangloss. I would be a sort of Voltairean master of ceremonies and do other roles.

Charles was superb as the much abused, much tried youth, who ran afoul of the iniquities, injustices, depravities, and inhumanities of the eighteenth century. He captured with great sensitiveness the pathos and naive charm of Voltaire's hero. Eleanor was lovely as the willing accomplice in Candide's loss of innocence. All of us gave it everything we had. The girls were lovely and worked like demons. The men did all the dirty work prescribed by Mr. Voltaire, all the marching, parading, slaughtering, raping, and pillaging, all the depredations of a chaotic century.

Mr. Michael Myerberg, a young man from Baltimore who had helped with the managerial end of *Americana*, was a person of sensibility, with a respect and appreciation for art and artists. To him the artistic incentive meant something; it was a phenomenon not only to be admired, but also to be helped and encouraged. He somehow talked the Shuberts into collaborating in the presentation of Charles's venture. Thus, these fabulous gentlemen inadvertently found themselves helping with the costumes, rudimentary scenery, and musical aspects of his ballet, and even more incredibly, with providing one of their many theaters—the Booth Theatre—which was idle at the time, for a week of performances. This last was a true *mirabile dictu*. The American dancers, as a rule, were able to play a single concert only, on Sunday afternoon or evening. This was true for Martha Graham, Humphrey-Weidman, Helen Tamiris, and the new crop of recitalists, such as Pauline Koner[57] and Esther Junger.[58] And here *Candide* was to play for one week! We found it beyond belief. But play we did, and it was a first-class catastrophe. Poor luckless Candide. Even in dance form he found the world cruel and heartless.

This was my first taste of artistic disaster. Until then I had known only the acclaim that greeted the works of my teachers. Even my own puny creations had been received with enthusiasm. I had become accustomed to it. In my innocence I was unprepared for the debacle that can greet even your best and most sincere efforts. I simply could not understand why this piece of Charles, with its many excellences, its wit, beauty, and imagination, its choreographic inventiveness and power, could fail so dismally and completely.

It was a hard lesson, learned in bitterness, and like all defeats and humiliations, carried like a heavy burden to the end of time. The irony was that my own performance was something of a personal triumph and somehow survived the general opprobrium. I learned from friend and foe alike that I had made a fine impression. All this was but ashes and gall. Failures such as this temper one. The hotter the fire, the harder the steel, I suppose.

*   *   *

When not at classes or rehearsals I had a living to make. I ran from one painter and sculptor and art class to another. Miss Anita Weschler,[59] fresh from art school, engaged me to pose for her in her Fifty-Seventh Street studio. Over the months, while I stood on the stand naked, and she worked on the clay model, we would discuss many things—heaven, earth, hell, the nature of man. Often she would bring lunch. This was a fine thing because those were lean, hungry days for me. We became good friends. Over the years Anita has been someone I can talk to on any subject; we have shared concerns about our respective arts, as well as aspirations, triumphs, and disappointments. She has always been kind, patient, understanding, and generous. So many people have come and gone over the decades, some forgotten, others remembered, but she has remained a friend, constant and staunch. This I cherish.

*   *   *

As the hour of crisis approached with *Candide*, Doris was summoned by Charles from her retreat in the family home in Vermont to help supervise the final dress rehearsals of his ambitious, ill-fated opus. She arrived, big with child, and everyone looked on with undisguised astonishment. Pregnancy was nothing new for me. My mother grew big as a house with monotonous regularity during my childhood and adolescence. But this was different. Doris was not the mother of a large family. She was a dancer, and I found it difficult to reconcile the splendid artist with this woman, burdened and imprisoned by the biological process.

Doris did all she could to help, then returned to Vermont. After the disaster, Charles, Pauline, and I escaped from New York for a little vacation in New Jersey. We had recently contracted to buy an old rundown farmhouse and surrounding land with the savings from *Americana*.[60] The house was completely unfurnished and tenanted by mice and squirrels. We arrived and found to our dismay that the moving van containing furniture, beds, bedding, dishes, pots, and pans, had failed to arrive as planned. The spot was isolated. That had been one of its charms. Now it was plain desolate. Nights in the hills of northern New Jersey, even in the middle of May, are glacial. We spent the night huddled on the floor, fully dressed, covered with topcoats and an old rug or two. Next day, of course, our lost effects arrived, and we swept the place and set up housekeeping.

Our return to New York was mandatory. We had to prepare for performances at Lewisohn Stadium. Doris returned, her pregnancy more advanced. The performances were to take place in late July. The child was due sometime in June. Doris would conduct rehearsals in her street clothes. I was in mortal terror lest she slip or fall, as she was quite active. She was putting the finishing touches to a suite of dances to music of Albert Roussel, the French composer.[61] The first was a formal dance in concerto style, the second a Sarabande, and the last a Gigue.

Even with the best of luck and propitious timing, Doris would never be in condition, by July, to dance the strenuous *La Valse*. Nevertheless, a personal appearance was mandatory. She designed the Sarabande for the girls and herself. But her own dancing was such as could be done by a woman newly risen from childbirth. No leaps, no dangerous extensions of the legs, no sharp bends of the torso. She taught Cleo Atheneos her part in *La Valse* and finished the choreography of the Roussel suite.

By now, June 1933 was upon us. New York was broiling hot. This was before the era of air conditioning. You just took it and melted with sweat far into the night. The merciless asphalt, brick, and concrete saw to that.

Roosevelt had brought the nation new hope. Things were still bad and would become worse before they got better, but at least one felt that something was being done to bring about a recovery. Strange, wonderful, innovative remedies were being concocted and applied to the ailing economy. The Hoover administration now seemed like a bad fever dream from which one was awakening with boundless relief.

One of the pleasant things was the repeal of the Prohibition Amendment. None of us were drinkers. Our one vice, as well as virtue, was our work. We knew nothing of bootleggers or speakeasies. But it was good to know that, as a transition to a more civilized dispensation where wines and liquors were no longer proscribed but could be enjoyed legally by those with the inclination and the means to do so, beer could be had. True, it was as yet only mildly alcoholic in content, but it was an exciting prospect and symbolic of a new freedom; above all, it was wet and cold. In the evening after rehearsals Charles and I would get a dozen bottles at the delicatessen, along with some Limburger cheese and pumpernickel bread. We would go to the apartment Doris and Pauline shared, have a very agreeable party, and discuss the progress of the day's work and the pregnancy.

Both seemed to be in good shape. Or at least in as good a shape as could be expected. Doris viewed her condition with pleasant good humor. By now I had stopped calling her "Miss Humphrey." Being a formal and diffident sort, I had only recently asked her for permission to address her by her first name. She laughed and said, "By all means." This in no way diminished my awe or my respect for her. To me, high artistry confers on those who possess it an aura of majesty, inviolate; familiarity is presumptuous and impertinent.

There were a number of false alarms. Pauline, Charles, and I lived in a state of constant alert. Doris's obstetrician had warned that zero hour was imminent. A car and driver, plus attendants (Doris was, after all, a kind of royalty to us) were to be on hand at all hours. I was the driver. Several times the trip was made to the hospital, and Doris deposited. When nothing happened, all would return home and continue the vigil.

I believe that on the third such unfruitful occasion the doctors finally decided that the human fruit was more than ripe for harvesting, and all that was needed was to give the tree a good shaking. They directed that we put Doris on the back seat of the car, find the bumpiest, roughest pavement in the city of New York, and drive over it a number of times as fast as the speed laws permitted. We drove to Tenth Avenue, which is paved with cobblestones and which decades of abuse by heavy trucks have rendered as uneven as the surface of the moon. Doris and Pauline were in the rear seat, Charles and I in front. I was at the controls. We pretended it was a dance rehearsal. We would find the roughest stretch of road. Fortunately, it was a Sunday or holiday, so there was no traffic. The street was empty. Someone would say, "And—," that imperious signal and command that dancers use to unleash their energies. I would step on the accelerator; the car would hit the bumps, and the occupants of the

Doris Humphrey in *Two Ecstatic Themes—Circular Descent.*

Doris Humphrey at Bennington.

Doris Humphrey and José Limón in *Four Chorale Preludes*, 1942.
Photo by Marcus Blechman.

Doris Humphrey and
Charles Weidman
in the 1930s.

Charles Weidman (left), Doris
Humphrey, and José Limón
in *Exhibition Piece*, 1939.

back seat would be bounced to the ceiling of the car, fall back on the seat cushions, and be hurled upward again, laughing and shrieking hysterically. It was great fun. We repeated this, I think, for about an hour, then, exhausted by the hilarity, delivered the patient back to the hospital, where Charles Humphrey Woodford was duly born early next morning.[62]

It was a scorching day. We paid our first visit to the infant. Through the glass partition the nurse showed us a naked, violently agitated shape, beet-colored, with bright orange hair, protesting with robust howls having been rudely dislodged from its warm, blissful abode and thrust, all unwilling, into this vale of tears.

Presently, Doris was discharged from the maternity hospital, where we had visited her regularly. She had appeared pale and wan at first. It had been a fine delivery, and the doctors were very pleased. "It's those dancer muscles that did it. That's what it takes," they told us. Bringing the mother and child home was an event. Everyone came to visit. There was a nurse, bottles, diapers, a nursery, crib, and all manner of cautions, formulas, and schedules. Nevertheless, Doris would often receive our delegation sitting up in bed, nursing the now reconciled little creature. The Titian-haired Madonna with the blond *bambino* sucking at her breast was a beautiful and touching sight.

But Doris was not one to let motherhood keep her away from the studio for very long. Besides, there was a perfectly good nurse. So, it was back to work. The doctors provided her with protective bandages, and she began to take part in rehearsals. It took real guts in more ways than one. The Sarabande in which Doris was to appear in order to fulfill the conditions of the contract with Lewisohn Stadium made progress. The Roussel suite, however, was not one of Humphrey-Weidman's best creations. The music was not terribly good, and this, I think, was reflected in the choreography. The opening Prelude had its good moments of formal invention and design, and also an exciting momentum, but was on the whole uninspired. The Sarabande was a dance of seduction, sinuous and voluptuous. Doris, in the central role, did her noble best, but succeeded only in coming as close to being obvious and banal as I ever saw her. The Gigue was a maypole dance with a real pole and ribbons in which we would invariably become tangled. I believe this was the only dance of hers that it literally distressed me to perform. I hated it. However, it seemed to go tolerably well with the public and remained in the repertory for a number of years.

* * *

A lovely person came up to the studio one morning. She had asked to see me, and I was waiting. Grace Cornell had recently returned from Europe and was looking for a partner to assist her in a recital she was planning. She was wearing a stunning leopard skin coat and hat, which were exactly the right things to set off her delicate, pale blonde coloring. I performed my solo dances for her. She examined us both standing side by side before the studio mirror. She said I would do, and presently we were rehearsing choreographies set for her in Germany by the famous Rudolf von Laban with whom she had been studying. They were quite different in technique and style from the dances we were doing on this side of the Atlantic, and found them difficult to assimilate. But Grace was sweet and patient, and we worked hard. She was a talented and beautiful dancer, and I found it a pleasure to work with her. By now I was irrepressibly composing solos for myself, *Danza*, to Prokofiev, and *Canción y Danza*, to Mompou. These were to be included in the program.

The recital was a big success, so much so that Grace invited me to work further with her. We rehearsed regularly after that, worked on new ideas, and before we knew it were playing engagements at the old Roxy Theatre. It was a successful collaboration, and it was suggested that we go to Europe together. The prospect was tempting, but I had made a commitment to Humphrey-Weidman and to myself. With much regret I declined. Subsequently, Grace found another partner, a young German, Kurt Graff,[63] another disciple of Laban's, whom she later married. The two have had a long career together, both here and in Europe. Often, I have speculated on my choice. Had I accepted Grace's offer, my life would have been far different.

The clash of artistic ideologies during this period occasionally had a tragicomical aspect. Martha Graham, during one of her extraordinary lecture-demonstrations at the New School for Social Research, was rudely heckled by an irate gentleman in the audience who, at a certain point, found the proceedings more than he could bear in silence. A spirited verbal attack, in heavily Russian-accented English, was hurled at the dancer and all her works. She proved to be more than a match for him. It was a scandal, and everyone was utterly delighted. The outraged conservative who had so strongly objected to Miss Graham's radicalisms was Michel Fokine. Evidently, the heresies of Isadora Duncan in St. Petersburg of 1905 were one thing. Graham's, in New York of 1933, were another.

* * *

Cleveland, Ohio, during the low point of the Depression, was the scene of a gallant effort and inevitable failure. A talented young man, Lawrence Higgins, conceived the idea of the Cleveland Opera Association. I believe there was some backing, but, as it proved subsequently, not nearly enough. Nevertheless, Higgins lacked nothing when it came to faith and valor. He produced *Aida*, *Carmen*, and *Die Walküre*. To do so, he assembled an impressive roster of singers, a symphony orchestra, dancers, and, to direct the ballets in the first two operas, Doris Humphrey and Charles Weidman.

The productions were a complete departure from the hackneyed ones of the past. Higgins directed everything with a refreshing and youthful iconoclasm. There was a mammoth set, an ingenious and tasteful adaptation of Norman Bel Geddes's for *Lysistrata* a few years previously. The

costumes were neither traditional nor authentic, but designed with originality and a superb simplicity. New use was made of inexpensive materials, dyed in bold and striking colors and combined superbly. The staging,
which used all the possibilities of irregular, angular steps and platforms
rising to several craglike eminences, was exciting. The choreography was
in the same revisionist spirit and quite effective. Dancers were recruited
from the area's dancing schools. Doris and Charles spent some weeks creating the various choreographies, and the work of rehearsing was left in
the competent hands of Eleanor Frampton.[64]

Frampton had been Charles Weidman's first dance teacher in Lincoln,
Nebraska. She had encouraged the talented boy to pull up stakes and go
to California to study with Ruth St. Denis and Ted Shawn. She and her
companion Helen Hewett had danced for years in vaudeville, making
quite a career of it and touring as far as Fiji and Australia. Frampton was
now associated with the Cleveland Institute of Music, in charge of its
dance department and making an excellent job of it.

Of the dancers participating in the season only two were importations,
Robert Gorham[65] and myself. Bobby was a contemporary of Charles
Weidman's at Denishawn. He was a handsome and talented dancer, and
Shawn had selected him to partner Martha Graham in his Aztec ballet
Xochitl.[66] This work, designed to tour the popular vaudeville circuits, was
spectacularly successful, and helped to launch the extraordinarily talented
Graham. Somewhere during the tour, in Seattle I think, Bobby sprained
an ankle, and Shawn, after a few hurried instructions, dispatched the
young Weidman to replace him. Graham took him in hand, hurriedly
rehearsed him, and pushed him onstage to dance opposite her as the Aztec
emperor. Bobby's lame ankle was taken to the French Riviera to recover.
The Crash of 1929 forced him to return to America, where he spent a season dancing in the touring company of *Lysistrata*. Now, like the rest of us,
he was feeling the pinch of the Depression. So he found himself dancing
in the Cleveland productions of *Aida* and *Carmen*.

It was murderously hot on the set, which was built in a baseball field
facing the grandstand. Rehearsing strenuous dances, exposed to the full
glare of the midsummer sun, was an unspeakable experience. The always
immoderate climate of the Middle West, too cold in winter, too hot in
summer, was the setting, perhaps the cause of another incident in the clash
of ideologies.

A local ballet master, one of the many Russian émigrés scattered
around the world from Shanghai to Johannesburg to Cleveland, had been
vociferously indignant at the choreographic outrages being perpetrated
nightly at the ballpark before an avid public. There were letters to the
press attacking the uncouth barbarities and deploring the violations of
sacrosanct traditions. How dare these ignorant Americans do thus and
such in *Carmen* and *Aida*, when the entire civilized world knew it should
be done like so?

The heat exacerbated matters. A crisis was inevitable, and it took a most disconcerting form. The distraught man disappeared, leaving behind a long and dramatic farewell letter, to the effect that with the world now fallen on such evil days, he would make a heroic end of it by plunging over Niagara Falls. The press had a field day with the story. There were headlines, interviews, conjectures, excitement, and the delighted necrophilia such things arouse. Where was the body? There was talk that he had never jumped, that it was all a hoax. The public, the papers, everyone demanded a body. It was never found.

Presently, an equally big sensation pushed the tragic disappearance of the unfortunate Russian into oblivion. The well-intentioned Mr. Higgins went bankrupt. He didn't have a dime, and many of us woke up the morning after the final performance to a bleak reality: we were broke and would have to get back to New York as best we could. How we did it I don't remember. To this day the dear man owes me several hundred dollars in unpaid wages.

Perdona nuestras deudas, así como nosotros perdonamos a nuestros deudores. (Forgive us our debts, as we forgive our debtors.) So runs the Lord's Prayer in Spanish. Defective Christian that I am, I have forgiven Mr. Higgins his debt to me for a selfish and, therefore, impure reason only. Thanks to him, I had the priceless experience of watching Mary Garden and learning an unforgettable lesson: do not bother to walk onstage unless you have the power to dominate it, to make it yours entirely. Unless you have that magic power, do something else with your life. Not that you should obliterate others—one's colleagues deserve respect and consideration—or be arrogant, indecently egocentric, or vulgar in your self-esteem. These failings should be left to pushy mediocrities unsure of themselves. But that power you must have. True artistry is an inborn incandescence, a diadem, nimbus, panoply.

On the scorching platforms in the Cleveland baseball park, I saw a petite, slightly plump, well-corseted, middle-aged woman in a modish summer frock with a diminutive hat perched on top of brilliant orange-vermilion curls. The company was rehearsing *Carmen*. Don José, Escamillo, the soldiers, girls, and crew—everyone was bellowing at the top of their lungs. Miss Garden whispered her part. She would walk here, stand there, and gesticulate in a species of minimal shorthand.

I was appalled. Was this the legendary Mary Garden? Why she was a worn-out old woman!

On opening night there was much commotion backstage. The dressing rooms were little cubicles built under the stage platforms. In front of Miss Garden's dressing room a crowd had gathered. There were photographers with flash bulbs, reporters, and other singers. In the center was a seventeen-year-old Sevillian gypsy slut. She was the color of mahogany. Heavy coal black bangs covered her forehead to the eyebrows. Her glasses were black tarantulas, her eyes violent red. The rest of her hair was braided into a single saucy pigtail that ended in a bright crimson bow. A white short-sleeved muslin blouse, low cut, barely contained a boldly pert bosom.

Heavy, indecent earrings. Naked arms covered with bracelets, chains, and bangles. The slimmest of waists, dark-brown shapely legs in tiny scarlet slippers. A skirt, bright green, with a profusion of ruffles and petticoats. In shameless abandon this hellion posed with her soldiers and her toreador for the photographers.

My eyes nearly popped out of my head.

But this was only the beginning. Onstage she became a rutting tigress. She growled. She devoured. She was wanton, voluptuous, and absolutely enchanting. Her voice, what did that matter? There were enough good voices surrounding her. But they served only as a background for the incandescent reality, the miracle of her performance. This I owe to Lawrence Higgins. I hope he never demands payment. I would be unable to meet it.

* * *

On Fifty-Fifth Street just off Sixth Avenue, on the third story of one of those brownstones that are fast disappearing from a city suffering from an obsessive giantism, Sammy Gluck and his wife Felicia Sorel made history.[67] They fixed up a theater and called it the Dance Center. It was as small as a theater can be, narrow, with barely enough room for ten rows of steeply banked seats, an intervening space to give the spectators some perspective, and a diminutive stage. There were curtains, wings, and spotlights. The whole thing done severely in black. It was compact and serviceable.

Here, in the early 1930s, Sammy produced, directed, and performed some of the most creative and exciting theater of the time in New York. He was a dynamo. Not a bundle, but a bale of nerves, restless, bold, and completely unafraid. He took good dancers, with well-established reputations, unknown but talented younger dancers, and aspiring beginners, and by the pure force of his indomitable will, molded them into stunning productions. Sammy was a martinet, a tyrant, impatient, tempestuous, and explosive. He was also lovable, warm, and human, with an irresistible sense of humor. But above all else, he was an artist. When the curtain went up, there was magic.

Two productions I will remember always. One was *El Amor Brujo*. It was set to Manuel de Falla's score and showed true originality in the treatment of Spanish atmosphere, costume, and decor. Sammy himself, with Felicia and Esther Junger, were memorable protagonists, full of fire, terror, and beauty. The other production, *Salomé*, to the Richard Strauss music, was Sammy's masterpiece. Felicia was unforgettable as the impassioned princess, an infinitely subtle blend of prurience and innocence, fire and ice, totally cruel, totally tender, and profoundly moving. I saw her performance many times. Sammy's portrait of the lascivious Herod was a masterpiece of the revolting. He depicted him as an obscene, impotent old lecher. My former associate Charles Laskey did fine work as the Roman captain who kills himself for love of Salomé. John the Baptist was done

with power by Harry Losee.[68] The encounter between him and Felici
was something to leave you limp and trembling.

I lusted, literally, and as it turned out, in vain, for this role of St. John.

When Sammy and Felicia had to give up the Dance Center, I had th
good fortune to become friends with these two extraordinary artists.
deplored the closing of their theater and expressed the hope that it woul
reopen in another location. When it did, in 1937, I accepted an invitatio
to join them. Sammy, to my delight, discussed reviving *Salomé* with me a
John. We even had a few preliminary rehearsals. He revived *El Amo
Brujo* and cast me as the young lover. In vain, Sammy sweated blood try
ing to make a Spanish dancer of me or even a modern dance adaptation o
one. I was like an elephant trying to be gazelle. I was dreadful. I wanted t
do the fanatic John the Baptist. Sammy did a commedia dell'arte piece an
cast Felicia as Columbine, himself as Pierrot, and me as Harlequin. It wa
not a great success. Sammy was a fine, rascally Pierrot, and Felicia wa
lovely as Columbine, but I was a mess. We never got to revive *Salomé*, an
I had to swallow my disappointment.

One of the young dancers in this second edition of the Dance Cente
was a lanky kid from Brooklyn. He was just beginning, and he looked u
to Sammy with true reverence. When he smiled, his face would light u
with a sweet radiance. This child was to become the great Jerome Rob
bins.[69]

* * *

The success of the new style of dance in the revue *Americana* did not pass
unnoticed by other producers of commercial theater. Almost immediately,
and despite the glaring fiasco of *Candide*, Michael Myerberg approached
Doris and Charles with tempting offers to do the choreography for this or
that show. Modern dance was "in."

Doris held herself aloof. She had had a skirmish with Lee Shubert during the final rehearsals of *Americana*. This potentate had been lurking in
the back of the house for days, making the ominous subterranean noises
of a volcano about to erupt. During a run-through of *The Shakers* he
became more and more irritated by what to him was its excessive length
and too slow progression to a climax. He contained the volcanic pressures
as long as he was able, and finally exploded. Now, this was a man of
almost legendary power in the theater before whom stars and directors
were known to tremble and grovel. I remember his imperious voice as he
charged down the aisle to where Doris sat. "Miss Humphrey, Miss
Humphrey! This routine is too long. It will kill the show. You have to cut
it! Cut it in half, cut, cut—!"

Doris stood up and in her cool, firm voice addressed the enraged,
quivering man. "Mr. Shubert, please keep your predatory hands off my
dances. I don't know whether you know what predatory means. In any
case, I am not going to cut them, and you will please not interfere." And

she turned her back on him and continued with the business on the stage. This was a totally new and baffling experience for the tyrant of Shubert Alley. Sputtering, he retreated to the shadows, no doubt to plan some dire retaliation. Someone must have dissuaded him, for *The Shakers* and the other dances remained intact and were the hit of the show.

Charles had had no such abrasions. He appeared good-natured and easygoing. Producers loved him. Besides, they wanted what he had. It was fresh and new. It would sell. Best of all, they could get him—and his dancers—for a song. So we found ourselves rehearsing Irving Berlin's *As Thousands Cheer*. Hassard Short, one of the most successful directors of musical comedies both here and in his native England, was to direct.[70] This alone would have been enough to insure the success of any show. His instinct for what would sell was phenomenal. But as though this were not enough, a glittering constellation of stars had been assembled— Clifton Webb, for years the most fashionable song-and-dance man; Marilyn Miller, the blonde daughter of Broadway; Helen Broderick, a leading comedienne, and most intriguing of all, Ethel Waters, the magnificent Negress.

This powerful top echelon was to be supported by an array of lesser actors and actresses. Letitia Ide and myself were to be leading dancers. Charles had by now promoted me to the post of assistant, and I found myself among the elite—Moss Hart and George Kaufman, the brilliant authors of the book; Charles and Mr. Short; and Irving Berlin, singing in a high squeaky voice the songs that were to become famous the world over.

This was in the late summer of 1933. It was very hot. In those days, air-conditioned theaters were unknown, and rehearsals on the stifling stages were an ordeal. I have often speculated on the fate of dance, and of the theater itself, if there were no people willing and even eager to immolate themselves so that theater in all its forms might survive and flourish.

Doris Humphrey once characterized the dancer's obsessive dedication as "a form of insanity, a sublime madness." I have seen battle-scarred veterans with beautiful, incredible faces on which every line, every wrinkle is a hieroglyph recording a disaster, triumph, or patiently endured agony. Their eyes have an opaque splendor; they have been blinded by powerful spotlights, pouring sweat, melted greasepaint, and running mascara; they have looked on visions and nightmares, on heights and depths unsuspected by ordinary mortals. They have endured what no athlete in possession of his wits would dream of enduring. Their muscles have transcended mere physicality and have become the luminous poetic vehicle of the spirit.

I have seen the unsuspecting young recruits, with their fresh untried vigor and their tremulous infant passion, wearing the ever-bright, ever-new dream, as a halo—like newly ordained angels. They are the promise of continuation. The destiny of the obsessed tribe is in their still inexpert hands. In good time, they will grasp firmly the halter of the divine Pegasus.

Commerce takes these eager devotees of a dream and puts them up for sale.

As Thousands Cheer made history.[71] It was an apotheosis of its kind. There had never been a revue as slick, as classy, as chic, as tuneful, as literate, as handsome, as sophisticated, as expressive, and as successful. From now on there was nowhere else for Broadway shows to go except down or in a new direction—like *Oklahoma!*.

Weidman did a fine job with the dances. Letitia, the other dancers, and I went on every night except Sunday and did two matinees, Thursday and Saturday. We took all we had learned in the studio and on the concert stage and "sold" it, with all the innocent ardor of young artistry, not knowing, in our ignorance, that we were working in a very plush, high-class whorehouse. Slowly, revulsion and hatred came to the surface from depths where it had lain amorphous and festering. The dances were brutally strenuous and demanding. Only young, healthy, and powerfully constructed human beings could endure the strain. By the end of six months life had become a nightmare. Often, I would lie awake at night, in a cold sweat, sick with abhorrence, because for seemingly all of an appalling eternity I was condemned to go to the Music Box Theatre, paint my face, limber up my muscles, and wearing the specious gaiety of a prostitute, dance to "Heat Wave," "Miss Lonely Hearts," "Easter Parade," and "Revolt in Cuba."

The show ran for a long, very long time—a year-and-a-half. There was even a tour that included Boston, Cincinnati, Detroit, and Chicago. I don't know what went on in Letitia's mind during this ordeal. This supremely beautiful woman, a goddess really, was endowed with an Olympian serenity I never once saw fail her. She walked through corruption untouched and uncontaminated. I never spoke to anyone about my torment, so that perhaps if she also felt any, she was in her turn reticent. And then came salvation. Letitia and I were recalled by Doris and Charles to be in new works. We trained our replacements, Grace Cornell and Kurt Graff, and returned to New York.

It was an exciting homecoming. It was a Sunday night early in 1934, and Doris and Charles were performing at the Guild Theatre. Our teachers had also had a fling on Broadway. But this had been for the Theatre Guild, which was something entirely different from crass commerce. Lawrence Langner, the director, had asked them to choreograph the dances for Molière's play *The School for Husbands*.[72]

Sylvia Manning and myself had danced in an earlier production of the play by Langner at his summer theater, the Red Barn, in Westport, Connecticut. I remember the pleasure of performing the beautiful duets Weidman had created for us to music of Couperin and Rameau. I remember the delectable irony of the great French master, his charm and urbane polish. The stars, Osgood Perkins as Sganarelle and June Walker as his wily niece, were superb, and I never tired of watching their performances. Such artists!

The New York production was more elaborate, of course. It had great style and sumptuousness. Doris and Charles created several elegant ballets for it and also performed in them. I saw a dress rehearsal only, because I was busy in *As Thousands Cheer*. I had known Doris and Charles only as revolutionaries. I was not fully aware that they had been trained in all the formal elegances of ballet and had not forgotten them one whit. What they did was to work in a sort of neoclassicism, and the result was utterly enchanting.

And here they were again, on the stage of the Guild Theatre, with *Rudepoema*, a long duet to Villa-Lobos, *Duo-Drama*, the main work of the evening, to music of Roy Harris, and *Alcina Suite*, to Handel.[73]

Rudepoema was a primitive rite of betrothal, incantatory and mysterious. Here Doris and Charles found new directions to explore. Their ability to create utterly fresh new movement always astounded me. There seemed to be no end to the ways in which they manipulated the human body to fill an austerely empty stage with excitement and beauty. The work was in a style of sculpturesque primitivism, consonant with the Villa-Lobos score.

Duo-Drama examined a man and a woman in three distinct historical moments. The first scene, which showed the couple in an elemental or primeval state, was robust and earthy in style. In the second, they danced with mincing step and gesture, emblems of rococo decadence. Last came the resurgence, which was dynamic and forward-looking. This final movement was quite brilliant in design and execution. *Alcina Suite* was in the preclassic or baroque style. It had grace and formal distinction. Viewed in retrospect, these works were significant as the final preparative essays for what was soon to come.

While the rest of us were fooling around with Broadway shows, Doris had been busy at the studio with strange new ideas. The abstract "pure dance" had always preoccupied her, and now, it appeared, she was exploring new horizons in this style. The work was entirely different from anything she had done before, and there was bafflement and disaffection among her girls. A number of them, unable or unwilling to countenance her experiments, left the company. It was a grave moment. The loss of almost half her dancers, all at once, was a serious blow. Doris was a courageous person and never complained. But we knew that during this period she had many sleepless nights.

A new crop of girls was auditioned from the classes and invited to join the company, enabling the rehearsals to continue. The new faces included Beatrice Seckler,[74] Eva Desca,[75] Edith Orcutt,[76] Katherine Litz,[77] and Sybil Shearer.[78]

A composer, naturally, must work with his materials and his instruments. His task is to use them in as creative a way as possible. He must know their capacity, potential, and limitations. A dance composer, especially, is subject to the properties of his dancers. He must know to what extent he can challenge and extend their innate abilities, or to what extent he has to conform to them. For example, a small, light, swift dancer will elicit from the choreographer one style of movement, while a bigger heavier, slower dancer will elicit quite another. The instruments that Doris now had at her command were younger, fresher, and quicker. Her ideas flew ahead, and these exciting new people kept pace. There was a ferment in the studio as slowly the new dance took place.

Work was interrupted by other obligations. In Philadelphia, at the Academy of Music, an event of historic significance in the world of art was being planned—the American premiere of Gluck's *Iphigenia in Aulis*.[79] How this superbly beautiful work had been neglected on these shores for over a century-and-a-half is hard to understand.

Marie Antoinette, Queen of France, born an archduchess of Austria, had known and admired the composer Gluck at the Hapsburg court in Vienna. As part of the festivities attendant upon her coronation she invited him to present a new opera in Paris. It was received with contempt and derision by the French, who resented what they called the barbaric German invasion. It was not a good augury for the queen and her reign.

We, not being French, found the opera exquisitely beautiful. It was by turns stately, noble, and dramatic, full of lyric beauty and enchantment. Doris and Charles were to do the choreography to the charming ballet music as well as perform. Our old friend Norman Bel Geddes was at the helm to stage and design the production. It was not his most original effort. The set seemed to me to be a somewhat inferior copy of his superb creation for *Lysistrata* five years previously. The costumes were also repetitive. Even great talent, I was learning to my consternation, was fallible. Finally, on the podium, conducting the Philadelphia Symphony and the singers, was the volcanic Alexander Smallens.

The dances were rehearsed at the New York studio. It was during these rehearsals that the new dancers were put to the test and proved themselves. For me, after the ordeal of *As Thousands Cheer*, the noble sound of Gluck was like water to a thirsty man. The performances of *Iphigenia in Aulis* were a redemptive experience. The impeccable, impassioned formality, the utter grace, the crystalline purity of this masterwork raised me from the depths. I was ready to begin anew.

Doris again made a deep impression on me with her dancing. She was bacchante, maenad, coryphée. She flew down ramps and up platforms with abandon. Charles did some fine dancing with the men. There was a lovely duet by the principals. At the end, a climactic dance for the full ensemble, there was always a stupendous ovation for the dancers.

One night after the performance I came face to face for the first time with a legend. I had accompanied Doris and Charles to a restaurant for supper and found that Martha Graham and Louis Horst were to join us. Remembering my first encounter with Graham, I was terrified and tried to find some pretext for escaping. To no avail. I had to sit in the presence of this strange woman who, over the years, was to frighten and fascinate me. On this occasion I listened to the conversation tongue-tied. I remember her commenting on the opera and on the dances. "Your dancing,

Doris, I was moved to tears by it." It took years for me to treat this great artist as human, to see her as a warm, loving, fellow being. I had watched her repeatedly in *Primitive Mysteries*. Her performance had a gemlike, diamond-hard perfection. Costumed in stiff, immaculate white organdy, she moved among her dancers as an infinitely remote planet moves in its orbit. The dance, a masterpiece of the American dance, was also evocative of astronomical perfections. It was cold, so cold, and distant.

Doris called her new work, when it was finished, *New Dance*.[80] It was the product of a mind that other times would have designated as "masculine." In those times women were deemed the inferior sex and denied the challenge of education. Oxford, Salamanca, and the Sorbonne were closed to them, and science and art were the exclusive prerogative of the male. On rare occasions a female would miraculously break the fetters that bound her sex and astound an incredulous world. Thus, Sappho, Joan of Arc, St. Theresa of Avila, Queen Isabella, Queen Elizabeth, Catherine the Great, and any number of others. Our times have inured us to looking at women with new eyes. Ability, comparable to and sometimes greater than that of men, has manifested itself in all human pursuits, with one laudable exception: there has been no female Bonaparte.

In the dance of our day there is no question as to the preponderant genius of women. Men are hard put to match the historic achievements of Anna Pavlova, Isadora Duncan, Ruth St. Denis, Martha Graham, and Doris Humphrey. This is not to deny the stature of such male luminaries as Nijinsky, Fokine, and Kreutzberg.

The American dance, as we know it, in the second half of the twentieth century is largely the product of two titanic artists, both women and both completely feminine women. There is no justification whatever for the old bromide of a masculine mentality in the body of a female. For fifteen years the Graham company was composed entirely of women. With these young, superbly trained girls, Graham created a miraculously expressive, technical vocabulary. This vocabulary was intensely, completely female, deeply rooted in the entrails, organs, and psyche of the female. It was used to compose a body of works unequaled in revelatory power, primordial rituals of mystical intensity celebrating an ancient, but consciously remembered matriarchy. The male of the species, during this period, was not even remotely alluded to. He simply did not exist.

Doris, on the other hand, worked with men. She cast *New Dance* for herself, her ensemble of twelve women, Charles, and four other men, William Matons, George Bockman,[81] Kenneth Bostock, and myself. *New Dance* was a work of symphonic dimension. Its theme—the relation of man to his fellows—would unite it with two subsequently composed works, *Theatre Piece* and *With My Red Fires*.[82] *New Dance* was a poetic vision of an ideal state, where order, grace, and beauty reigned.

The curtain rose to reveal pyramidal arrangements of blocks at the four corners of the stage. Standing or seated on these were spectators at an arena where a heroic spectacle was to take place. Doris and Charles stood

dead center stage, poised to begin. After a sonorous overture of percussion and cymbals, the two began a magnificent duet, full-bodied and affirmative, that evoked the strength and assurance that is man's, and the grace
and beauty that is woman's, and the heroic nobility of their joint destiny.
A summons and a credo, this duet was also a preamble to the fifty minutes
that followed. The quality of the movements, the beautiful off-balance
turns, the leaps that exploded into the air with no visible preparation, the
asymmetrical, contrapuntal rhythms, the intricate, dazzling patterns of
bodies and limbs intoxicated with space, always more space—all this
would permeate the fabric of the work.

There was a sudden pause. The women descended to the arena. The
men retired. In the passage that followed a myriad asteroids described a
spacious orbit. Doris was the central planet, whirling endlessly. Around
her the women encircled her circles. Centripetal. Implosive. The swiftly
whirling movement created an irresistible centrifugality, and suddenly the
stage was empty.

The men took over. Darting diagonals pierced the arena. There were
careening runs that climaxed in bounding horizontals and bodies bent
double backwards in the air; jagged, stamping rhythms; arms and legs
projected outward from an inner explosion; leaps that ended in long
strides on the knees. Here was all the dynamism and force of the male
nature unleashed.

And, again, the arena, pulsating with unbounded energy and anticipa-
tion, emptied.

The women entered in a slow and majestic procession, with long
slides, suspended balances on one foot, backs arched, faces raised, and
arms spread wide—like a celebratory and jubilant anthem. The men
joined them, and the procession became more exultant, until the *lento
maestuoso* overflowed into a fugal *allegro con brio*.

This fugue was one of those superb, contrapuntal edifices that Doris,
master choreographer that she was, liked to place in the climactic portions
of her works. It was a summation, a zenith, a dramatic cessation of all
movement and sound. The dancers pushed the constructions from the
four corners of the stage to the center, fitting them together to form a
large pyramid. Now, the "Variations and Conclusion" that were the coda
of the work began.

Order, clarity: these have been mentioned often as the twin goals of
artists, scientists, and philosophers. Ultimately, the cosmos is the supreme
manifestation of these concepts. The organization of the entire universe
from the gigantic stars to the minutest components of all matter is a work
of choreography, awesome in its structure and precision. All of sentient
life, as we know it, is subject to its pattern and rhythm. Only man, capricious, perverse, and fallible, seems intent on violating this order, creating
darkness where there is light. But architects, philosophers, poets, and
musicians compensate for this propensity to nihilism in man's nature.

The choreographic genius of Doris Humphrey was an affirmation of order and clarity. In this coda she created a dance that evoked the ordered congress of planets. It was most ingeniously wrought in its details, as elaborately simple as a snowflake or a many-petaled flower. From each corner of the stage, in ordered succession, a soloist would be projected diagonally to the central pyramid, and from there cover the stage with a choreographic variation, while the others progressed in a contrapuntal design to the next corner. The mathematical beauty and precision upon which the coda was built was a miracle of order and clarity. The work came to a climax in a centripetal gathering of energies into the central pyramid.

These are only words. Lightning is swift and dazzling. Thunder is sonorous. Only those who have been momentarily blinded by the one and deafened by the other can know what is meant by a verbal description of the phenomenon of an electric discharge from the heavens.

There is no cinematographic record of *New Dance*. There are only a few photographs and the recollections of those who witnessed the flash of its lightning and the roar of its thunder. For that is how *New Dance* was perceived by audiences, and that is what it was to me, who was shaped, molded, and tempered by it. I have not seen or heard its like since.

I performed the first variation, I thought of it as a gigantic drum, beat upon with restless flying feet. It had the slow, tilted turns of an eagle in flight, and sudden leaps, like explosions in the air. The second variation, which was danced by Beatrice Seckler, recalled jets of water, playful and glittering, in a fountain. One was aware only of the breathless ascent of a myriad crystalline drops, suspended, seemingly forever, in the light. Letitia Ide performed the third variation. Here was an Amazon, a goddess, now flying through the air, now lying weightless and recumbent on a cloud, describing a low, swooping spiral fall, while loose hair brushed the floor, only to leap up once again, sportive and jubilant. The fourth variation was a trio danced by Sybil Shearer, William Matons, and Kenneth Bostick. Shearer exploded brilliantly in all directions like a string of Chinese firecrackers, while the boys made a leaping, lunging accompaniment. Charles had a strong variation that recapitulated material from the opening duet and the men's dance. As for Doris, she was a flame and a whirlwind. And she was fecund, pregnant with further progeny, the second and third sections of her monumental trilogy—*Theatre Piece* and *With My Red Fires*.

My first elated steps as a choreographer had culminated in a group of dances to Bach's Suite in B Minor for orchestra. Eleanor King was my partner, and we slaved over the composition in the evenings and early mornings, whenever space was available in the busy studio. Eleanor had many facets to her talent. She was a superb comedienne in Charles's pieces. She was also capable of a heroic lyricism, which suited the formality of the dances in the Bach *Suite*. This work proved very successful in our little performances. Doris paid us the supreme compliment of inviting us to perform it for a gathering of students in her summer course. I always found it a pleasure to perform.

But the next level of accomplishment was now looming like an ominous barrier on the horizon. The fresh, pristine charm of a dancer in his early twenties, a charm that can and did, in my case, cover more than a multitude of deficiencies, could no longer be counted on. Audiences expect more, much more, when one reaches the middle twenties, and the first signs of a still distant decrepitude begin to show. Eleanor King left the company. Ernestine Henoch made a glamorous exodus to Paris, where she married the famous stage director Theodore Komisarjevsky[83] and danced for the uncomprehending Parisians.

Having seen Doris at work on *New Dance* and having had the experience of performing in it, I abandoned my early puerilities and became subject to a reign of discontent. I would spend day after day and night after night in the studio in solitary quest for the next step, the next development. Hundreds of movements and sequences were tried and discarded. A few dances were finished, rehearsed, and performed, then abandoned as failures, failures both to myself and that infallible arbiter, the public.

Early, very early in my life as a dancer, Doris, in one of her classes, in a discussion of art and the artist, mentioned that a dancer's movement was revelatory of the inner man, his nature and his spirit. "In the other arts," she told us, "you can hide behind words and facial expression. But it is impossible to deceive with the dance. The moment you begin to move you stand revealed for what you are." This admonition made a tremendous impression on me. It has followed me as a sort of artistic conscience throughout my long career.

The man who takes the trouble to buy a ticket to your performance is nothing less than a sacred responsibility and deserves your absolute best. He is interested in the same thing you are; otherwise, he would not be in the audience. He is looking for excellence in the ocean of mediocrity that surrounds him, for order in the midst of chaos, for beauty where there is squalor, for things that cannot be described in words and that, of all the arts, only the dance can give. For the dance is a lingua franca common to all men, white, black, pink, brown, and yellow. Human movement and gesture can cross oceans and mountains, rivers and deserts, bridge national frontiers and parochialisms.

When you consecrate yourself to be a dancer, spend your life sweating in the studio, and live obsessed with the things that bring new dances into the world—concept, costume, musical instrumentation, decor, lighting, accompaniment, rehearsals, and performance—yours is a heavy moral responsibility. If you fail the fellow-human sitting in the darkened theater out front, you have failed indeed. You have experienced the true nadir of defeat.

Perhaps this is the reason for the visage, the mask, that dancers acquire and wear. I have seen it over the decades. Painters, musicians, and poets do not have it. Their effort, their artistic travail is of another sort. The dancer's is that of the total man. The totality of his body, mind, and spirit goes into the crucible and is burned and tempered.

Doris Humphrey wore the mask of the most beautiful woman who ever lived. I saw that mask first when it was still young. But even then it was haunted. It was driven and tormented by furies and angels. Inherited from Puritan ancestors, from Elder Brewster himself, it came with too long and aquiline a nose, and in its proportions violated the conventional standards of beauty. But when Doris the dancer, tired, worried, worn, appeared in the arena, the mask was pure, translucent beauty.

* * *

What disciplines, what exercises were there to make the inner man a worthy source of that gesture you owed to yourself and to your fellow man? What rigors, what self-denials, what immolations? For the ascent to excellence and virtue is the travail of Sisyphus. Each man, each woman, each member of the dancer tribe has a heavy boulder to push up the steep mountainside. And each one seeks his own redemptive discipline and salvation.

For me, during this formative period, the solution was to follow blind instinct and give myself commands. *Work.* Unremittingly and obsessively. *Listen.* To the music of Bach, and as a sacrament of communion, eat his body and drink his blood, so that you will be hallowed and purified. *Learn.* Read biographies, histories, and works of philosophy; if you aspire to speak to man, know what man is made of. Look at other dancers, their works, style, music, costumes, and decor. Listen to poets, for they are dancers too, and your old friends, the painters and sculptors, and the architects and engineers who make such beautiful choreographies in stone. And work, always work.

A gesture, be it a leap, turn, run, fall, or walk, is only as beautiful, as powerful, as eloquent as its inner source. So take care. Purify, magnify, and make noble that source. You stand naked and revealed. Who are you? What are you? Who, what do you want to be? What is your spiritual caliber?

Work, listen, and learn.

* * *

The naive ardor of youth is perhaps the most beguiling of our human traits. Like spring, it is always a miracle. And while it lasts, this verdant time full of wild hope and tumultuous expectation, you think it will go on forever.

What were the results of this young ardor on my part? The consequences of this sacerdotal self-consecration? I became a better dancer.

* * *

Exhibition Piece[84] was a trio for Doris, Charles, and myself, which was an intoxicating honor for me. It was danced to a suite of witty piano pieces by Nicolas Slonimsky.[85] Pauline costumed us sumptuously in black velvet and mauve satin as Columbine, Harlequin, and Pierrot. I loved the delightful buffoonery, full of sparkling nonsense and brilliant choreographic innovation. That these two great artists chose me to be a third in such a piece was a formidable challenge, which I accepted with a mixture of panic and temerity.

My knees were quaking as the curtain rose on the premiere. Never in my short career had I had been so exposed. I can remember a cold daze, a sense of unreality during the performance. The other two, seasoned veterans at their peak, were giving it the consummate mastery of their medium that came with decades of experience. The work was a *commedia*, a satire and romp in high style. I had never been good at light things. Yet, to my infinite amazement and relief, I found myself getting roars of laughter and applause equal to those of the others. During the adagio section, when I lifted Doris on my back and carried her around the stage like a sack of potatoes while Charles executed a hilarious solo passage, she whispered, "See, you can do it!" The piece was given a noisy ovation. Again, the thunder from Olympus, the reward, precious beyond words. *Exhibition Piece* was a little gem, a graceful embellishment from the hand of the great symphonist. It was in the repertory for years and delighted audiences all over the country.

At the same time that Doris was composing *Exhibition Piece*, Charles was choreographing, almost as if by contrast, one of his best serious pieces, *Traditions*.[86] A gifted comedian, he was capable of fine achievement in this other vein. His earlier *Studies in Conflict*[87] I consider, in retrospect, a tour de force in imposing disciplined formality on a dramatic subject. A striking, dynamic, and violently dissonant piece by Dane Rudhyar was played three times. Charles danced in his strongest way a solo statement of the "conflict" theme. As in the ritual preparation for a duel, I, as the adversary, detached myself from a semicircle of eight men standing in the background. A beautifully developed two-part invention based on the thematic subject ensued. The men joined in for the third variation. This enlarged upon the theme while adhering scrupulously to the choreographic premise. It was a strong and arresting work.

Traditions proved to be one of Weidman's more forceful and effective pieces of theater. It was a trio for himself, Bill Matons (later replaced by George Bockman), and myself. The score, full of wit, irony and sarcasm, was by the talented, young Lehman Engel.[88] The three figures were used as symbols. There was a formal opening statement—a reiterated theme of fatuous, elaborate manipulations of the upper body, arms, hands, and head. The feet were planted in a wide stance firmly in place. "Here we have stood," they implied, "and here we stay." It was on the third monotonous repeat that I, as the first dissident figure, began to distort the hollow ritual. My gestures became increasingly twisted, more impatient of the fetters of tradition, until with a violent paroxysm I wrenched myself away, while the others looked on unctuously. It was Charles's uncanny talent for high comedy that made this passage, played with complete solemnity on my part, uproarious. Theaters in Omaha, Seattle, Los Angeles, and Atlanta, as well as New York, would shake to the chandeliers from the tumult.

From here the work mounted in comic suspense and intensity. The first figure would subvert the second, who would explode with violence, hurling himself across the stage, while Charles, the third figure, stood alone, spinning his empty futilities, oblivious to all except the past. There was a bold challenge, an attack by revolutionists that was ignored with hauteur or treated with contempt. Slowly, before one's eyes, he sank to the floor, his rococo panoplies aflutter, and expired with one last feeble flourish of an aristocratic hand. This episode never failed to bring down the house in a pandemonium of delight. There were howls and shrieks of laughter.

A grotesque funereal passage followed. The two triumphant assailants crawled like scavengers over the corpse. "Let's poke it, kick it, worry it, see if it's really dead," they seemed to say. The business was macabre, but for some reason very funny. The past was really as dead as a doornail. Charles could have made a living, falling apart and dying. When he chose, he could be very funny.

Finally came the rebirth. From ruin and ashes the "traditions," imbued with new energy and direction, returned to life. This concluding passage was full of dynamism, flying runs, leaps, and turns performed to a driving rhythm. The three resurgent traditions now returned to the positions of the opening, presumably, to flourish, fulfill their destiny, and face the challenge of the future.

Traditions was a serious work from the hand of a master of comedy. It came at a time when all our institutions faced an agonizing crisis. The revolutionary surge of the times was upon them, with its implacable, inescapable command, "Change, or be changed."

* * *

Late at night, during these middle years of the 1930s, coming home from performances of *As Thousands Cheer* at the Music Box Theatre, I would sometimes encounter at Tenth Street between Fifth and Sixth Avenues a lady walking a dachshund. The dog's name was Max, and he belonged to Louis Horst. The lady was Martha Graham.

Surely no dog was ever walked by a more distinguished personage. Even the highbred borzois of that pampered darling of Tsar Nicholas II, the prima ballerina assoluta Mathilde Kchessinska, were probably attended by a groom or lackey. But here was the great Miss Graham, very primly attired in tweeds, with a small hat perched on top of a severe coiffure, attending to Max's canine necessities. These were very pleasant meetings for me. We would discuss the weather, of course. I would stroll with her and await Max's pleasure, while he made a careful olfactory examination of each tree, lamppost, and fire hydrant for evidence of transgressions on

his territory, after which, with due deliberation he would raise his hind leg
in what dancers call an extension *à la seconde*, and reassert his claim.

We would discuss the dance. We observed a punctilious protocol. She
would comment with warmth and generosity on what Humphrey-Weidman was up to. I would speak with equal ardor about her works. One
night we discussed the dance critics. Recently, her audacious avant-
gardism had received what seemed to us all unduly heavy censure from
several critics. We matched our indignations. She closed the subject with a
remark I have never forgotten. "I have one answer for these people," she
said, her eyes narrowing in the light of the street lamp. "I say to them, 'I
would like to see you try it!'" On another occasion we had a good laugh
over Mary Garden's riposte to a persistently hostile music critic who,
after one of her spectacular triumphs, sought to make amends, only to be
informed by the singer, "I understand perfectly, my good man, perfectly.
You critics are like eunuchs. You know all about it, but you can't do it."

Graham and Louis Horst had apartments next door to the large establishment that Doris, her little boy, his nurse, Charles, Pauline, and I
shared. One night, pointing up to our respective windows, she said,
"Think, José, what would happen to the American dance if a bomb were
to drop and destroy these two buildings!"

Two blocks to the north, on Twelfth Street, also between Fifth and
Sixth Avenues, was the recently established New School for Social
Research. This institution quickly became a center where the American
dance functioned in several exciting ways. In the basement was a sort of
theater-in-the-round that was ideal for lecture-demonstrations. Charles,
Doris, Graham, and later other artists held forth on their precepts and
methods, assisted by their respective companies. It was here that the
memorable encounter took place between Graham and Fokine.

The auditorium upstairs was the frequent scene of exciting concerts,
with leading artists sometimes sharing a program. It was on these occasions that I saw Graham rehearse her company of girls in *Primitive Mysteries* and other works. I was struck by the sacerdotal authority with
which she rehearsed them, and by the hushed, almost religious atmosphere with which she seemed surrounded. Backstage, in the unbelievably
cramped wing space, we would "warm up" before performances. The
members of the Humphrey-Weidman company would look at the Graham dancers with a wariness and suspicion just short of overt hostility.
This was more than cordially reciprocated. With a curt nod, we only barely acknowledged each other's existence. I personally found some of the
girls absolutely fascinating. There were some spectacular beauties. One
was May O'Donnell.[89] Another was Dorothy Bird.[90] They had the fresh,
breathtaking radiance that blond, blue-eyed girls sometimes have, which
causes an involuntary wrench of the viscera in the enthralled spectator.
There was intense Anna Sokolow,[91] even then as explosive as dynamite;
Sophie Maslow,[92] straight out of the Old Testament; Gertrude Shurr,[93]
who had defected from Doris's group and, like all traitors, was fascinating

beyond words; Ethel Butler,[94] who exuded an intense, Slavic charm. These young contemporaries I was to know and cherish in future years. But now an insensate rivalry isolated us. Only later was I to discover, for example, that Lillian Shapero[95] was a delightful person with a rich sense of humor and a warm humanity. I did not know that the barriers we create between ourselves and our fellow humans are artificial, unnecessary, and what is worse, stupid.

These young women worked with my next door neighbor, the same Martha Graham I would encounter late at night being led by a willful and capricious dachshund. It was the reality of her greatness, and the blind, almost fanatical adoration in which her dancers held her that was at the root of our young hostility, our inability to look at each other with the casual friendliness of ordinary human society. No, we were contaminated; we were sick with that ancient malady, artistic jealousy.

For many years I have wrestled with this melancholy affliction. I have fought it every step of the way with every scrap of rationality and good sense I could muster. But so insidious, so subtle is its attack that, before one is aware, it has undermined and overrun the defenses, and one is at the mercy of a resentment—no, worse—a fear of another's excellence, and no jealousy engendered by the wiles of Aphrodite and Eros combined can compare to its abysmal torment. It is a cruel and corrosive experience. Woe to him who abandons himself to it!

Our masters, Graham, Humphrey, and Weidman, were on good terms. They had known each other as young people at Denishawn. They were the product of its school. As established artists, leaders of a movement that was to change the art of the dance throughout the Western world, they behaved toward each other with propriety. On occasion, Doris or Charles were critical of Graham's work; always, however, they expressed their criticism with the utmost respect and admiration. Graham always took great pains to tell me of her generous appreciation of the work of my teachers. We, their disciples, not having their background, experience, or maturity, felt free to give vent to our jealousies and hostilities. We reveled in the fetid miasma and spent endless hours ridiculing the rival camp. We were young, passionate, inexperienced, and stupid.

*   *   *

It was time for concerted effort. The stubborn earth had been broken, plowed, and harrowed. Individuals had planted the arid soil and irrigated it with their clean, copious dancers' sweat. The best cultivator known to man, the power of will and belief, had tended the young crop. And a harvesting was on the way.

Martha Hill[96] and Mary Jo Shelly[97] had seen the ripening crop. They found Bennington College, held the first Festival of American Dance there in 1934, and with the blessing and cooperation of the president, Dr. Robert Leigh, established the Bennington School of the Dance. These two ladies, practical and realistic as only inspired visionaries can be, organized everything with astonishing skill and efficiency. Bennington's small aggregation of white clapboard New England cottages, converted barn or two, old mansion, stables, handsome new brick Commons Building, and beautiful campus surrounded by the enchanting, verdant hills of Vermont in summer were used to accommodate dancers from all over the country. Each cottage had a good-sized, well-proportioned living room. From this all furniture was removed and stored away; rugs were rolled up and piled in hallways, and there you had a studio, that beautiful emptiness, that enticing space that makes a dancer's muscles ache with the desire to possess it and be possessed by it, to make the audacious and beautiful configurations in eternity that is dance. Upstairs were well-appointed bedrooms. The Commons Building contained the kitchen and dining rooms, and almost more important, a small stage and auditorium where performances were held the first year. This also served as a fine, ample studio for classes.

Bennington was an immediate success. A strong impetus was generated. The sickle, the scythe, and the reaper were in working order. It was a heady and intoxicating realization. The American dance had found a home—a summer home, that is—where its diverse forces, potencies, and potential could be concentrated, a place for climactic accomplishment.

Martha Hill and Mary Jo Shelly quite simply made possible a flowering and a harvest. There would be others, after the war, but for the present, a continuity was assured. It was important that the native art, as represented by Graham and Humphrey-Weidman, should work in conjunction and accord with its contemporary, the German modern dance, as created by the great figures of Mary Wigman, Rudolf von Laban, and Harald Kreutzberg, and as represented in this country by Hanya Holm. Holm, both as a teacher and choreographer, brought a fine distinction to the school during the years of her participation. Her methods of teaching young dancers were nothing short of brilliant. This was her greatest gift.

The directors devised a plan under which the four participating leaders—Martha Graham, Doris Humphrey, Charles Weidman, and Hanya Holm—would hold classes in their style and method, and give a recital or two during the session. In addition, there would be a workshop production under the direction of one of the artists, who would be given studio space, a composer, scenery, costumes, and maintenance for his or her concert company. Qualified students could apply for admission to the workshop and, on passing an audition, would find themselves in rehearsal and performing under the direction of a famous luminary of the dance world. It was a brilliant idea, and it came to a brilliant realization.

Martha Graham conducted the first workshop, in 1935. Her production was called *Panorama*, and it was a substantial work, using a large ensemble and a specially composed score by the young Norman Lloyd. It had ingenious stage props by Alexander Calder and sets by Arch Lauterer. The minuscule stage in the Commons Building was far too small for a production of this magnitude, so the directors, resourceful and indefatigable as always, obtained permission to use the Vermont State Armory in the center of town, an imposing edifice built in the last century that contained a not-too-cramped stage and ample seating capacity on the ground floor and in the balcony.

Graham made stunning use of the Armory's resources. She devised a choreography using an upper and lower level, that is, for the smallish stage and the more than ample floor level, with transitional levels between the two. Lauterer designed a fascinating array of vertical panels that were used as stage wings and manipulated by the dancers during entrances and exits to exciting effect. Calder provided mobiles in circular, ovoid, and other shapes that were suspended from the fly gallery and integrated into one of the episodes.

The company acquitted itself with its customary discipline and distinction. The young apprentices, having walked on air all summer, had the experience of their young lives when the audiences almost blew the roof off the Armory with their acclaim. My good friend Evelyn Davies, who would become a distinguished teacher in Washington, D.C., was one of those young girls, and she has described this summer as one of the unforgettable experiences of her life.

For me it was an electrifying one. I had not been present during the 1934 Bennington summer session, as I was busy with *As Thousands Cheer* in New York. But this year I was one of Charles's assistants in his classes. I remember the irrepressible excitement that, along with sweat, saturated the atmosphere of the college. Occasionally, I would find myself at a table in the dining room with Martha Graham and Louis Horst, those awesome presences, and John Martin, the puissant dance critic of *The New York Times*, who was in attendance giving lectures on dance history. With his distant, reserved manner, Martin is one of the few men who have frightened me. His eyes had the clear, cold brilliance of a blue diamond, a hardness that could congeal the very marrow of your bones. He was the maker and unmaker of reputations. At his Olympian pleasure, or caprice, as it sometimes seemed to us dancers, you rose or fell. Dancers fawned upon him, or paled, stammered, and cringed in his presence, or avoided him as one would the dreaded Fates. As the hawk is to the rodent and the typhoon to the navigator, so was this man to us.

And the frustrating thing was that he could not be dismissed as an opinionated ignoramus. He was a man of parts, a brilliant man, educated, cultured even. He could write superbly. With an urbane, literate English honed to as fine an edge as that of the finest surgical instrument, he would make his incision, open the visceral content of the dance over which you had slaved and sweated countless days and lain awake countless nights, spread it out, carefully dissect it, and discuss it with a cold impersonal detachment with the world as witness. These were your guts, and you were without benefit of even a local anaesthetic. It was years before I could look him in the eye without tremor or rancor, before I could place him in a rational perspective. In coming years he would praise me to the skies and damn me to hell. The time would come when we could talk, man to man, laugh and be friendly, eat and drink together, and he could forgive me for being a dancer, and I him for being a dance critic. But much was to happen to me and the world before that.

The morning after the premiere of *Panorama* I made a breathless dash for *The New York Times*. My fingers were trembling, my eyes greedy and expectant. Then came the blow, low, to the solar plexus. Martin's comments were devastating. The brutal exertion of six weeks, the creativity of the choreographer, composer, artist, and designer, the clamor of the ovation: all this was nothing. For him the work was pretentious, boring, and worse. I did not show up for breakfast, but Ruth, Norman Lloyd's wife,[98] recounted the epilogue to this unhappy affair. John Martin sat in splendid isolation when Martha Graham entered the dining room. All breathing ceased entirely. She walked firmly and directly to his table, and said in a clear, cold, cutting voice, "Thank you, John, thank you. If I never see you again it will be much too soon," and walked away, leaving Ruth Lloyd and others weeping into their scrambled eggs.

* * *

Doris and Charles, back in New York at the studio, began the autumn round of classes and rehearsals, faced, as always, with the need to balance artistic creativity with survival. Among Doris's best works was one that never saw the light of day. One might say that it miscarried, or, in that old Anglo-Saxon word, so final and pathetic, that it was stillborn.[99]

Darius Milhaud had composed an arresting and evocative score, *The Eumenides*, to Paul Claudel's translation of the Aeschylus play. It was a substantial work for orchestra and large chorus, and for over a year, on designated evenings, Doris had worked with us on the choreographic setting of several scenes. These included the opening, where the chorus of women fled in terror from Agamemnon's ghost only to be confronted by the mournful figure of Elektra in the palace courtyard; the confrontation between Elektra and Orestes, the murder of Clytemnestra, and the concluding scene. Doris used Eleanor King as her "stand-in" in the role of Elektra, and myself as Orestes.

This work again put me in awe of the grandeur of Doris's genius. She renewed herself with each effort. I marveled at her instinct, discernment, style, her capacity to discipline and give formal shape to tumults, and her seemingly inexhaustible choreographic resources. She made the dancers evoke, in their movement and appearance, the earliest Mycenaean art. There was violence, panic, and terror in the first scene, as the women fled through the portals of the doomed house of Atreus; deranged, loping runs, sudden pauses, and contorted wrenches of the entire body. What appalling phantasm had terrorized them? The scene was handled with consummate mastery. The women tore their hair, clawed their faces, fell to the ground in a frenzy, all this in a most stylized formality and contrapuntal architecture. The dance recreated the crime committed against the honor of the warrior king, and now his ghost was haunting the palace, calling for vengeance.

The tormented Elektra entered. The chorus engulfed her, clamorous with pity and compassion. Eleanor King was unbelievably moving as the ravaged princess, helpless in the clutches of monstrous iniquity and degradation. Doris molded her carefully, with the patience and precision of a dramatist-sculptor, into the patterns of agony and obsession. She made Eleanor over. It was beautiful to watch.

She labored to turn me into the vacillating Orestes. It was a tough assignment on both sides. I was not as experienced an artist as Eleanor. I did have one indisputable characteristic, what John Martin called at about this time "a great strength, a leonine intensity." In other words, I was a sort of half-grown lion. Orestes did not come easily to me. But where Doris was concerned, I was ready to go to any lengths, and, so, I became a weak, bewildered boy, the creature and instrument of an insanely vengeful sister. Eleanor pushed, dragged, lifted, cradled, cajoled, tormented, and took entire possession of me. Finally, abetted by a chorus of demented furies, she forced me through the portals of the haunted palace, there to murder my depraved mother and her paramour.

There was pandemonium. Elektra and her sympathizers went insane with an unholy expectation and joy. Watching this dance from my safe corner behind the gray blocks piled up to indicate the portal of the palace through which I had made my exit was a revelatory experience. I knew Doris's girls well, or thought I did. They were "nice" people, from decent, respectable homes and families. I had met their parents, brothers, and sisters, and the husbands of those who were married. Ernestine Henoch's mother was a gentle, sweet soul. Katherine Manning's parents were eminently respectable citizens of Saddle River, New Jersey. Dorothy Lathrop and Virginia Landreth were gently bred young ladies. Ada Korvin[100] was a great lady, an emigrée Russian baroness, who had escaped as a young girl from the Bolsheviks via the Trans-Siberian railroad, Vladivostok, and China. And so it went—these were nice people.

And yet, in this last scene, led by Eleanor King, who herself came from an impeccable Brooklyn family, they turned into atavistic furies. They terrified me, and I could see that the old mythic rite of ancient Greece, where women, led by the priestesses of Demeter, tore a male victim to pieces and devoured him, had left a disturbing residue. Serene, cool, and possessed, Doris never once raised her voice, even under trying circumstances.

The Eumenides was a labor of love if there ever was one. All of us sensed that Doris was opening new paths, leading us to unsuspected horizons. The work was tough and demanding. Doris turned us inside out, pulled us apart, and put us, all aching muscles and strained ligaments and tendons, back together again. Yet we could see the savage, brutal piece taking shape. We felt ourselves part of a vibrant, impassioned orchestration. The rhythms and patterns dominated you, hurling you like the angry surf. You were left panting and exhausted, with the knowledge that blind powers had possessed you.

Doris appealed for help to bring the work before the public. Money was needed. *The Eumenides* could not be presented with a small ensemble of instruments and two pianos, as were most concert works of that era. The Milhaud score called for a full-sized orchestra, a large vocal chorus, and soloists. We gave numerous showings at the studio for important people, including orchestra conductors. They were impressed. They were enthusiastic. And nothing came of it. The work was put away and forgotten—stillborn.

* * *

But the maternal womb was fecund and again heavy with child. *Theatre Piece*, the second work of Doris's epic trilogy, was on the way.

Here, as in all her works, Doris's artistry was inseparable and indistinguishable from her humanism. She cared. Although, in many ways, she was far removed from her Protestant, even Puritan, bourgeois heritage, this could have pushed her, as it did some of her fellow artists, to rebellion, to sloppy artiness and bohemianism, or to political radicalism and even bolshevism. But hers was too complex a mind, too fastidious a sensibility to allow herself such predictability. Doris, I came to understand, was an elitist. Her personal demeanor and deportment had the utter simplicity, serenity, and elegance of an aristocrat. Her art, both towering masterpieces and failures, revealed this ambivalence in her nature—an utterly unsentimental compassion for her fellow humans and a steadfast, patrician contempt for their vulgarities.

New Dance was her choreographic ode to the nobility of the human spirit. *Theatre Piece* was to explore the derangement of that spirit. Mankind, as she saw it, was capable of reason. This was amply proven to her by philosophers and artists. Where they could go, the rest of us could follow. Being as she was a supremely rational individual, she saw no reason for others not to be, or at any rate, not to try to be as rational as she was. The world had need for man's respect for the dignity of his species. He must cherish his fellow human beings. Hers was a poetic and noble vision of the universality of love. I gathered from listening to her over the decades that all this was not just sentimental twaddle. It was an expression of her love of order. It meant better choreography. A peaceful, orderly world would be man's transcendent work of art, his masterpiece. *Theatre Piece* was her excoriation of competitive society, its follies and vulgarities. The work began with a formal prologue introducing the cast of characters. This passage was brief and led immediately to the first episode. A curtain opened, revealing the gray blocks we had used in *New Dance*. (This was the Depression, and grave austerities were mandatory in all departments.) The blocks, which were of various sizes, were arranged into ingenious designs and shapes to suggest the skyline of a modern city, to serve as bridges, towers, stages, and many other things.

This scene showed human fragmentation. The spectator saw only parts of the performers. Hands, demanding, grasping, predatory, protruded from the massive horizontal block, seemingly suspended in midair. Above, a head was visible and, below, two pairs of feet that belonged in some monstrous way to the disembodied head. The feet were traveling in one direction. Then the head would turn and face the other direction, while the feet continued their progress, until, as though surprised to find themselves going the wrong way, they switched direction and encountered the by now returning head. But the head and feet never managed to catch up, nor could they agree on what direction to pursue. This created an eerie effect that was also very funny. There was a scene in which a fatuous and unsuspecting male (Charles) was pursued by a pack of predatory females. Panting, pushing each other aside to gain the advantage, they would fling themselves in his path in lewd abandon. At last, he casually selected the most aggressive, threw her over his shoulder, and exited with the rest of the pack in pursuit.

Another scene was set in a stadium. The pile of boxes now became bleachers. Two athletes (George Bockman and myself) would engage in a contest that at times resembled soccer, football, wrestling, and various track sports. The response from the spectators in the bleaches was every bit as mindless as the puerilities of the contestants, every bit as corrupted by the mania for competition as the sports themselves. At this point the dissident (Doris), who had looked on with alarm at the demonstrations of the herd, made some protest, only to be ignored or brushed aside.

A scene in a theater followed. Now, the boxes served as a stage, and the rest of us became the audience. Charles, Katherine Manning, and Katherine Litz performed a memorable parody in two parts. The first showed the actors concerned neither with excellence nor with artistry, but only with outdoing each other. Tender love scenes would be played to the gallery. The actors would go to any and all lengths to "upstage," eclipse, and trip a rival.

The second section was a frantic scene in a music hall. I remember this as a small masterpiece of absurdity and pure "corn." It was the competitive principle brought to a maniacal pitch. To Wallingford Riegger's insanely jazzy percussion, the performers knocked themselves out "selling" themselves, Charles as a song-and-dance man and the girls as a leggy chorus. There was much pushing, jostling, and wriggling to get to center stage front. There was a moment when the man would overpower the girls and use them as props to put his song across. In retaliation, the girls would use their legs, bosoms, and derrières, all the undulating paraphernalia of sex, to attract and hold the public's attention. This section was burlesque turned pandemonium, played to the shrieks and roars of the audience.

Suddenly and inexplicably, the stage emptied, and the "protestant" found herself alone. To a beautiful recitative passage for solo clarinet, Doris performed one of her most eloquent and moving dances. It was a meditation, a credo, done with spacious, liquid gesture invoking sanity and equilibrium. There were lovely leaps, from which she landed with the softest of pliés, and delicately poised suspensions and balances. All of Doris's dances were incantatory. This solo passage was a rite exorcising crudities, malformations, and bestialities. There were thematic allusions to *New Dance*, movements of a crystalline luminosity recalling a distant, noble vision. The dance scaled the platforms, a *gradus ad Parnassus* that ended with Doris poised in precarious serenity atop the highest eminence.

Over the years I have speculated on the position she chose to finish this passage. I have seen representations of the Buddha in many places in the Orient—in Bangkok, Taipei, Kyoto, Seoul. The figure sits in absolute, ineffable serenity. The symmetry and balance are perfect. Doris, however, sat on the very edge of a vertical construction twelve to fourteen feet above the stage floor; the lighting, dimmed elsewhere, isolated her, so that she seemed to perch dangerously at the very edge of a chasm. Her torso leaned sideways over the blackness with one of her legs extended on the opposite side at a high oblique to balance this dangerous tilt. One arm reached out parallel to the extended leg; the other curved in front of her in a placatory gesture. Her gaze seemed to probe a distant horizon. This was the balance, or lack of it, of the Western mind. I know that in her thinking she was irrevocably of the Occident. Her art had its roots in the "agon" inherent in human destiny. She used this term often in her discussions. To her the Eumenides were real, but man, in a savage, pitiless century, poised over the abyss, could yet redeem himself through the power of his will and his spirit.

A confrontation followed. The horde, the insensate mass, burst from behind the structures and began what Doris referred to as "the rat race." All of us, in waves of three, a man flanked by two girls, progressed up some steps behind the set so that we seemed to emerge from the distance, climbed to a summit, and moved at a heavy trot interspersed with intricate choreographic maneuvers, to the footlights, where we exited, each group alternating to stage left and right, ran as fast as possible, crawled under the curtain at the rear of the stage, and reappeared to continue the race. This produced the effect of a massive, irresistible torrent.

As the dissident, Doris attempted to arrest the headlong impetus. She arranged several passages with me when I came around. These were crude and violent, encounters between the rational and the irrational. I would lift her high, toss her out of the way, and then continue the race, which promised to last forever, but was interrupted by an imperious musical fanfare. All motion was arrested. There was a call to order. The participants moved formally to their places at the opening of the piece and, as the curtain fell, bowed to a central focus.

Early in my experience I learned about competitiveness in the theater. Not being of an especially competitive nature, I was unprepared to encounter it in the raw, and when I did it gave me quite a jolt. During the run of *Lysistrata*, I was standing in the wings waiting for my next cue to enter. Violet Kemble Cooper, as Lysistrata, and Ernest Truex as Kinesias, the distraught husband, were making their exit after an animated dialogue, both perspiring and panting with the exertion. Miss Cooper pounced, verbally, on Mr. Truex, and in her very precise British diction said, "Mr. Truex, don't try that on me again. Remember I know two tricks to your one, TWO TRICKS TO YOUR ONE!" This last was flung over her shoulder, as she disappeared, offended majesty personified, to her dressing room, slamming the door in the confounded face of Mr. Truex.

Miss Cooper's professional probity had been outraged by Mr. Truex's attempts to "steal the scene." Her successor in the play, Blanche Yurka, had a scene with Miriam Hopkins, who played the vixen Kalonika delightfully. Lysistrata had caught her red-handed, with the helmet of the goddess Athena under her robe, feigning pregnancy, in order to escape confinement within the Acropolis. She was supposed to chase the miscreant back within the gates, and give her a purely symbolic swat in the rear with the helmet. Miss Yurka, carried away with artistic zeal, would supplement this with one or more good resounding slaps on the fleeing Kalonika's thinly veiled buttocks. These would elicit loud guffaws from the audience. The blows grew nightly in intensity, accuracy, and number. We ribald characters, watching in the wings, would count, speculate, and lay bets on the next performance, and watch Yurka, a hefty woman, enjoying herself tremendously, and Hopkins's discomfiture and mounting indignation as she rubbed her burning posterior on her way to the dressing room. One night came the breaking point. Hopkins turned on her tormentor. "Miss Yurka, don't you dare do that again. I won't have it!" "But darling, it finishes the scene so beautifully." "I don't care. Mr. Bel Geddes directed that there should be one slap only, and that with the helmet. My behind is black-and-blue from your sadistic treatment. If you don't stop I'll complain to the stage manager." Sad to relate, Miss Yurka was obliged to desist. Thereafter, there was to be only a light, anemic tap on Miss Hopkins's bottom during her flight back to the Acropolis, and the play was robbed of one of its most delightful moments.

Theatre Piece was in violent contrast to the noble formality of *New Dance*. There was a memorable occasion when both works were performed at the Guild Theatre. They were received with wild enthusiasm by the audience. We felt very rewarded. Doris was now regarded as an incomparable master of the difficult art of choreography.

No matter how formidable your talent and achievement, there are inevitably those who will dislike what you do, resent your success, and envy you. At the height of Doris's powers as a dancer and choreographer, when she was creating works of an artistic magnitude, formal integrity, and dramatic power never before seen in this country, a commentator in the *New Masses* denounced her as "a dancer having only the remnants of a once good technique" and her works as being those of a "decayed bourgeois." I, her staunch and dedicated partisan, found this a galling outrage, and was dumbfounded when my indignation was met by her cool and dispassionate rationality. "Anger is not the best response to criticism," she said. "One must examine it carefully and try to discover where that criticism may be justified. One must, and can, learn from one's enemies."

It is difficult to believe now, after thirty-five years, that there was a time when millions of Americans were permanently unemployed, and hunger and misery stalked the land. Disaffection led many to rebelliousness, and they found in the doctrine of the Communist Party a panacea for the troubles of mankind. The solution was as simple as it was cogent. Capitalist society and all its corruptions and iniquities must be liquidated, and the millennium, modeled after the Workers' Fatherland, would bring justice, equality, and decency to humanity.

Certain members of the Humphrey-Weidman company were quite convinced of this and spoke as though the time had come to raise barricades along the avenues of New York City. After all, the heady triumph of Lenin and his Bolsheviks in the streets of Petrograd was still fresh in many memories, and stirring accounts were not lacking. One was John Reed's *Ten Days That Shook the World*, so memorably translated to the screen by Sergei Eisenstein. American writers, poets, dramatists, painters, sculptors, and dancers were swept by this revolutionary fervor. All that was needed was the solidarity of right-thinking men, concerted action, and one good push for the decayed capitalist system to join the tsarist regime in well-deserved oblivion.

There were numerous company meetings instigated by a sort of committee composed of our more militant colleagues. Doris and Charles were formally enjoined to place their talents at the service of the imminent and inevitable world revolution. The meetings became tempestuous when Doris would point out, in that calm way of hers, that she disapproved of injustice and the exploitation of the poor by the rich, but saw no cause for nor possibility of armed and bloody insurrections, Russian style; conditions here were not what they had been under the tsars; the Roosevelt administration showed an enlightened concern for the plight of the suffering; her works, and those of Charles, were works of art, not propaganda tracts. They were based on a humanistic concern with man and his condition. She reminded them of *New Dance*, *Theatre Piece*, and Charles's *Traditions*. She did not want to live under any sort of dictatorship, whatever its political orientation. She preferred not to have official sanction for her work. She demanded absolute freedom to do as she saw fit. I never knew how she held her temper during these meetings, when she was subjected to impertinences that would have made me explode. I learned a great deal about self-discipline. The creative momentum in the converted machine shop on West Eighteenth Street was not to be retarded by politico-ideological turbulences, the genuine distress and privation everywhere, and the ever-present necessity to function on excessively limited artistic budgets.

Charles composed one of his most mature and coherent pieces, *This*

Passion.[101] The work was a species of three-part fugue. Each component "voice" was based on a contrasting idea in concept, style, and treatment from the other two. The first dealt with a tawdry *crime passionnel*, where an unprepossessing husband was done to death by his sluttish wife and her lover. The second voice was a nightmarish vision of a world inured to living underground with gas masks and the threat of annihilation by poisonous gases. The third was, again, the artist's call for order and sanity, the ever-recurring vision of an impossible Utopia. Each "theme" was broken into three parts—a statement, development, and conclusion. These parts were juxtaposed and performed in sequence. The by now indispensable blocks, supplemented by doors, curtains, street lamps, and other ingenious pieces of scenery, were used very effectively.

Charles created strong theater. The opening scene, an imaginary interior, showed the husband (Charles), as an uncouth, unlovable creature. The wife (Doris) waited on him, barely concealing her revulsion, rejected his advances, and lewdly consorted with her lover (myself). The music underlined the bleak monotony of discontent and boredom.

The three protagonists melted into the shadows, and the performing area was transformed into a street scene, with nervous, jittery figures moving to a frenzied tempo. Every face was that of a grotesque insect or a goggle-eyed beast with an ugly snout that was actually a gas mask: the costumes were prophetic. The men wore jackets much like the "mod" style now current, and the girls wore micro-mini skirts.

Suddenly, the stage was empty. The atmosphere became serene, with lights and music in consonance and a dance that was like a heroic sarabande. The wife and her paramour stole a clandestine moment together. They moved like furtive reptiles, plotting the murder of the husband. Charles used a powerful, slashing movement to indicate the crime, a sort of brutal shorthand. The husband was enticed, all unsuspecting, and gruesomely murdered, his corpse dragged into the shadows.

The masked troglodytes took over, diverting themselves. They danced, got drunk, made unlovely love. A stripper appeared and went into her routine of titillation. She took everything off, except for her gas mask. As a final, climactic tease, she removed the mask, revealing the ultimate indecency, her naked face, an act that sent spasms of obscene delight through her audience. Again, the Utopian vision appeared, as remote and intangible as the cool, abstract beauty of a fountain or a mirage.

The police, like monstrous frogs, hopped off the boxes to apprehend the guilty lovers in the crude style of a tabloid. A black-robed judge appeared above a tribunal; there was a grotesque indictment, to which the pair responded with craven accusations of each other. The judge pronounced sentence. The policeman dragged the two away, but the condemned adulteress-murderess had some final words. Here, Doris performed a beautiful passage. It spoke of the loathing, suffering, and infinite boredom of the miserable woman's life. She addressed judges, juries, the universe, challenging, defying. She was guilty, she was glad she sinned and would gladly sin all over again. Then, exiting, she went to her doom, still a slut, still tawdry, but with a peculiar majesty.

Now, the masked creatures hurled themselves across the stage in wild panic. The attack had come, and there was no place to hide. They died horrid, comical deaths, twitching convulsively like cockroaches sprayed with a lethal insecticide, expiring on top of boxes, in the dark recesses, out in the open. Charles could make even a scene like this laughable. And then, came his final vision—the sarabande, more serene and heroic than ever, and even more of a mirage.

As companion piece to *This Passion*, Doris composed *Race of Life*. It was based on a series of cartoons by that master of humor, James Thurber. The score, witty and delightful, was by Vivian Fine.[102] It was the story of a family—father (myself), mother (Doris), and child (Charles)—embarking on a journey to a mountain top, there to plant a banner inscribed with the word "Excelsior." Pauline Lawrence, with the assistance of a young artist, Betty Joiner, costumed us as nearly as possible to resemble the Thurber drawings.

Thurber's genius for capturing human absurdity with devastating directness and deceptively crude economy of line, was matched only by his subtlety, insight, and compassion. Clearly, he did not despise his human fellows for their foolishness or frailty. He laughed not in derision but with them and for them. Perhaps he sensed the impossible dream locked tightly inside even the drabbest fool; certainly, he knew that only the cruel laugh at his foibles. Thurber seemed to say, "Oops! That was fun. Maybe I'm next. Let's wait and see."

Doris knew that Thurber posed a serious challenge. The episodes in *Race of Life* were clearly indicated. There were incidents, adventures, dangers. How to give the drawings a continuity and translate them into movement without making animated cartoons was the problem. We sweated blood, as they say. An entirely new manner and style of movement had to be invented. Doris took us apart and put us together again. And more than anyone else, she completely made herself over. She became a gross, strident, harassed female, a woman no longer young or attractive; me she made into a fat fool of a husband, stupid and dull. Charles took to this piece like a duck to water. He became a noisy, mischievous brat of nine, unruly but completely delightful.

The family began their confused journey by disagreeing on which direction to follow. Each had his opinion as to the right one and insisted on following it. It was only after much confusion, done to violently asymmetrical rhythms in the music, that some consensus was reached, and the family advanced, literally, by leaps and bounds. In the distance a band of Indians, obviously on the warpath, could be discerned; the three took cover, and the Indian chief (George Bockman, later Lee Sherman) flew in, looked over the terrain, and called to his three squaws (Katherine Litz, Beatrice Seckler, and Edith Orcutt). There followed a very funny parody on the tribal dances of the North American aborigine that included imaginary smoke signals, elaborate sign language, stalking the enemy, and of course the hunt. It was magnificent nonsense, and the dancers showed great skill as comedians.

The Indians, restless nomads, made their exit; the family, delivered from danger, cavorted and pranced with childish delight. The little boy scurried about, looking under imaginary rocks for bugs, lizards, and other things little boys like. Papa danced like a middle-aged elephant, and Momma remembered what she used to do, decades ago, in a meadow covered with buttercups and daisies. It was idyllic.

Exhausted with simple pleasures, the family fell asleep. The Beautiful Stranger appeared. Papa was enticed and enmeshed. Momma, who had seen all, knocked her errant husband cold with a rock conveniently provided by the Boy. The Beautiful Stranger made a disdainful exit. Quite possibly the next scene was a figment of the father's imagination as he lay unconscious. The Night Creatures appeared (the same cast as the Indians), disturbing the family's slumbers with their strange shenanigans. Like all bad dreams, they disappeared with the sunrise. Refreshed, the family now continued its journey. Finally, after a curtain opened upstage to reveal the ever useful cubes, demi-cubes, quarter-cubes, and double-cubes, now arranged to suggest a craggy incline, the three hardy pilgrims—after an arduous ascent performed prestissimo—reached the summit and triumphantly planted the banner with the inscription "Excelsior." Curtain.

These recollections of my tutelary decade with Humphrey-Weidman are not, unfortunately, an unrelieved rhapsody in praise of their artistry. I was not without reservations. These two, my masters, were artists, not machines. They had their ups and downs. Toward the end of the 1930s Charles permitted himself to be seduced by the siren song of Broadway, and it was perhaps inevitable that his product, as the decade approached its close, should suffer. There is no doubt that the early austerities, which had presided like uncompromising muses over his *Happy Hypocrite*, *Candide*, *Studies in Conflict*, *Traditions*, *This Passion*, and other fine works, had unlocked a rich reservoir of creativity of the first order. For this the American dance is in his debt. These works were seminal to the subsequent flowering of dance on these shores.

Doris, on the other hand, saw that the commercial theater was not for her. After *Americana* and *School for Husbands* she steadfastly refused to permit herself any deviation from artistic rectitude. Both artists, however, faced different economic circumstances. As a man, Charles had to support himself and his endeavors. Doris was fortunate in having the support of her husband, Charles Woodford. This quite automatically insulated her from the blandishments of commerce. She could enjoy the privilege of undiluted, uncontaminated art. I learned, again and again, that great talent, even genius, is not infallible. I saw my teachers undergo the genetic cycle—the act of conception, the exaltation of gestation, the travail of birth. I saw them tremulous with the excitement of a new idea; I saw and shared with them the drudgery and often the torment of mind and body; I was there, jubilant, when things seemed to go right. There was no feeling on earth like it, this attainment of will and spirit, this transcending of obstacles and limitations. I saw their obsessed dedication.

And I saw failure, dismal beyond words, merciless and irrevocable. Heroic failure often carries with it a cathartic aftermath. One can find a somber solace in a superlative debacle. But how to endure living with half-success, half-failure? With the knowledge that you failed to move, to transfigure the spectator? That he left your performance untouched, unravished, merely lukewarm?

The years gave me, inevitably, experience, and with it, increased capacity, which led to greater artistic responsibility within the company, and this awakened latent critical faculties. The years of innocence were ended. Blind worship of my artistic heroes gave way to a more discriminating and far from total acceptance of their works. And, stirring uncomfortably in a dim recess of my awareness, at first unrecognized, then by slow degrees more palpable, was a persistent question, a challenge even. "Can you do as well? Do you think that, some day, some year, you could do better?"

* * *

The Bennington summers became a way of life. It was accepted among us that we would be participants in one way or another. The Graham company would be in residence, then the Humphrey-Weidman company, and then the Hanya Holm company. It was a fine plan. Those of us not "in residence" would be teaching classes. The weeks in July and August were intensely busy. The vernal landscape and the humid heat did not intrude. They were only a background, seen and felt dimly. The sweat, the sore muscles, the violent exertion, the almost fanatic dedication were the only reality. Only on rare occasions would we venture into the outer world, and then with a feeling of guilt. There were expeditions into remote, enchanting valleys walled in by verdant hills, to towns and villages belonging to another century. I have never forgotten the breathtaking beauty of these places, the austere grace and simple elegance of cottage, mansion, church, barn, or bridge. The architectural genius of the Anglo-Saxon flowered with incomparable distinction in Puritan New England and in the Cavalier South, but was gradually corrupted, neglected, or destroyed as he pushed westward. The dreary, monotonous ugliness of the Middle and Far West, of Chicago, Denver, Dallas, and Portland are perhaps a judgment and a penalty. He took too much too suddenly, and in his greed and hurry forgot the dignity and proportion left behind, condemning himself to live and proliferate in ugliness.

Architecture has always offered a close parallel to the dance: to me choreography is a form of architecture. Great dances—*Les Sylphides, Primitive Mysteries, Passacaglia*—are monumental pieces of architecture. They are miracles of planning, construction, and beauty. My impassioned response to the architecture of the Vermont hills springs from the same source as my devotion to the dance. The use man makes of sticks and stones is closely related to how he puts together the movements of his body to create the concatenation called choreography. Gorged with beauty, I would return to Bennington from an excursion, asking myself, "Can I make a dance as fine, as tall, as noble as the church spire in that impeccable village to the north? Let me try." Failure, then or later, would not deter me. I would lick my wounds, then return, undaunted, to the task of erecting a noble architecture in movement.[103]

During the summer of 1936 I was to be witness and participant in a work that showed me how sublime a structure could be created in movement, how little I knew, and how long the road I must travel. The destructive power of possessive love was the central motif of *With My Red Fires*. Here, Doris, now on the threshold of middle age, devised for herself the role of the Matriarch, while Charles and Katherine Litz were the young lovers. The rest of us, both men and women, were to play the part of a chorus in the style of a Greek tragedy. The music for this monumental work, a companion piece to *New Dance* and *Theatre Piece*, was by the gifted Wallingford Riegger, and again he matched Doris's concept. The score was beautiful, strong, eloquent.

The work opened with a "Hymn to Priapus." In a hushed, mystical silence, broken only by the patter of bare feet, began a canon-fugue in four voices, each "voice" being performed by a dozen or so dancers. The movement was archaic in style. Each group, on entering, added to the rhythmic and visual momentum. At the climax, the dancers came to a dead stop. They dropped to their knees, expectant, and a lovely sensuous melody, an invocation to young love, was heard. The hymn resumed, mounting in fervor and intensity. There were bold running and leaping phrases in diagonals, circles, and parallels. Young men and women found each other, paired off, and danced their joy. In transcendent rapture they walked, ran, and flew, upright, horizontally, upside down, à la Chagall, with the initial fugal premise as their background—a superb choreographic architecture.

At the height of the ritual the protagonists were introduced—Charles, young, strong, escorted by the girls, and Litz, golden and radiant, accompanied by the men. The dance that followed was a celebration of their first magical encounter. There was a joyful de-escalation of the fugue, voice by voice, then a farewell and a blessing. The lovers, alone, performed a wildly elated episode, which ended sinisterly with the raising of a curtain at the center rear of the stage. The Matriarch appeared, a somber figure in gray and black, and beckoned to the young girl. Reluctantly, the lovers parted. A chilling scene followed in which the mother violently upbraided her daughter. Passive and sullen, the girl submitted to the histrionics, which alternated between lamentations and accusations.

Doris was incredible as the wily, tyrannical mother. Pauline had dressed her in one of her most stunning creations, a stylization of the high-necked, tight-bodiced, wide-skirted dress of the late nineteenth century that gave Doris a predatory look, half-hawk, half-vulture. The choreographic style was a curious blend of the pathetic and the odious. The range of gesture was amazing—minute flutters of the hands, jerks of the head and shoulders, fragmented isolations and contortions of the pelvis and extremities—all of which created the effect of a feathered creature intent on some baleful ritual.

The mother, finally dominant, cradles her child. Both fall asleep. A blue nocturnal light descends. From the shadows the lover silently summons her. The girl disengages herself from the maternal embrace and joins him in the soft night. There is an idyllic, erotic episode. The two flee. Three fatelike figures appear and surround the family abode. Their slow, solemn dance is full of portent and malediction. They disappear into the shadows whence they came.

The Matriarch suddenly awakens. Finding the girl gone, she flies into a rage and sounds the alarm. The furies respond, joining her in a species of war dance, a cyclone gathering momentum from the deranged woman whirling at the center, her enormous skirt billowing like the winds of a hurricane, her torso and arms cutting the air like lightening. The choreographic technique here was masterful. The lust of the hunter intent on tracking down his prey was worked out in a complex sequence of jagged, asymmetrical phrases of varying durations—no two were alike—that alternated between violent action and sound and the sudden cessation of both. The massed dancers would hurl themselves upward and forward, run and drop on their haunches, like predators searching for the scent of their quarry. Tension, suspense, and menace filled the air. The furies exited. The Matriarch, hoisted on the shoulders of two minions, was carried back and forth like a monstrous effigy of doom and deposited on top of a jutting pillar or eminence. Here she perched precariously, thrashing and fluttering, an infuriated bird of prey, hackles bristling dangerously.

The mob reentered, half-carrying, half-dragging the fugitives, whom they deposited at the feet of the old woman. Her vengeful fury rose to an incandescent climax, and after a final malediction she made a slow exit, gorged with venom, leaving the guilty pair to the implacable judgment of the chorus of furies, which retreated with a heavy, punitive gesture. Merging with the gathering dusk, the chorus disappeared as the lovers comforted each other in their desolation.

With My Red Fires was presented in August 1936 at the Vermont State Armory. It was received clamorously. Also on the program was *Quest*,[104] a work by Charles in which a figure reminiscent of Candide, finds himself in the inhospitable world of the middle 1930s. The piece had its good points, notably the episode in which the protagonist (played by Charles) confronts a pyramid of haughty dowagers who end up using him as an ashtray for their cigarette butts, and the scene in which he is forced to submit to a crudely humorous inquisition by grim, uniformed Fascists, who dissect, weigh, measure, and probe his mind and body, leaving him, so to speak, in pieces, rejected as a "non-Aryan." It would be senseless to compare the two works. Each was founded on different premises and used a different style. One was the work of a tragedian, the other that of a comedian. On the program they served each other well.

* * *

One morning I was giving myself a "workout" in one of the small studios, when Wallingford Riegger knocked on the door and entered. The ordinarily cheerful composer looked pale and serious. "The radio has just announced that a junta of generals have launched an attack on Spain, from Morocco. It looks well armed and well organized. They seem to have help from Italy and Germany. This may be the beginning of World War II."

Thus began a period in my life from which I would emerge years later spiritually scarred and in some ways maimed. From that day on I carried a pressure, a weight inside my skull, squarely between my eyes. Carefree innocence was ended. There was no joy, and pleasure, taken with a sense of guilt, offered neither solace nor relief. So began what I have heard described as the dark night of the soul.

There was a swift concatenation of crimes. The most Christian, most Catholic Generalissimo Franco, champion of Western Civilization, let loose on the ill-prepared Spanish Republic his barbarian legions from North Africa to slaughter, rape, and pillage. Early in the holocaust, with the wanton assassination of Federico García Lorca, he silenced one of the sweetest lyric voices in the Castilian tongue. In emulation of his Fascist and Nazi mentors he burned books, murdered, imprisoned, or banished philosophers, poets, dramatists, and pedagogues. His ceremonials were graced with the Fascist salute and cries of "¡Viva la muerte!" and "¡Abajo la inteligencia!"

Atrocities abounded on both sides. But to me the Republic was defending an incipient and unpracticed democracy, even if the aid of anarchists and Stalinists was accepted in that defense. Franco aimed to destroy the impulse toward a just and rational society, to reestablish an archaic feudalism and to impose a Fascist tyranny. The ferocity and brutality of the Spanish Civil War appalled and horrified the world. Battles, sieges, and massacres became daily occurrences. The Western democracies, including the United States, maintained a fatuous and what turned out to be a disastrous neutrality, while the Fascist dictators, with armaments and men, aided Franco in his destruction of the Spanish Republic. Only Russia helped, but not enough. Only the Bolsheviks, and thousands of young men from Europe and the Americas, who out of detestation of the necrophiliac menace to the human spirit gave generously of their courage and their blood in defense of liberty.

The artists and intellectuals, so feared—with good reason—by the Fascists, everywhere rallied to the cause of the beleaguered Republic. We knew, much earlier than our governments, who the enemy was, and that the Fascist tide, horrid and pestilent with death, would attempt to engulf the world. It had begun with Spain. For the duration of the Spanish Civil War, and even after the surrender of the Loyalist forces to Franco, we did whatever we could able to help the Republican cause. All branches of the performing arts gave of their time and energies. Music, drama, and dance were generous. There were benefits, many of them, with prestigious figures making appeals for money.

When your house is on fire, you do not question the identity or motives of those who come to put out the flames. When waves are about to engulf your boat, you do not reject the assistance of those who offer to bail water. We found ourselves working with outright Stalinists in a common cause. I am careful to say "working with," because the Communists were as a rule not only the instigators, but also the most impassioned workers in the various projects and enterprises. If Satan himself and all his fiends had been as active as were the Bolsheviks in opposition to Fascist Franco, I would have been more than happy to be their ally.

It was a busy autumn and winter for us. Rehearsals began in September. Both *With My Red Fires* and *Quest* were in need of directorial reconsiderations and meticulous rehearsal. The works were to be performed at the old Hippodrome, that now extinct arena on Sixth Avenue and Forty-Third Street. The huge stage was propitious for both productions. The expanded orchestra was to be directed by Norman Lloyd. The International Ladies' Garment Workers' Union was our sponsor. The cavernous barn was packed to the rafters for the performance, and it was a fine occasion. The reception was tumultuous.

* * *

Martha Hill, that indefatigable "handmaiden to the art of dance," as she would sometimes call herself, divided the busy weeks of her life between Bennington College and New York University. Four days there, three here. She taught her classes with the dedication and skill of the inspired. I, for whom teaching was either a chore or a bore or both, regarded her with admiration but not envy. I was content to be a performer.

Periodically, she would invite some colleague to fill in for her at Bennington on the days she spent in New York. One year she asked me. I was happy to accept for two reasons: I needed the money, and I thought it would be interesting to see the college in session during the winter. A busy but comfortable schedule of classes was worked out for me.

I have always grumbled about the privileged rich, their ostentation, greed, gross self-indulgence, and callousness. My wife, bored and irritated by this quirk of mine, tells me that I suffer from "the taint of poverty." This I'm sure is the exact truth. I have never been afflicted by the acquisitive mania. Money is something one needs to pay for food, shelter, studios, costumes, dancers, musicians, and other costly things. One works hard to earn that money, but one doesn't devote one's life to making money just to put in the bank or make more money.

I arrived at Bennington for the winter session prepared to find myself in enemy territory surrounded by the pampered female progeny of the rich and their professional lackeys, obsequious, servile, and contemptible. Quickly, very quickly, I was disabused of my ignorance. True, the college was a sanctuary for the privileged. But the students were also intellectually select: preparation, capacity, and ability counted as much as background for admission. An academy, laboratory, atelier, forum, and theater rolled into one, the school was a boldly innovative venture in preparing an elite, in the finest and fullest sense of that word, to enter and grace human society. The young ladies with whom I worked were of fine caliber. They were not afraid of hard, very hard work. There was a great deal of talent.

Martha Hill, modest as always, had not prepared me for any of this. She preferred to have me find out for myself. The faculty was in all respects superior. I came in contact with Ben Bellit,[105] Francis Fergusson,[106] Gregory Tucker,[107] Julian de Gray,[108] and many other fine artists. After a full day, the college community would assemble for evening concerts, lectures, and seminars. There was an excitement, a turmoil even, in the way the intellectual, cultural, and political state of the world was examined and discussed.

After the activities of the dance department, those of the department of drama interested me the most. I saw a great interest in avant-garde experimentation. A high point was a production of Sophocles's *Elektra*. Fergusson directed the speech, and Hill the gesture and choreography. The result was a superbly stylized work of compelling power. The drama students (a group that naturally included some men imported on scholarships) and the dancers transcended, thanks to talent and fine direction, the limitations of youth and inexperience. Arch Lauterer[109] provided inspired settings and lighting. I have never forgotten this moving experience.

* * *

In 1937 Hanya Holm was in residence at the Bennington School of the Dance and presented the major work at the Festival in August. At the same time, the School awarded three fellowships to young dancers that provided them with production facilities and allowed them to present their works at the end of the summer. The recipients of these awards were Anna Sokolow, Esther Junger, and myself.

I found this stroke of good fortune exciting beyond belief, and since the announcement was made early in the year, I began to dream about and plan a work more ambitious than anything I had previously attempted. There was a young composer at Bennington named Henry Clarke.[110] He was a member of the music faculty, and one of his works, Sarabande for Oboe and Piano, was performed at an evening concert. The oboist was Robert McBride,[111] a fine instrumentalist, also of the music faculty. I had found the work hauntingly beautiful. The oboe melody appeared to soar, disembodied almost, in a tragic ecstasy, sustained and driven by the contrapuntal impetus of the piano.

I asked the composer for permission to use the Sarabande for my new work, and he was most cordial and generous in assenting.

The piece was too short for a dance of fifteen to twenty minutes such as I was planning. There was much insomnia, much worry, and a few headaches, before the form of the work became clear. I had known for several months that I had to do a work based on the Civil War in Spain, a sort of lyric ode, an anthem in praise of the heroic Republic. The Clarke music would be performed twice, as a preamble and as an epilogue. However, I still needed music for the middle section. This Norman Lloyd agreed to compose. I was set—and avid—to begin.

The opening days set the tone for the entire summer session. It was to be a time of almost unbearable tension and excitement. The three Fellows held auditions and selected their casts. Anna, at this point deeply embedded in the Graham company and its repertory, selected dancers adept in the style—about fifteen, if I remember correctly, all girls. Esther planned a choric work with almost thirty dancers. I needed six girls and four men.

Once they were chosen, I got to work. The dancers were to take their daily classes in technique, music, and other subjects in the morning and to be at my disposal in the afternoon and evening. After much thinking I found a title, *Danza de la Muerte*, in Spanish of course, which seemed appropriate to the subject. The opening dance, by the company, was called "Sarabande for the Dead." There would be three solo dances, done by me, "Hoch!," "Viva," and "Ave." The closing dance, again by the company, was "Sarabande for the Living." Here at last was the testing ground. There was no parental, tutelary support on which to lean. I was on my own.

The style of movement was of a rugged sculptural formality. The opening was a solemn commemoration of brave men fallen in battle, an elegiac tribute by comrades who would follow in their footsteps and by women bearing a double burden of mourning, both for the dead and for those about to die. Into the central solos I poured all the venom and detestation of which I was capable. "Hoch!" was a brutally repellent storm trooper, an automaton swift as lightning and efficient as death, a goose-stepping barbarian stamping out Teutonic marches. "Viva!" was a creature of bombast, a bogus Caesar, wrapped grandiloquently in a purple toga and crowned with a gold laurel wreath declaiming Latin pomposities. "Ave!" was a death figure, all black-velveted Spanish decay, posturing with sinister elegance. Norman Lloyd composed three very effective pieces here, a march, a recitative, and a pavane. The finale, predictable but inevitable, was a ritual of rededication.

I remember this as a good, strong, young piece. It was full of my immaturities but also of my virtues. It was a stepping-stone across the torrent that must be crossed and recrossed endlessly. The decades would give me surer footing, better balance, more wariness. But the danger of slipping and being carried away by swift, merciless waters is always present. We poor mortals imagine ourselves scaling the heights to Parnassus, when in all reality our triumphs consist of deferring, as long as we can, the final tumble into the dark Styx.

Anna Sokolow also had an anti-Fascist piece, which she called *Façade—Esposizione Italiana*.[112] At dress rehearsals I looked at it with admiration and envy. It was replete with stunning imagery and passages that moved me to say, "I wish I had done that!" Already, in 1937, Anna possessed that singular power of communicating with unerring directness, of using the abstract in gesture to create almost brutally impassioned drama. She was on her way to becoming what she is today, the most advanced of the advance guard, the most disturbingly human of choreographers.

Esther Junger, for all her undisputed talent and accomplishment as a performer, was not a practiced choreographer. Her piece, a primitive ritual of betrothal, with herself as the bride and me as the bridegroom and a large group of girls as a chorus, was, as I remember, competent but uninspired. Esther was brilliant in her solo passages. I served her well, supporting and lifting her.

During one of the final dress rehearsals I inadvertently bumped my toes (we were dancing barefoot) hard against her leg. There was an ugly, cracking sound. The two small toes of my right foot were dislocated and stuck out at a complete right angle to the usual alignment. I limped to the edge of the platform, sat down, and pulled the toes back into place. There was considerable pain. The girls squealed. The rehearsal came to a terrified stop. Mary Jo Shelly ran up, pale but calm, her usual efficient self. Quickly, she drove me to a doctor. No bones were broken; it was just a bad sprain. Bandages and complete rest were prescribed, and above all no dancing.

I had tumbled into the black river. I spent the night in acute torment. The following day I limped to the studio, tried this and that, and decided to disobey the doctor's orders. It would hurt, but it wouldn't kill. I changed all the difficult balances and jumps so that the major strain would be borne by the left foot. The right foot would function in an auxiliary capacity. It was painful but possible.

Opening night I went on. My colleagues assured me that the incapacity was not apparent. Fortunately, there was an intervening evening after the premiere, when Hanya Holm, the Festival's major attraction, presented *Trend*. This was a work of gigantic proportions by a master choreographer. She used an enormous ensemble and filled the two-leveled stage of the Vermont State Armory with a dazzling kaleidoscope of movement. Her principal dancer, the magnificent Louise Kloepper, danced a superb solo interlude. This beautiful creature was one of the ornaments of the modern dance of that era. Merely to watch her move was a ravishment. She and Hanya Holm earned a resounding triumph.

My stalwart collaborators of that summer included two well-remembered people. One was Pauline Chellis,[113] a Boston native and a distinguished dancer and pedagogue in that city for decades. The other, Alwin

Nikolais,[114] in good time would arrive at his own unique form of theater and create astounding kaleidoscopic visions, in which movement, costume, decor, sound, and lighting would meet and cohere in ways undreamed of before.

The dance was more than ever the nexus between me and existence. I lived for it. Everything else was shadow and echo, an intrusion on the one reality. There was a curious relationship between ordinary human experience and this inner life: the first was a sort of truancy, a defection, while the second was the school-temple-sanctuary to which one had perforce to return. The dance was my one reason for being and my justification.

This obsession was to receive confirmation from an event, a revelation that was to shake me to my very foundations. This was a solo concert by Martha Graham. Her program, made up of her famous dances, included, if I remember correctly, *Imperial Gesture*, *American Provincials*, and *Ekstasis*.[115] I came prepared, as always, to be impressed, to admire, and to confirm certain presumptuous reservations.

Her one premiere was *Immediate Tragedy*, with music by Henry Cowell.[116] She had arrived on campus about a week before with Louis Horst, who was to play for her. I had heard the sound of the Cowell piece as she rehearsed in a studio adjacent to where I was working. It was scored for clarinet and piano. Since she rehearsed this piece daily, I became familiar with the music, and also with the sound of a rapid stamping of bare feet resounding through the wooden partition. I was curious to see what this dance would be like. I saw.

A woman with a heroic stance, symbol of multitudes of women, made an entrance diagonally on stage. She was dressed austerely in a white, skintight bodice, with a black, ankle-length skirt that flared from the hips. Her black hair, pulled back severely and knotted at the base of her skull, was fastened with a black ribbon, the ends of which fell down her back. Her arms were held high overhead, as Spanish dancers hold them. This introductory passage was like a tightly wound spool of thread that, as it unwound, conveyed what Picasso's apocalyptic "Guernica" would convey to me later. For this dance was nothing less than a vision of embattled, tortured, heroic Spain. Translated in some miraculous way into a modern American idiom were the grace and fury of the Spanish dance. Here, with a supreme and fiery incandescence, was distilled the Goyaesque defiance, the Quixotic gallantry, and the heartbreaking, bellowing desolation of the *cante jondo*.

The consummately sinuous torso, the supple, beautiful arms; the hands flashing like rays of lightning; the head held high like a Queen of *todas las Españas*, thrust forward in defiance, or flung back, far back, as in a despairing cry; the restless legs churning high the skirt like the cape of a bullfighter; the frenetic turns, the leaps, the falls; the feet, the stamping, pawing, hoofing feet, beating the floor in an ever-mounting crescendo—all this went to make a spectacle such as I have never witnessed again.

To say that *Immediate Tragedy* was a tour de force in concept, expressive gesture, theatrical effectiveness, and plain human endurance is not to do it full justice. For me it was a supreme experience, if not *the* supreme experience, of dance. Next day, crossing the grassy Bennington quadrangle in front of the Commons Building, I encountered Graham, accompanied by Louis Horst. The evening before, at the end of *Immediate Tragedy*, a demonstration had taken place. The entire audience had risen and roared, clapping, stamping, whistling, and yelling. I remember being too benumbed by emotion to applaud. I later realized that, had I abandoned myself to the frenzy around and within me, I would have run blindly to the stage, thrown myself at her feet, clasped her knees, and cried. Since such behavior was unthinkable, I controlled myself and escaped as soon as I could from the crowd, so that, alone, I could try to understand what had happened to me. This morning I managed to thank her most formally for a magnificent performance.

I do not know why *Immediate Tragedy* disappeared from the Graham repertory. It was never repeated. I kept expecting to see it again, as I would her other works. On various occasions I have asked her why she gave it up, a dance that in my estimation, as I was careful to remind her, was the apogee of all her works. Her answers have been vague and enigmatic. It is conceivable that quite unconsciously she knew that the performance in the Vermont State Armory was a moment of rare transcendence for herself and the audience, which had responded with such delirium. I know that for me it was a transcendental experience, and I am grateful.

In this period, her group choreography, while acclaimed with enthusiasm by the public, was received quite coldly by the press. One evening on West Tenth Street, as we waited for the fastidious Max to make up his mind what to do where, she seemed dispirited and somewhat inclined to disparage her work. When I demurred by expressing my admiration for her solos, especially the fabulous *Dithyrambic*, she laughed. Yes, everyone was in agreement; she was no choreographer. Doris was the great one, the only choreographer. "I am the flashy soloist, the personality girl!" I have never forgotten her light laughter, and the ironic, almost bitter tone in which she spoke these words. It disturbed me deeply that this great woman should feel herself vulnerable to the opprobrium of those who were vastly her inferiors.

That winter *Danza de la Muerte* was danced in a concert at the Kaufmann Auditorium of the Ninety-Second Street YM-YWHA. For me this was a pleasure. I had had time to make choreographic repairs, which is always such a luxury, and my sprained toes had mended completely, which compounded the luxury. I could do all the stamping, balancing, and jumping with entire confidence.

* * *

The Humphrey-Weidman company, having no enterprising impresario to handle it, in consequence found its touring activities confined to neighboring cities and colleges and the public universities of states adjacent to

New York. It was not much, but we played to fine, appreciative audiences of dance *aficionados*, and it kept the company busy.

Pauline Lawrence, speculating on the success we encountered in these places, saw no reason why the company shouldn't expand its tour itineraries. When she found the big booking concerns disinclined to take us on, she simply determined to do it herself. She engaged a secretary-typist and used the living room at 31 West Tenth Street as her office. The two put in a full day's work for months writing to concert managements in every town and city, to every college, and to every museum in this country and in Canada. The response went beyond her most sanguine expectations, and early in 1938 she took the company on its first transcontinental tour.

Pauline functioned as company manager and representative, business manager, press agent, stage manager, and lighting director. When the curtain went up, on her cue, she would double as one of two pairs of hands at the piano, give the electricians at the switchboard their cues as needed, jump to the percussion instruments when these were indicated in the musical score, and return to the piano. Intermissions meant supervising and directing changes of scenery, refocusing spotlights, and changing colored slides. After the final curtain she would supervise the crew in packing the curtains, lights, props, and costumes, accompany the loaded trucks to the railroad station, check the baggage to the next destination, tidy up a bit, and join the company at whatever reception was being held by the local sponsors.

All of us, being completely absorbed in the task of performing, keeping ourselves fit, and fighting the ever-present fatigue and exhaustion of a protracted tour, took Pauline and her services very much for granted. Being, on top of everything else, the company's wardrobe mistress, which meant seeing that the costumes were kept in good repair, and cleaned and pressed before each performance, she had to deal with all the complaints, big and small, of nervous dancers who, usually just before curtain time, discovered a rip or some other defect in their costume that demanded instant attention.

That first tour, in early 1938, was undertaken by railroad. It was still possible, in those days, to find trains running. A few years ago, while on tour with my own company in Toledo, having arrived by chartered bus, I found myself during the day on an errand near the railroad station. I had remembered it as a place of incessant activity. I walked in. The big, ugly building with its Beaux-Arts pomposities, huge columns, enormous cupola, pediments, allegorical statuary, and plaster scrollwork was a sad sight—the empty carapace of a long dead turtle. Of the many ticket windows, each one once the destination of long queues of ticket buyers, only one was open, with no one at the wicket. The Western Union and the Traveler's Aid booths were dismantled. The waiting rooms were empty save for a few seedy-looking bums stretched out on the benches, sleeping off a bout with an empty pint bottle of rotgut discarded on the floor. The arcade, once full of shops, was a desolation of boarded-up windows. Lit-ter was everywhere. Every corner had become a public urinal. The large black board announced the arrival of one lonely train in the morning and another in the evening.

On the 1938 tour, more often than not, the railroads would put at our disposal a whole coach. There were good Pullman accommodations for overnight jumps. The itinerary for this and subsequent tours was roughly as follows: Hartford, Providence, Boston, Albany, Syracuse, Buffalo, Cleveland, Montreal, Toronto, Detroit, Ann Arbor, Chicago, Milwaukee, St. Louis, Kansas City, Vermilion, Denver, Salt Lake City, Berkeley, San Francisco, Los Angeles, San Diego, Phoenix, Denton, Atlanta, Birmingham, Tallahassee, Savannah, Charlotte, Greensboro, Richmond, Philadelphia, and back to New York.

In-between we played many small localities with colleges. This became known as the "gymnasium circuit." Pauline was an intrepid pioneer in bringing modern dance to places that had no theaters but only the gymnasium of the local college or high school. She was equal to the challenge. On arrival, having seen to the unloading of the scenery and lights and to the women who were to press and repair the wardrobe, she would have the black velour cyclorama and "legs" hung at one end of the hall. She would direct the placement of spot and floodlights and focus them. She would drill the electricians on the entire sequence of cues for each production. By the time darkness fell and the performance began, Pauline had created a theater. One lost the chilling awareness of playing in a gymnasium and felt, instead, surrounded by the civilized and urbane amenity of the theater.

Doris and Charles knew the territory into which they ventured. Years of touring with Denishawn had given them an intimate acquaintance with it. Both had sprung from the inner core of the continent, Doris from Oak Park, Illinois, Charles from Lincoln, Nebraska. They knew that the cultural desolation was only a matter of surface, that there was a substratum of receptivity, appreciation, and even enthusiasm that awaited the artist.

To my amazement, I saw that dance lovers would drive hundreds of miles, sometimes in snowstorms, to attend a concert and afterward present themselves backstage to express their appreciation. There was a hunger in these people. Very often, in some college or university, a lecture-demonstration was held on the day or afternoon before a performance. Doris conducted this with masterful ease. She had a superb command of language and a presence of great simplicity and distinction. With utmost lucidity, she would discuss the origins and the essence of the modern dance, its principles and technique, its content and form.

The rest of us, in handsome costumes designed by Pauline for such occasions, would demonstrate. Both masters had devised ingenious studies intended to give the spectator unfamiliar with the dance a fairly good understanding of what we were all about. There were studies in physical technique, movement dynamics, spatial design, rhythm, the great reservoir of dance gesture inherent in the human muscular system and in such familiar actions as walks, runs, leaps, falls, and turns. Doris would introduce and explain.

I used to enjoy these lecture-demonstrations and found them exciting to perform. They were infinitely instructive as well. Here was an intelligence of a very high order revealing its motives and processes. Listening to Doris I completed, so to speak, my higher education, something I had abandoned a decade earlier at the University of California. I was constantly impressed by the depth and breadth of her culture and the rationality and discipline of her thinking. She seemed to encompass so much not only with the mind but also with intuition and instinct.

Pauline organized a number of transcontinental tours for the company. We became familiar with Baton Rouge in January, when the camellias bloomed, while the northern prairies, just one day's train ride away, were swept by frigid gales from Saskatchewan. We would leave Denver during a blizzard and awake next morning to the miracle of spring in Seattle and Portland, with apple and pear orchards in full bloom. It was on one of these tours that I fell in love with San Francisco. The location was incomparable, the people friendly, relaxed, and likable. The brutally ugly and depressing characteristics of Detroit or Chicago were here transmuted by a singular alchemy, something that can be understood only with the bones, viscera, and skin—a vibrant excitement akin to pure joy.

*   *   *

After eight years I confronted my father once more. The man had aged. Heartbreakingly. The tall, robust carriage was gone, the frame stooped and shrunken. I towered above the fallen enemy. My vigor, pride and, arrogance were annihilated, quite literally, by a compassion and tenderness more terrifying than all hatred and hostility. I knew then what I had only suspected before that moment, that forgiveness and love were possible only when I saw him destroyed.

In his beautiful, formal Spanish, in a voice only the echo of the assured, sanguine tone of his heyday, he sought to find a way to reach me. I, in turn, did everything in my power to convey that I wished no longer to be a stranger to him, that we could at last be friends and face each other without enmity and rancor. My brothers and sisters, some of whom I had last seen as mere infants, were quite grown up. I saw their solicitous affection for the old man in their looks, their voices, and their behavior. I saw that they were fine, decent people and that my father had not failed in their upbringing. They were well-bred, the boys tall and full of a man's dignity, the girls of a grace and delicacy beautiful to see.

I invited them all to the Philharmonia Auditorium for our concert. It was a packed house and as wildly enthusiastic about our dances as anyone could wish. We had ended with Doris's "Variations and Conclusion," which always "brought down the house." That evening, before my own variation, I said to myself, "This is for my father." The applause at the end was prolonged, and there were innumerable curtain calls. At last, Doris ordered me to take a solo bow. It was a heady moment. I remembered, as a boy, sitting out front to hear the Los Angeles Philharmonic Orchestra play Tchaikovsky, Brahms, Schumann, and Beethoven. Now, here I was being most noisily acclaimed.

Afterward, I saw many of my old friends, including my wonderful schoolteachers. They were all very proud of me. At last, my family came to the dressing room. They looked shyly at me as if I were a creature from another planet. And my father, looking very pleased, said, "*Muy bueno, Pepe, muy bueno.*" Never, in my recollection, had he addressed me by the familiar and affectionate diminutive used by my mother and my brothers and sisters. It had always been the formal "José." Tonight, for the first time, it was "Pepe."

*　*　*

In 1938, Martha Graham made a totally unexpected overture in my direction. She asked me to work with her in her new production for Bennington. She needed a leading man. Would I be available and willing? I was agog and dizzy with excitement. What was being offered me was an opportunity beyond my most extravagant fantasies.

Naturally, I went to Doris and Charles for advice and guidance. They were both quite dispassionate. They said the choice was entirely up to me. But they asked me to remember that accepting the offer would be an inconvenience to them and their work, of which I was already an important part. Moreover, my collaboration with her, if successful, would of necessity lead to others, and to inevitable conflicts in rehearsal time, performances, and tours. Finally, they reminded me that she was a formidable and all-consuming personality. I would run the risk of being swallowed up artistically. They told me to think it over carefully. I did.

I had no fear of being "swallowed up." On the contrary, I rather imagined that it might be a not altogether unpleasant experience. But I have, even now, a Quixotic streak in me. One does not abandon one's loyalties, no matter what. One does not live for gain, but for belief. I owed Doris and Charles a debt. This obligation was concocted of archaic notions having to do with loyalty and honor.

It would have been wonderful to accept Graham's offer. I would have loved working with her, every instant of it. Yet I told her, with the deepest regret, that I could not. I have often speculated on the course my life would have taken had I made the opposite decision. As it was, Erick Hawkins appeared on the scene and became her partner and her company's leading man.

The work she was planning was *American Document.*[117] It was a most propitious and distinguished debut for Erick. I tried very hard not to be consumed by a black envy.

*　*　*

In New York, Charles completed one of his finest works, *On My Mother's Side*.[118] In it he looked homeward to his roots and his beginnings, with nostalgia, irony, and compassion. A poetic figure, almost a young Walt Whitman, took us back to the rugged Weidman ancestors who laid claim to the Nebraska prairies. These included an old pioneer woman, an aunt who had gone on the stage, his own tenderly recollected mother, and a dour entrepreneur who, when faced with the ruin of his enterprises, hanged himself. This gallery of ancestral portraits was one of his most sensitive and poignant works.

Each of the remembered figures was introduced by a spoken text written by William Archibald[119] and recited by members of the company that established, with a curious eloquence the scene about to be played. The apt and perceptive score was written by Lionel Nowak.[120] This extraordinarily talented musician had come to work with Humphrey-Weidman fresh from a brilliant career as a student at the Cleveland Institute of Music. He had replaced Norman and Ruth Lloyd, after these two went their way to raise a family.

The first decade of my artistic infancy was coming to a close. It seemed to accelerate in tempo, and I was carried with it as a bird is borne aloft in a strong gale. My wings, figuratively speaking, were stronger, and I realized that they were becoming bolder, more venturesome, and that the time was near when I would leave the security of the parental nest and taste the joy of doing battle with the beautiful, terrible winds.

I asked leave to accept a teaching and performing engagement for the summer of 1938 at the Colorado State College of Education, in Greeley. Miss Jean Cave, head of the Department of Physical Education for Women, was a dance enthusiast and had asked me to come. I was to share the teaching load with Evelyn Davies, and both of us would join forces and put on some works at the conclusion of the session. We were to use as many of the students as we liked and to perform as well.

The school was a great contrast to Bennington. In Colorado I was on my own and not overshadowed by the great figures who dominated the Vermont program. I had full responsibility. Working with Evelyn was a pleasure. We planned and worked furiously, in spite of the altitude and the punishing heat. The students were a pleasant group of girls, of varying degrees of skill and capacity, and this was a stimulating challenge. We gave several performances in the gymnasium that were well attended and well received.

After this I spent a short period at the Perry-Mansfield Camp in Steamboat Springs. My old friends Charlotte Perry and Portia Mansfield[121] were as always kind and hospitable. I taught a series of classes in the mornings and in the afternoons rode up to the stunning mountains in a gay, noisy cavalcade, very much the dude rancher. And before I knew it, I was on a plane, an archaic flimsy thing it seems now, flying the midnight skies back to Bennington and escorting Martha Graham into the Armory, which was packed by an expectant multitude. We took our seats in the balcony as the house lights began to dim. She leaned in my direction, "Do you suppose Doris and Charles will be angry with you for sitting with me?" she asked.

The new work was by Charles, his *Opus 51*,[122] so titled because it defied all attempts to find a name for it, so he simply made a list of all his dances, from the earliest compositions to the most recent, and found that this would be his fifty-first, hence the title. It was a work of delightful invention, the grandfather, I think, of dadaism in the dance in this country. It was concocted from a species of nonrepresentational doodling. Things had a charmingly unexpected way of coming out of nothing and going nowhere, and exploding in-between into brilliant fragments of pure nonsense. His mastery of wit, irony, and slapstick was given full rein, and tore off like a bronco roaring, kicking, and raising all sorts of hell. The work had been composed and rehearsed with scrupulous care, yet it had the saucy spontaneity of an improvisation—an early "happening." Charles used an impressive range of gesture, movement, and dynamics. Nothing meant anything, and it was all explosively funny.

Charles presided over the pandemonium with a detached and demented pomposity. He was the focus, crux, and apotheosis of the purest absurdity—and entirely in his element. The company performed with the absorption of acolytes at some unholy Sabbath in Bedlam. Memorable performances were given by Harriette Ann Gray,[123] Beatrice Seckler, Katherine Litz, George Bockman, William Bales, Lee Sherman, Eleanor Frampton, and Pauline Chellis. Vivian Fine wrote one of her wittiest, most successful scores. Altogether, it was a high moment in the Master's career.

Doris Humphrey presented her choreography to the Passacaglia and Fugue in C Minor of J.S. Bach.[124]

It was, incomparably, a masterpiece.

A zenith.

Ineffable.

* * *

The Humphrey-Weidman company took off again that winter on a transcontinental tour. Pauline had done it again. Class accompanist, costume designer, uncompromisingly acerbic critic of her two colleagues' dances, governess to the infant Charles Humphrey Woodford, lighting designer, stage manager, business manager, second pianist at performances, she was now again our impresario. It was a fine and busy tour, and it took us again to the West Coast. *Passacaglia* and *Opus 51* proved to be great successes. Other works went along in the repertory. I was given a great honor: Doris let me replace Charles in *Passacaglia*. It remains one of the most profoundly rewarding experiences of my life.

Martha Hill and Mary Jo Shelly conceived the notion that in 1939 the Bennington School of the Dance should be held in another part of the country. The success of the School and Festival had surpassed all expectations. Students and dance audiences had flocked to the Vermont hills to study with the masters of the American dance—Martha Graham, Doris Humphrey, Charles Weidman, Hanya Holm—and to attend the premieres of their works at the Festival.

Perhaps the time had come for the School and Festival to seek a broader orientation and present itself, since it lay claim to the name "American," elsewhere than in New England. Mills College, in Oakland, California, was selected as the site for this experiment. The campus, as distinct as can be from Bennington, proved hospitable, and the four masters, with their assistants, arrived for the intensive six-week summer course.

The Misses Hill and Shelly performed miracles of improvisation and conversion. Drawing rooms, refectories, terraces, and patios became dance studios. Fortunately, there were enough dormitories and faculty accommodations. The musicians, among whom were Louis Horst, Norman Lloyd, and Lionel Nowak, conducted classes outdoors under the eucalyptus trees.

There was to be no Festival, however. None of the leaders were planning new works. But a "second string" Festival was a possibility, and some of us—Marian Van Tuyl, Louise Kloepper, Ethel Butler, and I—leaped at it. We spent every moment away we could spare at rehearsals, preparing works to be shown at the end of the session.

I had been planning, for some years, a rather ambitious work, a series of solo dances on a Mexican subject. I had made a number of false starts and had learned in the process what not to do. I was given the use of a classroom, from which the chairs and desks had been cleared, and here I spent my afternoons and evenings, including Saturdays and Sundays. Lionel Nowak agreed to compose the score. Slowly, the work—which I called *Danzas Mexicana*—evolved and took shape. There were five solos, five symbolic figures from Mexican history—the Indio, Conquistador, Peón, Caballero, and Revolucionario.

The cruel, heroic, and at the same time beautiful story of my native land has long held a singular fascination for me. It is never entirely absent from my thinking. I am certain that it has been a strong influence in shaping me into the person I have become. The confrontation of the blood and the culture of the European and the American Indian, resulting in centuries of unremitting conflict, has been resolved within me into something harmonious, into an acceptance and an understanding. I find myself quite at home in any metropolis or village of the Hispanic world, in sympathy with the people, the language, and the way of life. They are important to me; they made me what I am.

Indio. A figure from Mayan and Aztec sculpture—hieratic, half-man, half-pyramid; a rite of invocation to benign and destructive powers; a creature long since risen from the savage state into a culture of barbaric splendor; existing in and because of a compelling rhythm, primitive yet complex; an adoration of the sun and the earth; a canticle to Quetzalcoatl.

Conquistador. The vision of Hernán Córtez, as seen by José Clemente

Orozco. An apocalyptic apparition, bringing doom and destruction, wielding the double-edged symbol of redemption and death.

Peón. A creature of infinite pathos, lying in degradation on a bright crimson blanket, which is also a pool of his blood. His dance is a lament, the despairing cry of three centuries of bondage and servitude.

Caballero. A creature of fastidious elegance and preciosity, the decayed descendant of the conquistador, with all his cruelty and none of his strength.

Revolucionario. The contained fury of centuries finally unleashed; wildly explosive; an exultant crude shout of triumph.

The rare and blessed solitude I found in the improvised studio that summer gave me, such as I was, to myself. I embarked on the most precarious of journeys, that into one's interior, the "terra incognita" of the spirit. There was no compass, no starry constellations or chart to guide me. There was only a blind tropism toward an unknown and distant goal. What I would find there I did not know. All I knew was that I wanted to find out who and what I was. For almost ten years I had been a pupil, disciple, and follower. Now the time had come for me to assume full stature.

My only visitor at the studio during those weeks of sweat and travail was Lionel Nowak. He would come at intervals with music paper and pencils. I would perform sections, fragments, phrases, thematic movements, and improvisations. We would discuss the sort of music that was needed. He would play something he had written as a result of a previous session. We would be very critical. Sometimes he would improvise. I would jump up and exclaim, "There, that is the sort of thing we need." Then, I would be alone to continue these introspective forays that were often fruitless and disheartening, but sometimes exciting beyond words, when I would experience, as if in recompense for the dull and even despairing hours, such pure rapture that I was suffused with energies and powers I did not know were mine. Living became a sublime adventure. There were moments when I seemed to explode, and the fragile, fleshly envelope and the four confining walls were shattered into oblivion, and the only reality was a convulsive, blinding consummation. I worked like a madman. While making these dances, I grew up.

Becoming adult meant augmenting the range and scope of my sensibility. As a human being and as an artist, I had reached a turning point. The challenges, the ordeals in store for me would be greater, but so would be the implements at my disposal. It was fortunate that the appalling events of September 1939 found me prepared and alert.

When the Nazis invaded Poland the world knew that the Armistice signed on November 11, 1918 had ended, and the long-expected, long-dreaded cataclysm was upon us. The dull, painful pressure inside my skull between the eyes, my constant and faithful companion since the Fascist attack on Spain, now took hold in earnest. It impinged upon my every living moment, awake or what passed for sleep. It poisoned all existence and made it into a nightmare. The torment consisted mostly of the realization that against this monstrosity I was utterly impotent. There was nothing could do to stop it. I was more than helpless; I was lost.

Lost and confused. The life I had made for myself with inflexible undeviating will was thrown into panic and chaos. I could not remain undisturbed by the fateful ordeal, the horror let loose upon humanity Much as I sought to escape or to insulate myself from it I could not. This inner turmoil was bound to have its outward manifestations, and in due time it exploded and disrupted my life.

In the autumn of 1939 I accepted once again an invitation from Martha Hill to teach at Bennington on the days she spent at New York University. Once more I found myself commuting between New York and Vermont. The campus was agog with news of the war in Europe. There was a new crop of young ladies, every bit as intelligent and dedicated as the ones I had known during my previous assignment. There was the usual ferment and excitement, with poetry, music, and politics very much in the air. As before, I took a great interest in the activities of the drama department This year they were busy with a theatricalization of Hart Crane's poem *The Bridge*. Again, Francis Fergusson directed, with Martha Hill in charge of the choreographic action. Arch Lauterer was doing the sets.

Again, I was struck by the imagination and boldness of their approach to theater, a creativity unknown in the commercial theater in New York The directors used the devices and capacities of the stage and its performers in an entirely revolutionary manner. There was no timidity or caution. no need to think of box-office appeal. The audience would be there, and it would be an avid and intelligent one. And it would have a rich and rewarding experience, for so this production of *The Bridge* turned out to be.

For the 1940 summer session, the Bennington School of the Dance was returning to its home base. The Graham and the Humphrey-Weidman companies would both be in residence. Hanya Holm had accepted an offer to teach at Colorado State College. Mills College had invited Marian Van Tuyl, Louise Kloepper, and myself to hold a summer session on its campus. I made plans to be there.

I had sworn never again to have anything to do with a Broadway show. A weak will, the economic pinch, and the skillful persuasiveness of one Milton Bender, theatrical agent to the prestigious and the aspiring, caused me to go back on my oath. Milton assured me that George Balanchine was anxious to have me as the leading dancer after Ray Bolger in *Keep Off the Grass*.[125] The other stars were to be Jimmy Durante, Jackie Gleason, and Ilka Chase. Martha Hill was very kind and understanding when I asked to be relieved of my Bennington commitment. In my place she invited William Bales, who now began a long, distinguished tenure at the college.

The music for *Keep Off the Grass* was dismal almost beyond endurance. Still, the show had its rewards. One was the presence of Betty Bruce as the leading dancer, a superb tap-toe-ballet type who more than compensated for the overall dreariness. Irrepressible, like a braid of Chinese firecrackers, she made a pandemonium of rehearsals, mocking, teasing, and insulting, with saucy good humor, everyone in sight, from Mr. Balanchine, Ray Bolger, and myself, to the last of the chorus boys, one of whom was Jerome Robbins. These high jinks in no way interfered with the concentration and intelligence that she brought to the work at hand. She was a true professional.

Balanchine had recently done a superb job of theater in *On Your Toes*.[126] His dances for Ray Bolger and Tamara Geva, especially "Slaughter on Tenth Avenue," had distinction and charm. Balanchine's was a highly sophisticated European mind that viewed such American simplicities as hoofers and stripteasers with delight, irony, and great wit. And here he was, trying—not too successfully—to conceal his infinite boredom with the assignment. He had very little with which to work. Ray Bolger, aside from some rather raucous scenes with Jimmy Durante and Jackie Gleason, had nothing deserving of his very special talents as a dancer. Betty Bruce and myself worked hard on some completely unrewarding dances. Mr. Balanchine tried hard on the "production numbers." He had a competent corps de ballet from his school. He would arrange them in a semicircle and give them "combinations" to the execrable music. I was to be in the center, a concupiscent faun in hot pursuit of Daphne Vane, playing a winsome nymph. Days would pass, the semicircle would go through its paces, and I just stood around idle. Finally, I approached Mr. Balanchine and asked him what he wanted me to do. "You go in center and do Modern Dance," he responded.

Once, during a lunch break, we had a conversation about the situation in Europe. The war seemed to have come to a halt after the defeat of Poland. In the press there was much disappointment, as if an eagerly anticipated fireworks display or a baseball game had been canceled because of rain. Much was being made of the unexpected and shocking treaty between Hitler and Stalin. I asked him what he, as a Russian, made of it. He laughed as though it were a tremendous joke. The Western nations, Britain, France and their allies, including the United States, had expected the Nazis to attack and annihilate the Bolsheviks, but Stalin, astute and wily beyond words, had spoiled this little stratagem by coming to an understanding with his supposedly implacable enemy. It was, he assured me, a most delightful and typically Russian joke.

The dreary business moved to Boston for the final rehearsals and tryouts. I found myself sharing a dressing room with a young man whose sole function was to impersonate a gorilla. His costume was massive, topped by a mask with the most malevolent expression. In this appalling getup he was supposed to chase Jimmy Durante, playing the part of a boastful circus lion tamer, off the stage and up the aisle to the delight of the customers. On his return to the dimly lit dressing room he had a habit of entering stealthily and throwing his hairy arms around me from behind and letting out an indescribable noise, half-growl, half-howl. The unnerving part of this charade was his always unexpected timing. My other dressing room companion was a midget, who played Mickey Mouse in another scene. He was a middle-aged man and a dipsomaniac. He would stagger into the dressing room every evening and on matinee days, poke his disconcerting face close to mine, his breath reeking of stale and perpetual binges, and ask. "Bist du yidl?"

It was the first week of May, and Boston was miserably cold. Walking through the Commons at daybreak after an all-night rehearsal, I would curse my folly and stupidity. Exhausted by the endless repetition of sickening dances and dispirited by the degradation in which I found myself, I would reflect that there is nothing more galling, come the dawn, than the realization that your whoring is neither high-class nor well-paid.

But worse was to follow. On the bright, sunlit morning of May 10, 1940, the Boston papers announced in large headlines the Nazi invasion of the West. The press seemed obscenely jubilant. At last something was happening. The real show was on, and there would be monstrous headlines every day with extra editions. Circulation would be catapulted sky-high.

At the theater we went through the motions of performing, but everything was curiously empty and meaningless. For me the entire mess became insupportable. I don't know why or how I stayed on, but presently we got to New York. It is to the credit of the metropolitan public that they saw through the cheap vulgarity of the enterprise. Nothing, not the clowning of Jimmy Durante, the delightful humor of Jackie Gleason, the inspired hoofing of Ray Bolger, or the talents of Ilka Chase, could give the thing any substance, coherence, or validity. Mr. Balanchine's hands had been tied behind him. Betty Bruce's best efforts and my own undistinguished contribution went for nothing. The thing was a dismal and well deserved failure. It ran for a few halfhearted months during which the unthinkable disaster became a reality: the Nazis were victorious in the West. In a spring of nightmares there was even a choreographic climax, a newsreel showing a veritable *Totentanz*, Adolf Hitler prancing in malevolent rapture on receiving news of the capitulation of France.

Having been born and reared a Francophile, this, plus the news photos of the Nazi troops parading in triumph down the Champs-Elysées, was almost more than I could bear. I hit bottom. So began for me years of desperation. Nothing seemed real; living was one long, taut, aching nerve. There was no mind, no spirit, no will, only a feverish lump inside, weighing me down. I resigned from the show, trained a replacement, and left for California and Mills College.

Crossing the continent by train gave me time to think and try to collect myself. Moving away physically from the chaos and debacle that New York had become for me put matters in a less feverish perspective. If the world had gone insane, I wasn't entirely culpable. If France had gone down in catastrophic defeat, I wasn't to blame. But I was responsible for my graceless and ignominious traffic with commerce.

Mea culpa, mea culpa, mea maxima culpa.

I arrived in California, hollow-eyed, contrite, and chastened, prepared to dedicate myself, miserable sinner that I was, to virtue and good works. Repentance, I had been taught, was the road to redemption. Purified, detesting sin as only a recently reformed transgressor can, I began my duties at Mills.

A drowning man not only clutches at straws, but he simultaneously makes plans for the time when he is safely back on solid ground. All my torments during that black spring had not kept me from thinking about my responsibilities the coming summer. I was to teach classes in the technique of modern American dance, or at least that sector of it with which I was familiar. I was further expected to produce a work, and this, I now suspect, is what kept me from totally falling apart when I struck bottom. I had a function. I could continue to be of service to my great love, the dance.

All dance, all choreography, is autobiographical, whether or not one knows it, likes it, or intends it. What was more natural, and inevitable, than *Le Spectre de la Rose*? At the very zenith of his glory, Nijinsky, gifted as almost no other dancer, summed up his era in Fokine's infinitely charming ode to a society whose elegance and urbanity were about to be lost forever. Later, toward the end of World War I, his radiance extinguished, Nijinsky groped blindly toward lucidity in somber, mystical visions danced in a world convulsed by an insanity far more appalling than his own pitiful derangement. The young Isadora Duncan danced the dawn and early spring; as a heartbroken mother, she danced Niobe; finally, the woman ravaged by age and dazzled by a revolutionary mirage danced the "Internationale." I, with all humility and reverence, could do no less.

My effort was to be *War Lyrics*. Quite predictably, I was to continue my flight on borrowed wings. I had admired William Archibald's poems for Weidman's *On My Mother's Side*. Now, at my request, he wrote the "lyrics" for my new piece. With these in my hand, I pounced on the composer assigned to do my music at Mills. Young Esther Williamson[127] was a Bennington alumna. I had first encountered her at the college, a gifted musician and a lovely person. Now, I gave her no rest.

I plagiarized myself shamelessly. The form of *Danza de la Muerte* had proven satisfying. I gave Esther the plan. There was to be a prologue, three central episodes, and an epilogue. The Archibald text would be recited and danced by a choric ensemble. And I plagiarized Doris Humphrey. What I had seen, heard, and performed in her powerful *Orestes* I now put to use as model and guide in a venture new for me—the use of speech with dance movement.

For years in New York I had looked covetously in the direction of May O'Donnell of the Graham company. She had only recently resigned and returned to San Francisco. I needed a female dancer as a partner for the three central duets in the new work. I asked her to do me the honor,

and to my intense delight she agreed. And so began a fine and distin
guished—though brief—collaboration. Every day May would travel al
the way from San Francisco to rehearse with me. There were three duet
to be composed—"The Wife," "The Blonde," and "The Nurse." May wa
to dance each role, and I would be the soldier.

War Lyrics began with a formal processional of figures suggesting
Greek chorus. Lee Sherman was the leader. This led to the first text, whicl
was danced and spoken to a solemn measured accompaniment played or
percussion instruments. It was addressed to the wife. She was pitied fo
her sacrifice, extolled for her stoicism. The choric mass parted revealing
low platform on which the soldier slept with his wife. A bugle wok
them, and the two confronted the anguish of parting. The scene endec
with the soldier's heroic departure, with the wife, brave and desolate, lef
behind.

The chorus reentered, and to a lively, jazzy rhythm, danced and recitec
the second poem, dedicated to a dance hall floozy. She was praised fo
giving the weary soldier a moment's solace and forgetfulness. Again, th
platform was revealed, this time with the soldier and his companior
carousing in drunken abandon.

A third poem, danced with compassionate foreboding, was an admo
nition to be gentle to the woman who was to see him die. The platforn
now became a battle scene. Mortally wounded, the soldier fell in slov
motion. The nurse, a vision perceived through his final delirium, half
mother, half-ministering angel, rocked him with infinite tenderness on he
lap, like a Mater Dolorosa. The chorus now reentered and to the violen
cacophony of percussion danced and chanted the last poem. A grave wa
to be dug, and dug deep, for it must contain many, infinitely many deac
soldiers.

War Lyrics was a stirring experience for me and, I am happy to remem
ber, for the audiences that saw it. It was also quite gratifying that a persor
of the distinction and discernment of Alfred Frankenstein[128] found it mer
itorious and gave it a more than generous appraisal. The work wa
rewarding in many other ways. Having composed and performed it some
how fortified me and prepared me for the vicissitudes that I knew I mus
undergo. For I sensed that the coming ordeal would leave no on
untouched. It was important for me to say what I had to say, in that way
at that particular moment. My return to New York was a shambles. I saw
that my association with Humphrey-Weidman was ended. We had quit
simply outgrown each other. As quickly as possible I took the train back
to San Francisco.

533 Post Street:
San Francisco, California

May O'Donnell, Ray Green, her husband, and Gertrude Shurr, the third member of the team, met me at the Embarcadero Terminal. I had crossed the beautiful bay from Oakland by ferry. We drove to the studio and over coffee and toast began to lay our plans. These were very simple. We were to resume where we had left off after the performances of *War Lyrics* at Mills College and do new works. We were as sanguine and enthusiastic as one can be in the gentle October climate of San Francisco.

May and I worked well together. We made a handsome team. We were eager to make further progress. There was constant discussion. Ideas were presented, examined, discarded, accepted, deferred. This went on endlessly, from morning to night, in the studio and even during meals. The air was charged with excitement and expectation. We stimulated one another to a high degree. We were very serious young people, yet we had moments of great good humor. All of us had a healthy sense of irony and a fine appreciation of the absurd and the bawdy. We needed this. We lived in a world perched precariously on the brink of chaos and disaster. At any moment our fine plans, our precious artistic aspirations, and our entire lives might topple over the edge.

Before leaving New York, I had seen a portent of what was in store for me. An Act of Congress now required that all aliens resident in the United States register and submit all pertinent data: date and port of entry, list of residences, occupations, etc., etc. With a jolt I realized that I was an alien. I did my best to supply the required information and received my Alien's Registration Card. There was more to come. As an able-bodied alien male I was subject to the recently enacted draft law. There was a symbolic raffle in Washington. A high dignitary was blindfolded: from a huge container filled with the numbered destinies of young men, he drew out the first number.

I have never had any luck with games of chance. I have never won anything in a raffle and have always lost money to the machines and gaming tables in Reno. But this time my number was near the very top. In disgust I concluded that injustice, also, wears a blindfold. Very shortly, I was ordered to report to the military authorities for a physical examination.

High above Grand Central Station is a labyrinth of passageways and galleries. Here I found myself, with numerous other men, lining up, with only a dossier held self-consciously in front to conceal a humiliating public nakedness. The lines moved slowly from gallery to gallery, where mili-

97

tary doctors and assistants gave us thorough, if somewhat brusque, physical and psychological examinations. One of the doctors, after hefting, flexing, and poking to his satisfaction, disposed of my case with the pronouncement, "Oh boy, what a soldier you're going to make!" I was classified 1-A.

My colleagues at the Post Street studio were aware of my draft status. Ray Green himself had a similar classification. We knew that every plan we made, every step we took, was subject to the caprice of the local draft board. We were marked men, in a very precarious position. To speculate on the plight of the artist in the warring nations of Europe was of little help. We clung to the fact that the United States was not at war, and at this juncture we sincerely hoped she would not join the fracas.

War or not, we were an irrepressible crew. We had work to do. We decided to retain and improve the duets from *War Lyrics*. We began two new works. *This Story is Legend*, a poetic allegory, was based on a poem of William Carlos Williams, in which the explorer Hernando de Soto follows his destiny into the heart of the virgin North American continent, there to find his end in the waters of the mighty Mississippi, which he had discovered. A humorous folksy dance about Casey Jones and his engine was the second new piece.

May and I worked with intense and total concentration. We began early in the day, took time off for lunch in the apartment she shared with her husband across the hall from the studio, and continued for the rest of the day, stopping only in the late afternoon for May's classes, which she held on odd days. Meanwhile, across the hall, Ray Green was busy at the piano composing the scores.

Slowly, the works took shape. May and I gradually found a method that served us well. Our ideas complemented and stimulated each other's. We would criticize, evaluate, and modify with full appreciation of the other's efforts and abilities. My admiration for May had begun years before when I first saw her perform with the Graham company. She was no stranger. I had studied her for years, and now found her more stunning than ever. Her solo recitals in San Francisco with Ray had created a fine impression; she had achieved artistic independence and had matured. She was a ravishing woman and a superb dancer. Her temperament was serene and assured. I never saw her angry or distraught, although she was capable of a good, strong "Damn it!" She had a fine Irish sense of humor. Laughter came easily. Often, after trying out a new lift, we would end up in a heap on the studio floor, bellowing with laughter.

Legend began with a beautiful solo by May. She represented the great Mississippi. Her movements were fluid and flowing. Clare Falkenstein, a young artist then living in Berkeley and a good friend, designed a stunning dress that suggested blue waters. The dance was seductive, a siren song of the far-off, irresistible, and unknown. May wore water lilies in her long honey-colored hair. In each hand she held a lotus flower. She was an alluring vision, as heroic as the great water course.

De Soto entered, holding aloft a draped banner. He embodied the rest-less dynamism of sixteenth-century Spain. All points of the compass, all horizons, and new worlds were his for the taking. His dance was made up of powerful thrusting and reaching movements of the legs, arms, and torso. Archibald's text depicted the continent as an alluring woman and the explorer as an obsessed lover in search of her. To convey this, we entered and exited, crossed and recrossed the stage forming all manner of patterns—diagonals, zigzags, curves, circles. The more elusive she became, the more ardent he grew. There were instants when she would hover over him, full of enticement and promise. There was the inevitable confronta-tion, an impassioned love duet, which in retrospect seems one of the finest passages in the entire work, containing some quite original and lovely choreography. The piece ended in a very moving and effective manner. The river-continent, having tested the courage and constancy of her suit-or, finally yields herself to him. He dies cradled in her arms, and she buries him, lovingly and tenderly, under a long trailing blue veil, brooding over his watery grave as the curtain falls.

The style of gesture and movement was worked out to give each pro-tagonist an expressive domain as different as possible from the other's. May's movement was curved, flowing, fluid. Mine had a hard, irrepress-ible drive; it was angular and turgid. The piece was a fine vehicle for both of us, suiting us as dancers and as individuals. It had some fine music, and a fine range of dramatic and poetic evocation.

Casey Jones was set to music already in the Green repertory. A lively ballad about the larger-than-life railroad man, it had some witty and sprightly variations. May and I had a fine time composing a real romp of a dance here. There was the engine, danced by May, in a stunning red-and-black tutu, and the engineer, Casey Jones, danced by myself in very funny railroad engineer's regalia, complete with oilcan. Clare Falkenstein paint-ed a delightful backdrop of an old-fashioned choo-choo train. It set off the dance admirably and gave it the aura of a child's drawing. The dance was full of ingenuous capers such as delight children of all ages, and when we performed it for school audiences, as we did on a number of occasions, we had a howling success.

I had arrived in San Francisco with very little money, which did not last long. The Greens and Gertrude Shurr came to my rescue, economical-ly as well as morally and artistically. I was given a couch in the studio to sleep on. I had my meals with them. Their generosity, considering that they themselves had to struggle to make ends meet, I find unforgettable. After a hard day's work, spent but content, we would treat ourselves to dinner in the Italian quarter or Chinatown, and an evening of gay, animat-ed banter, a serious evaluation of our day's accomplishments, and plan-ning for the future.

The artist Clare Falkenstein and her husband Richard McCarthy, a young lawyer, would often invite the four of us to their delightful home in the hills overlooking Berkeley. Their hospitality was kind, warm, and lov-

ing. For us hungry artists an evening at the McCarthys was always joyful-
ly anticipated and fondly remembered. There was wonderful drink, magnificent food, laughter, and good cheer. Clare was beginning a quest that
would lead to the Left Bank in Paris and artistic distinction on both sides
of the Atlantic. Dick was an irrepressible and charming Irishman, full of
fun and whimsy. They were a handsome couple. And how enchanting it
was to sit on their terrace while the sun set over the Golden Gate and the
entire bay and city surrendered, swooning almost, to crepuscular magic.

It was in this setting that I first learned about martinis. Our delightful
host would shake a large pitcher-full in front of you, assume a ponderous
Irish brogue, and say, "Sure, and you've got to take another, for snakebite.
These hills are crawling with the vermin!" I have ever since taken precau-
tions. There are likely to be snakes anywhere, including penthouse terraces in New York.

Also, most memorable, are Sulgwyn and Charles Quitzow. I first met
them at Mills College. Sulgwyn and her young teen-age daughter Oeloel
came to the classes during the Bennington School summer. Charles would
drive them over from their home in Berkeley, and he was an indefatigable
spectator. They became my staunch friends and admirers. And so began
the most constant and rewarding of friendships.

Sulgwyn Quitzow's mother had been a contemporary and disciple of
the young Isadora Duncan. This was enough to put me on the scent. Alert
and avid, I began a long chase to learn everything there was to be learned
about the early years of the woman whose history had been so significant
to us dancers. First of all, my friends drove me to a decayed section of
Oakland. We found the house where the young Isadora had lived as a
child and young girl with her mother, Augustin, and Raymond. The
neighborhood, seventy years ago, was a typical middle-class residential
district. The houses were one-story cottages designed by delightfully confused and naive romantics, part-Victorian Gothic, part-Hudson River
Valley Gothic, part-Grimm fairy tale, and part-Gold Rush lunacy, the
whole of the structure—which was covered with gables, verandas, bay
windows, and cupolas—literally encrusted in a gingerbread decor. The
result was so unbelievably absurd as to be charming.

One such a house, fallen into disrepute and decay, was inhabited by a
Negro family that was quite patient with us and our inquisitiveness. There
was the usual front yard and a lawn where even the weeds were struggling
to survive, much less flourish. Two sad remnants of palm trees stood on
each side of the walk like sentinels guarding a dead past. We walked
around to the back and saw another building, a one-time carriage house,
stable, and hay loft. Here the young Duncan brood had run wild. My
guides pointed to a beam protruding from the apex of the roof. From this
a rope used to hang, and with it the young Isadora, something of a
tomboy and a daredevil, would invent as many ways as possible of swinging through the air in long, flying arcs. The interior of the shed was the
first of the Duncan dance studios. Here Isadora, high priestess of Terpsi-

chore by grace of instinct and by virtue of atavistic powers conferred upon her from the cradle, began her career.

This was a profound experience for me. I have subsequently been privileged to visit places suffused with the aura of human genius, such as Sainte-Chapelle in Paris and Beethoven's house in Bonn. This sad, rickety remnant in a forgotten corner of Oakland, California, produced the same awe and wonder. Here was a repository of miracles. Our innocent Republic will no doubt permit it to pass into oblivion without suspecting that one of its most unique cultural treasures had her beginnings here.

High on a hillside overlooking Berkeley is a house built like a Greek temple. It was the home of the Boynton family. Mrs. Boynton, Sulgwyn Quitzow's mother, was a contemporary and disciple of Isadora Duncan, and she carried her conversion to Duncanism to its most logical conclusion. The Hellenic ideal that was the cardinal tenet of Isadora's crusade for Truth and Beauty in life and art was practiced by the Boynton ménage in ways that would barely cause a ripple in our present emancipated age, but were nothing short of scandalous in the early decades of the twentieth century. Since, unlike Isadora, Mrs. Boynton could find glory beneath the columns of the Parthenon, she built her own temple. She dressed the children and herself in Greek tunics and sandals. The Temple of the Winds, where the family ate, danced, lived, and slept, was to be a monument to the exaltation of the spirit. The food was Spartan—fruits, nuts, vegetables, milk, honey—and nothing was artificial or adulterated. Everywhere was fresh air, sunlight, wind, and rain, since the temple had no walls, only curtains. The children, boys and girls alike, were sent to school in Greek tunics. One can only imagine the reaction of the neighbors to all this. Mrs. Boynton, dedicated as only Duncanists can be, opened Temple of the Winds to all who would dance. She taught, preached, and practiced, presiding over Hellenic rites and festivals.

When the Boynton boys entered adolescence, the Grecian masquerade became too much for them. The jeers and taunts of their schoolmates drove them to rebellion. Being good healthy American boys, they wanted to be like everyone else, so Mother had to give in and allow them to adopt the crass and unaesthetic pants, shirts, shoes, sweaters, and jackets of their fellows. The girls seemed content to continue to dress in the flowing tunics and draperies à la Duncan.

As part of my education in Duncanism, Charles and Sulgwyn Quitzow arranged for me to visit the Temple of the Winds. Mrs. Boynton would receive me. She had been made aware of my veneration of the great Duncan and was eager to talk to me. So, one afternoon we drove up the twisting avenues that climbed to the house. By now the Temple had lost some of its pristine austerity. Walls had been built because the hills could be chilly even on summer nights; fireplaces had been installed, along with staircases, bathrooms, and modern kitchen facilities.

We waited beneath the front columns. Presently, down a curving staircase, descended a lady in a long Grecian tunic over which was draped a flowing mantle. Mrs. Boynton was most gracious. We sat on the terrace and tea was served. The entire occasion was devoted to the life and art of Isadora. Mrs. Boynton had a wealth of memories on which to draw. As sunset approached, Mr. Boynton came home. He was a lawyer and spent his days at an office in San Francisco. He joined us on the terrace and entered into the conversation with gusto. To him, Duncan was the most fleet and graceful of creatures. On her rare visits to San Francisco she had sat with them on this very terrace. He remembered her performances. She was unbelievable. "Why, she was like a coyote!" he said, paying her the Westerner's supreme compliment. Mrs. Boynton, now elderly, regretted not having been able to come to my performances. Would I as a great favor dance for her sometime, right here on the terrace, overlooking the lovely bay? I demurred. There was not enough space; the floor was solid concrete. She would not be put off. Isadora always danced, anywhere, any time. She transcended the limits of space and the inconvenience of cement floors.

The result was that some weeks later and as a result of much urging on the part of the Quitzows, I found myself one balmy evening in a pair of black tights, standing on the terrace, facing the lovely bay and an audience of Mrs. Boynton, her daughter Sulgwyn, and the latter's two children. Charles Quitzow sat at the grand piano. We were lit by tall candles. All this was in honor of Isadora Duncan. It was unrehearsed. We would do as she would do. There would be music, and the dance would follow. It was as simple and natural as that.

Charles began. He was a superb pianist. He played the Chopin preludes, all twenty-four of them. It felt very strange to me. I had never improvised dances before. I didn't know how. All dances had to be created and rehearsed with much thought and great care. Now I tried to follow Duncan's manner. Listen to the music with your whole self. Give that self to it, utterly. Become one with it. Lose yourself, and then you will dance.

I discovered a strange and wondrous impetus. It carried me as a leaf is borne by the winds. There was no will, no calculation. There was a surrender to fury and exaltation. I have no idea what I did nor what it looked like. But suddenly there was infinite space and no cement floor. Beyond was the bay, the stars, and the night. The panting breath, the movement, the sweat were one cataclysm and one rapture. Four pounding bass notes brought the final prelude to a conclusion. I stood immobile where I had finished. The terrible pounding continued. It was my heart trying to break through the walls of bone and muscle, through eyes and ears and brain. I had danced for the mother of us all.

The Quitzows knew that I was in financial difficulties. They began a campaign to persuade the authorities at the University of California to invite me to teach in the Department of Dance. This would take much time and conniving. Meanwhile, they opened the Quitzow studio to me; it was a going concern, and several days a week I would cross the bay and hold classes there. These were always delightful occasions. There was the usual assortment of students, from total beginners to more experienced dancers. All were eager and full of energy, and the classes were a pleasure. The studio was handsome, of a kind that is possible only in California. It was spacious and concealed from the street by a lush profusion of the region's semitropical flora. Having become accustomed to the rigors of New York winters, I never ceased to be astonished and delighted by roses and calla lilies blooming in December and January.

After classes I would be invited to dine, *en famille*, with the Quitzows. Charles, who not only played accompaniment for the classes but also performed all the other tasks connected with the running of the school, was a fine cook. He would prepare strange wonders from whole cereals and other foods undefiled by commerce. The diet seemed to work beautifully, for the family was as sturdy and handsome as could be. Sitting with them by the light of lanterns and candles, one had the impression of being immersed in a Rubenesque ambience, all ruddiness and gold.

After dinner we would sit and listen while Charles played—brilliantly—Schubert, Chopin, and Beethoven. Sometimes Sulgwyn and the two children—Oeloel the girl and Durevol the boy[129]—would perform charming Duncanesque dances. I was happy to be there. Never having seen Duncan, I could only imagine how she danced from reading accounts of her performances. My beautiful friends stood, so to speak, in direct descent from her. The technical vocabulary was of the utmost simplicity. But there was grace, roundness, and harmony.

*   *   *

Betty Horst,[130] a leading dancer with Ruth St. Denis and Ted Shawn, had one of the most prestigious dance schools in the Bay Area. I had known Betty in New York, which she would visit every summer, studying with Humphrey-Weidman. She was the wife of Louis Horst. They lived with the continent between them, but were not divorced, and continued to have an amicable relationship. Betty was a handsome redheaded woman of great charm. She was vivacious and gay, a delightful person to be with. Her studio was full of lovely children and young ladies who came to study with her. It was also swarming with Siamese kittens, the progeny of her two adult cats, and these enchanting creatures were the apple of Betty's blue eye.

Occasionally, Betty would have friends over for a Sunday supper. These gatherings were a lot of fun. She would have some exotic delight— Chinese, Tahitian, Mexican, Italian, even San Franciscan, from Fisherman's Wharf—all served buffet style. It was on one of these occasions that I met one of Betty's best friends, Pauline Alvarez. This imposing lady was the wife of a man reputed to own extensive coffee plantations in El Salvador.

Pauline Alvarez was most affable, and we would converse in Spanish. Suspecting that I was somewhat down on my luck, she would invite me to her home for dinner. Her munificence was heaven-sent, for at times I was down to my last dime. Her dinners were invariably festive and sumptuous. There were always other guests. She had a superb Chinese cook. Her two daughters, Peace and Carmen, were delightful girls, both in their teens. One never saw Señor Alvarez. He was upstairs in the master bedroom, having suffered a massive stroke that had left him a helpless paralytic. Everyone referred to him as Daddy.

At the Post Street studio work continued in earnest. By now we had an immediate objective. Ray Green had been busy booking a tour. We were to play Seattle, Portland, San Francisco, Riverside, and San Diego. Meanwhile, Clare Falkenstein had painted another handsome backdrop, an abstract wilderness for *Legend*. The costumes were finished, and we were ready. There had to be a preview, naturally. We invited an audience. My guests included Betty Horst, the Alvarez ladies, and the Quitzows. The McCarthys were there, of course, and so were a number of May's favorite students. May and I danced our entire repertory, with Ray Green at the piano. The preview audience was enthusiastic, and presently we were on our way to the Northwest. We traveled in the Greens' coupé, with our costumes and scenery and personal luggage packed in the rear trunk.

We were very well received. It was a good program, and we were in fine form. Everything about the tour seemed to point to a propitious future for the new venture. Still, we were aware that nothing stood on a firm foundation. It could be swept away at any moment. All we could do was put on a good front and go on for as long as we could.

Southern California has a disconcerting way of affecting me. There is an ambivalence in my reaction to the region that is baffling to the extreme. I am happy to see my family and my old friends, for whom I have the greatest affection, yet the memory of past miseries makes me dread the place, and I find myself impatient for the moment when I can once more escape, see its landscape no more, and breathe another air.

At Riverside, set among the orange groves, is an outdoor amphitheater. The stage is handsomely enclosed by tall clipped cypresses, which form the backdrop and wings for entrances and exits. One beautiful evening our small troupe found itself giving a performance before a most agreeable audience. Things had gone well, and we had reached the high point of our program, the moment that as a rule was compelling to an almost hypnotic degree. May, the seductive virgin-continent, was kneeling with her arms cradling the rapturously expiring adventurer de Soto. There was a hush in the audience. The music was tender as well as sweet, half-lullaby and half-love song. It was a touching scene.

From the somber depths of the cypresses trotted two dogs, making what was obviously their accustomed nocturnal round. Sniffing carefully, they let go on the nearest wing, then solemnly proceeded to dead center stage, where May and I, drenched in a pool of violet and steel blue spotlights, were dancing. They circled our little pyramid, giving us a leisurely olfactory scrutiny. We were aghast, for the audience, which had begun to titter when the dogs had first made their entrance, had now abandoned all effort to control itself. There was uproarious laughter. "What'll we do?" May whispered between clenched teeth. Close to her bosom, I whispered back, "Just keep on going."

We went on to the bitter end. The dogs, having gone to the footlights to investigate the noisy pandemonium and finding it harmless, made their exit. De Soto was buried beneath the waters of the Mississippi to what was by now extreme hilarity. There was a merciful blackout, and May and I ran offstage, collapsing on each other in hysterical laughter. It was some moments before we were composed enough to take our bows, for by now the audience was applauding as clamorously as it had laughed. We bowed, again and again, with all grace and formality.

I lament that theater is moribund in this land. It has not quite reached the state of rigor mortis, but it does give forth a mortal stench of decay. On occasion it has tremors and twitches, which is astonishing in an entity so close to being a cadaver ripe for burial. These feeble reflexes are sometimes taken, breathlessly and hopefully, by the few remaining theater lovers as signs of a miraculous resuscitation. Would that this were so! But nobody cares, outside of the few dedicated fanatics. The obscene ghouls who rule what passes for theater in New York merrily and lucratively preside over a grotesque and necrophilic debauch where putrefaction is shoved down the gaping gullets of the mindless.

Once upon a time, life and creativity did flourish in the American theater. There were theaters in almost every town and city, and they were alive with plays, actors to perform them, and audiences to enjoy them. In that Golden Age, as it has been called, there were great playwrights and superb actors, both native and foreign. The remnants of those days are the sad, dead theaters and opera houses left stranded, specters haunting the dead or dying core of towns and cities scattered over the huge continent.

San Francisco has its share of these once glorious and living vestiges. These theaters, located downtown, were now usually closed. On occasion some touring company would cause the marquees to light up, and a desultory public would partially fill the house. Actors and spectators alike seemed to be participating in some hollow rite, no longer valid nor cogent. People looked as though they were surprised to be there. The excitement, the expectation, the electricity was lacking. This was anemia, theater as anachronism.

May O'Donnell, Ray Green, Gertrude Shurr, and I held staunchly to the belief that the future destiny of the arts lay in the West, and by that we meant San Francisco. The East, that is New York, was corrupt and decayed—finished. My three colleagues had preceded me by a few years in abandoning New York. They would contribute their youth, talent, and energies to creating this western renaissance. I was in complete agreement with them on this. That is why, when it became necessary to leave the

Humphrey-Weidman company, I headed West. The four of us had animated discussions about a golden future. We were full of dedication and ardor.

It was a happy and exciting time. To contemplate a splendid new beginning is intoxicating. Knowing that you have the capacity to help bring it about is even more of an intoxication. At the studio each of us went about our labors with almost mystical exaltation. We were a band of obsessed true believers. We looked neither to the left nor to the right. Only the distant luminosity held any reality for us.

That is why we failed to see that the idea of San Francisco as the new Athens, the fecund womb of the arts of the future, was only a delusion, and that our little band, along with many others, was destined to fail. San Francisco and its surroundings had only one desire, and that was to lie content and somnolent in the mists and radiant sunlight. An Athens, a Florence, a Paris, a New York needed rigors and ordeals, physical as well as spiritual, to give birth to artistic splendors. This charming place wanted only comfort and peace. We gave our one performance at the Veterans Auditorium. It was well advertised, well attended, and well applauded. We were quite beautiful. There was excellence, fire, power, imagination— all the ingredients of good theater. For a brief moment, we nudged San Francisco awake. It smiled sweetly, then rolled over, and returned to its slumbers.

When I fled New York, there was something I had left unresolved. Like all unfinished business it haunted me and gave me no rest. Pauline has since told me that the moment she saw me walk into the Humphrey-Weidman studio, she knew that here was what she had been waiting for all her life and that nothing else would do, ever. For years, if she gave me any sign of this, I was too busy and too blind to notice. As company manager, secretary-treasurer, and general slavey, she could be extremely acerbic when it came to any infraction of discipline or presumption on my part. Still, I rather liked her and thought she could be fun when she wanted to be. On the whole she seemed to ignore me and went about her duties, as I went about mine. I rather thought she didn't like me.

She never existed as a human being for me until some years after I had joined the company. The realization came very suddenly. It was during one of our previews at the Eighteenth Street studio, where my colleague and I were showing our teachers and a few guests the dances we had made. I had just shown my first effort and, astounded at the warmth of the applause, had retreated to the dressing room. Pauline entered, rushed to me, embraced and kissed me with fervor, told me I was magnificent, and rushed out.

Pauline has never suffered fools with any patience, and I could be foolish at times. During a dress rehearsal for one of the company's performances, I made some fatuous comment about her handling of things, and she exploded with her Irish temper and told me that someday she would

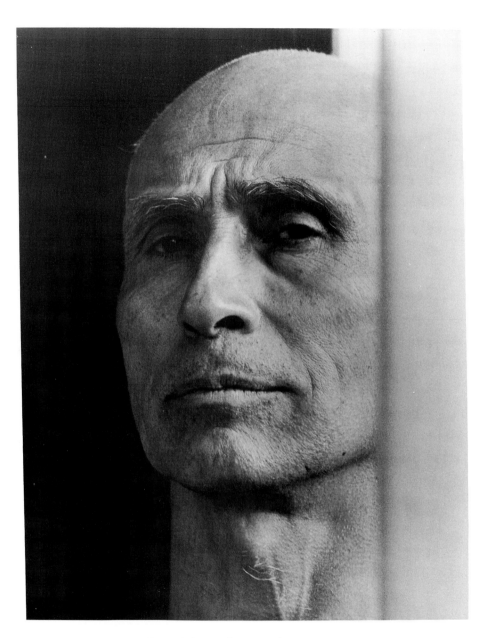

Portrait by Paul Draper, late 1960s.

José Limón at Bennington.

With May O'Donnell, early 1940s.
Photo by Barbara Morgan.

In Doris Humphrey's *Lament for Ignacio Sánchez Mejía* outdoors at Jacob's Pillow.
John Lindquist photograph © The Harvard Theatre Collection, The Houghton Library.

In *Danzas Mexicanas*.

In *The Emperor Jones*. Gjon Mili © TIME Inc.

With Pauline Koner in *There is a Time*. Gjon Mili © TIME Inc.

In *The Emperor Jones*

With Pauline Koner
in *La Malinche*.
Photo by Walter Strate.

With Lucas Hoving in *The Traitor*.
Photo by Arnold Eagle.

With Ruth Currier in Doris
Humphrey's *Night Spell*.
Photo by S. Enkelmann.

In rehearsal.

With Betty Jones in
The Moor's Pavane.

The Moor's Pavane.
These photographs were taken by
Daniel Lewis at the Brooklyn
Academy of Music during Limón's
last performance of this work.

With Betty Jones and Ruth Currier in *Ode to the Dancer*, 1950s. Photo by Arnold Eagle.

With Pauline Lawrence Limón at their New Jersey farm, late 1950s.
Gjon Mili © TIME Inc.

push my teeth down my throat. I gave her a wide berth after this, until, at a party, where I was carefully avoiding her, she drew me aside to ask why. When I explained that I made it a practice to avoid people who disliked me, she answered that I was gravely mistaken, that she loved me very much. She looked radiant, sweet, and beautiful as she said it, and I took her in my arms and kissed her, quite foolishly, for the first time.

From then on there was an understanding between us. But I was determined to maintain my independence, something she found incomprehensible. As we came to know each other, our relationship veered between the extremes of harmony and discord. Marriage had been discussed over the years, but I was in no way ready for it. This, I think in retrospect, was at the bottom of our often stormy relationship. There was also a subconscious awareness on my part that Pauline's chief loyalties lay with Humphrey-Weidman, that Doris, Charles, and their activities had first claim on her.

My break with the company, and the perspective acquired by the three thousand miles between us, helped me to resolve the matter of loyalties. Then, one day, a letter in the familiar, impetuous handwriting arrived. It described an appalling situation. She was writing, it said, from the empty living room of the apartment at 31 West Tenth Street, which we had all shared for years. Doris and Charles had found other living quarters. All that was left were filing cabinets and objects left behind by the others. That was all she had, she wrote, with quiet dignity. The brief, momentous lines transformed me. I knew instantly what I must do, and I sent her a telegram asking her to be my wife. Very shortly after came a telephone call. Incredulous, she asked me to repeat my proposal. Did I really mean it? I did.

An immediate wedding was out of the question. She had her commitments to the company, and she must comply. It was not until late September that I met her at the Embarcadero. It was a lovely experience. I saw her for the first time with new eyes. Here was someone to whom I would devote myself and be responsible for until death. I think she sensed my feelings, and she has been, ever since, secure in the knowledge that no matter what, I would be there and could be counted on. It was in some respects reckless of me to propose marriage at this time. I was not doing at all well financially. My bride had often not only to chip in but on occasion to foot the entire bill. This was embarrassing to me, but it was now or never, and besides I knew that eventually I would be able to assume full responsibility.

Pauline Alvarez very generously offered us her warm and ample hospitality. Her commodious town house had more than enough room. My fiancée and I went through the legal formalities of getting a marriage license and, while waiting the prescribed few days, went about enjoying the enchantments of the city. It was a strange period. It was like walking on air, and I felt a serenity and happiness in knowing that something very beautiful was about to happen in my life. There would be a resolution, a completion. I was to abandon boyishness and irresponsibility and accept a man's estate.

The morning of the third of October 1941 was full of ripe, mellow sunlight. Our wedding party consisted of Ray Green and May O'Donnell, who would be our witnesses, and Peace and Carmen Alvarez. While waiting for the judge who would officiate at the ceremony, Pauline said to me in a quiet voice, "There are two doors, large ones, at each end of this room, and there are one, two, three, four large windows. There is still time, if you want, to escape."

The judge, a kindly, paternal gentleman began very simply by asking us to reflect carefully on the step we were about to take. Did we fully understand its gravity and significance? Upon our affirmative response he proceeded with the ceremony. It was very simple. There was an infinite sense of irrevocability and finality.

The Greens gave us a gay wedding luncheon, and more generosity followed. We were to have their car for a wedding trip. We left immediately and headed for Carmel, where the Byngton Fords had invited us to stay at their beautiful home. Ruth Ford and Pauline had both been members of the Denishawn company. The house was spectacular, one of the many the Fords designed, built, sumptuously furnished, surrounded with enchanting gardens, occupied for a while to give it a homey touch, and then sold, in order to build another, even more attractive one further up the magic mountains facing the Pacific.

Ruth had not given up her connection to the dance. Each house would have a large, handsome room that, during the Ford incumbency, would serve as a dance studio. Ruth would hold classes and keep herself in shape. She would join us for breakfast or lunch dressed in her studio attire, and we would talk about the things that dancers enjoy. Pauline and I spent long hours at the beach and went for drives along the magical shore and in the countryside. There was much humor and gaiety in learning to become a married couple, but also a brooding seriousness. We knew that shortly we would have to part. Pauline had to go back to New York and manage a tour for the Humphrey-Weidman company.

Our nuptial flight was all too brief. I saw Pauline to her train and returned to my work with May. By now the Quitzow influence had gotten me some teaching at the university in Berkeley, and I had the pleasure of once again being my own man financially. Pauline Alvarez proposed that I repair and use the empty apartment over her garage as my home. In return, I was to help with the care of "Daddy Alvarez," who was bedridden and had to be lifted and helped around. Being strong, I could be useful. The apartment consisted of a studio-living room, kitchen, and bath, and was in need of repair and redecoration. I spent all my spare time scraping, plastering, painting, and doing other repairs.

One morning Carmen burst in. The radio had just announced the Japanese attack on Pearl Harbor. I ran to the main house, where by now the family was gathered in the music room on the second floor. They were listening to the radio. Toscanini was conducting the New York Philharmonic in the First Symphony of Shostakovich. The adagio was coming over the radio, tragic, lost, portentous. Everyone leaned forward, eyes wide with panic, to hear the repetition of the terrible announcement. The words of the announcer and the anguished desolation of the music answered one another like a litany of doom.

We had known that the plague raging over the earth would engulf us sooner or later, but none of us was prepared for this appalling news. The girls were in tears. Captain Kearns, Pauline Alvarez's father, a retired old sailor, was choleric as only the Irish can be.

Across the street was a handsome mansion that housed the Japanese consulate. Suddenly, one of the girls called us excitedly to the window. We joined her and saw an amazing sight. From every chimney poured heavy clouds of smoke. Our neighbors were hurriedly burning things, not only in their furnace but also in all their fireplaces.

One alarm followed another. Japanese planes had bombed or were about to bomb defenseless cities on the West Coast. A blackout went into effect. The Alvarez girls and I ran to the stores and bought heavy black cloth and spent days cutting and nailing it to every window in the large three-story house. We were instructed to put buckets of sand on the roof and landings. They were to be used to extinguish incendiary bombs. Everyone was to go to the cellar in case of an air raid. Betty Horst, living alone in a large studio apartment, was terrified. Always solicitous, Pauline Alvarez instructed me, in case of an alert, to take the car and instantly fetch Betty. Betty was relieved. She said that being alone with those screeching sirens would drive her mad.

A few nights later, very late, the dreadful wail woke me from a sound sleep. Instantly, I jumped into some clothes and ran downstairs, started the car, and sped toward where Betty lived. The city, ghostly and deserted, with no street lights, was bathed in the eerie light of a full moon. It was chilly, and my teeth were chattering. Out of nowhere a police car swooped down on me, its siren making an ungodly accompaniment to the other intolerable shriek. I was stopped. No cars were allowed during an alert. I explained my errand. The law was inflexible. "Park the car, Mac, and continue on foot." This I did, running frantically up and down the hills to her house. Panting with exhaustion I rang Betty's doorbell. There was no answer. I went around the side of the building, under her bedroom window. I rapped on the windowsill and called her name. The infernal din drowned my voice. Still there was no response. Alarmed, I pulled myself up and looked in. Bright moonlight illuminated Betty. She was serenely asleep.

The entire Japanese population of San Francisco was evacuated and interned in concentration camps located in the arid interior. The enormity of this act on the part of the government of a nation that prided itself on its enlightenment and humanity did not strike me at the time as anything extraordinary. The previous years had accustomed us all to violence, injustice, and barbarism. After the horrors in Poland and Western Europe, followed by the Nazi attack on Russia, the treatment of the Japanese, many of whom were born citizens of this country, seemed mild by comparison. The Japanese quarter became a dead city, with the streets empty of vehicles, and stores and homes devoid of all life except for a few prowling dogs and cats. There is something infinitely melancholy in the spectacle of abandoned human dwellings. Life went on without the Japanese.

The Ballet Russe de Monte Carlo gave a season at the large new Opera House at the Civic Center. As always, the season was lively and spectacular. The stars—Alexandra Danilova, Tamara Toumanova, Frederic Franklin, and many others—were full of glamour. I found myself deeply moved by the Massine works. This master, the mainstay of the revival of the Ballet Russe in the early 1930s, had created a most impressive roster of works. I had been fortunate in seeing performances, in New York, of *Choreartium*, to the Brahms Fourth Symphony, *Les Présages* to Tchaikovsky's Fifth, and ballets to Beethoven's Seventh Symphony and Berlioz's Symphonie Fantastique. This formidable group of symphonic works proved to be the zenith of Massine's career. And, of course, there was his confection of confections, *Gaîté Parisienne*.[131]

Massine's choreography tended toward the lavish and the spectacular. He had at his disposal a fine corps de ballet and first-rate soloists. Decor and costumes were, of course, in the grand manner. Sometimes this abundance of means would stand in the way of his creative faculties. Often his solution to a choreographic problem was to fill the stage with the entire cast and let them go, fortissimo. There is no denying the impact of these massive mob scenes. They enchanted the provincial and the simpleminded, but were unworthy of his finer capacities.

On this occasion there were two works new to me. One was *Rouge et Noir* to the First Symphony of Shostakovich.[132] This exciting piece of music, at the time almost as fashionable as Beethoven's Fifth, Massine brought to exciting choreographic realization. The ballet was done in his "modern" manner, that is the dancers wore severe all-over tights and leotards, in contrasting colors. The women were, of course, on pointe, but did not wear tutus. The style of movement and gesture was angular, sharp, and acerbic. There were many arresting and inventive figurations and sequences. The work was a distinct contrast to Massine's neoromantic symphonic works and seemed his response to the travails of Mother Russia. A devoted son, he was voicing, in lyric and poetic terms, his anguish at her ordeal, his pride in her heroism.

The other new work was *Bacchanale*, to the Venusberg music of Wagner.[133] I found this work the apogee of Massine's achievement. Here, at last, he had ascended to the apex of a great pyramid, the base of which had been prepared by his other symphonic works. Here was unerring mastery. All the components seemed to mesh and coalesce into a structure of great formal and dramatic power. The result had the beauty and eloquence of great theater. And, like all great theater, it devastated, purged, and exalted.

Again, the master seemed concerned with the terrible holocaust rampant over the earth. To him it was proof of our derangement as a species. We were, quite simply, insane. He chose as symbol and protagonist Mad King Ludwig II of Bavaria. The monarch, dressed in regal panoply, wandered among his hallucinations, the source of the ballet's phantasmagoric atmosphere. There were monsters of beauty, the grotesque, and the repellent. The complete roster of Freudian obsessions seemed to pass before him, to surround and submerge him—with obeisance, menace, and mockery—in a demented saturnalia. At times, he embraced his madness and gloried in it; at others, terrified and appalled, he sought to escape from it. To his feverish imagination, the Goddess Venus appeared, all fire and ice, tormenting him with visions of glory and damnation. Formal elegance of gesture was contrasted with brutally explicit dissonances. Massine had taken the grand manner and given it the grandeur of eloquence.

The role of the King was danced unforgettably by Casimir Kokitch.[134] This superb artist gave a heartbreaking performance. As a symbol of tormented humanity, fatally flawed yet gallant and heroic, he confronted the hellish visions of his insanity with the same blind nobility with which young men face the madness of battlefields. I wept, helplessly, for him, for Venus, for the monsters, for young men at that very moment dying in the war, and for myself.

My old school friend Owen had settled with his wife and two children in a small rural community some distance to the south of San Francisco. The family had gone through the long ordeal of the Great Depression but, being young and intelligent, had survived, none the worse for the wear. Owen now had a ranch in Atascadero and was raising turkeys. It was a precarious business. The young poults were extremely delicate creatures, vulnerable to diseases, any one of which could wipe out an entire flock and its unfortunate owner as well. It was a nerve-racking and exhausting occupation, the crux of which lay in constant, backbreaking labor both to rid the premises of ever-accumulating excreta and to abide by the stringent health measures required for feed and drinking water. My friend and his wife worked early and late, yet their combined efforts barely sufficed to keep the anxiety-ridden enterprise from turning into a shambles at any moment.

On a number of weekends, and sometimes for longer periods when my activities in San Francisco permitted, I would go down for a visit. My friends welcomed me for two reasons: they were happy to see me, and I added to their labor force. I spent days scraping dung off cement floors and loading it onto a truck for disposal. The infant turkeys, who were kept under huge, circular, metal canopies heated electrically to a carefully prescribed temperature, needed constant surveillance, night and day.

After a hard day's work Owen and I would sit at the kitchen table and recall with nostalgia the idyllic joys of our school days. Sometimes, we would adjourn to the living room, and here he would urge me to play the music we loved during our adolescence. He never seemed to tire of the Rachmaninoff and Scriabin preludes. I had long ago given up my high school preoccupation with keeping up and improving my piano technique, so my playing was very rusty. My friend, however, seemed oblivious of my ineptitudes and listened with enjoyment.

There was a crisis of sorts when I had announced my coming marriage. My friend always professed never to understand why I had left California to follow the career of a dancer, living with all those questionable people, when I could have remained in God's country and gone into partnership with him. Now, on acquiring a wife, I would be forever unable to do that. He was hurt and bewildered. His friend Joe, as he called me, was a fool.

The infant turkeys, soft and fluffy, stood under the suffocating heat generated by their mechanical foster mother. Under them were old newspapers to catch their droppings. These had to be replaced daily to minimize the danger of disease. Owen would go into town for supplies that included bales of old newsprint. One morning, on beginning my daily chores, I was astonished to discover a whole batch of papers announcing a dance performance. A huge and rather handsome photograph of May O'Donnell and myself adorned the first page of the second section of the *San Francisco Chronicle*. I was struck by the irony and incongruity of the situation. Here I was, standing in the din, mess, and stench of a turkey pen, expected to line the floor with a photo showing myself and my dance partner as beautiful, radiant beings. I hesitated. My procrastination was ended by my ever-pragmatic friend. Amused, he spread the papers on the cement and lowered the brooder over the poults. The next day it was my task to remove the many reproductions of the picture, now thickly encrusted with the previous night's accumulation.

At the Post Street studio the awareness grew upon us that the days of our artistic activity were numbered. By the spring of 1942, the war was gathering a hideous momentum, and it was only a matter of time before both Ray Green and myself would be, as some writer put it, called to the colors. How long before such a call came was the tantalizing question. Added to this was the unacknowledged certainty that the present San Francisco was not headed for a cultural and artistic rebirth. Tensions engendered by our anxieties made tempers short, and Ray Green and I had several undignified rows. Under normal conditions our relationship was rational enough, but the incertitude that seemed to darken every prospect was enough to bring to the surface a basic incompatibility.

We resolved all this by planning a final tour, this time to the despised East. We played Detroit. It was June, and for the first time I saw the city without snow. We played New York, one performance at the Kaufmann Auditorium of the Ninety-Second Street YM-YWHA and another at the Humphrey-Weidman Studio Theatre. Our success was moderate. The bottom had fallen out of things, and I was dispirited.

My colleagues returned to California. I stayed behind in New York to look for a home for Pauline and myself. We found a place on Thirteenth

Street just off Fifth Avenue. It was minimal, but decent. Pauline decorated it in her superb, austere taste. We marked time waiting for the febrile summer to spend itself and allow us to get back to work. I took classes with Doris. She knew that matters were uncertain for me and suggested that, in the interim, we work on a program to be given at the Studio Theatre in the fall. I was happy to join her in this, and work began. The project was an all-Bach program, to consist of one old work, the *Passacaglia and Fugue in C Minor*, and three new ones, *Partita in G Major*,[135] *Four Choral Preludes*,[136] and *Chaconne in D Minor*. Having danced *Passacaglia* for a number of seasons, I was happy to be rehearsing it once more. After my fling at independence in the West, I was once again under the discipline of a great master, and I saw Doris in a new light. One neatly rounded decade had been lived under her tutelage. I had come as a young ignoramus of twenty-two. I had been molded, tempered, and tested. Breaking away had been a necessity. The perspective of time and distance had been salutary. Now, I was a man nearing his mid-thirties, and I was being treated no longer as a disciple but as an equal.

The *Four Chorale Preludes*, which Doris was to choreograph, were "In Thee Is Joy," "Man's Fall from Grace," "Love and Mercy Shall Restore Thee," and "Awake, the Voice Is Calling." She composed them for a group of her girls—Maria Maginnis,[137] Gloria García,[138] Molly Davenport,[139] and Nona Schurman.[140] Doris and I had the leading roles. She used a style evocative of medieval religious art suitable to a work meant to recreate an allegorical passion play. Pauline designed costumes of a sumptuous simplicity; we were like figures in stained glass windows. The four preludes were held together by a loose dramatic thread, more implied than explicit. "In Thee Is Joy" was a celebratory entrance, with lovely formal configurations, using fleet runs and airy suspensions. "Man's Fall from Grace" followed. To the anguished beauty of this prelude, the two protagonists unfolded a vision of man's fall from innocence and divine grace. Here Doris's choreographic inventiveness narrowed the focus of the work to the fall of the body. She devised intricate ways for us to fall, at times singly, at times simultaneously, at times sharply and quickly, or smoothly and slowly. Sometimes we supported each other; at other times we fell free, away from each other. In "Love and Mercy Shall Restore Thee" the ensemble brought solace to the abandoned. With compassion, they half-led, half-carried them up two curved ramps that met upstage center. The final prelude was a formal recapitulation. The allegory ended as it began, as a joyful celebration of the human spirit. It could not, danced to such music, have ended in any other way.

As proof and measure of my newly acquired status, I was given the responsibility of devising a substantial solo work of my own. I had lived with Bach's Chaconne for a number of years. It had been a constant and beloved companion. It had seen me through some dark moments, and I had come to sense the grandeur of its architecture and the sublimity of its concept. Composing a dance to it seemed an act of presumption, even impertinence. Nevertheless, the idea persisted, an ever-present urge and temptation. There were two abortive attempts, both abandoned when I saw that they weren't ready. Now, two cogencies, my own time limit and the all-Bach program, drove me. It was now or never.

The first series of rehearsals were held in the living room on Thirteenth Street. By pushing chairs, tables, and other furniture against the walls, a not-too-constricted space was made available. I would set the phonograph, listen, and try movements. My first problem was to establish a seminal dance phrase from which the entire work would flow. In this I was following the style of the music, which is a series of variations on a theme. This theme persists throughout as the basis for elaboration and invention.

Bach's theme has a somber and austere majesty. It is also one of the master's most profoundly beautiful utterances, impeccably formal and elegantly baroque. Day after day I struggled to compose a phrase of movements, eight bars in slow three-quarter tempo, that would somehow reflect what is in the music. It took a tremendous amount of sweat—not only of the body but also of the mind—and intuition. There was no dramatic idea or story on which to lean. Here was the challenge that had to be met and transcended if totally abstract, formal beauty were to result.

After days of effort I arrived at a sequence that seemed to stand the test of those formidable eight bars and to flow in kinesthetic consonance with them. I had the choreographic premise, and from this all else had to emerge and develop.

There is a miraculous fecundity to the art of Bach. In this Chaconne, the fecundity seems inexhaustible. The work has a logic, radiance, and purity. Each variation creates its own perfect little universe, yet joins its successor to create a mighty impetus that ascends ever higher to regions of rapturous sonority. I met each variation with the utmost reverence and attempted to reflect in movement what the music seemed to imply. No, much more. Because, locked up in this room, with these sounds penetrating my sensibilities and my bones and tissues, the music took full command. At times I would abandon myself to a kind of trance, stand totally motionless, and say, inaudibly: "Tell me, tell me what to do here, and here, and there." Then, the will and the intelligence would take over, and what the intuition had gathered from the music was carefully and rigorously formalized to comply with the thematic premise. The dance emerged, formal, majestic, elegant, and above all beautiful.

There are things that one not only remembers but also cherishes with all fervor, for they are indispensable allies in the cruel yet splendid battle that artists must wage for their survival both as human beings and as artists. One of these is the moral support and regard of certain persons. For me Doris's regard was the "magnum desideratum." When my dance was ready, I showed it to her privately at the Studio Theatre. It was a long and demanding work. Performing a new dance is always exhausting, for one usually pushes too hard, and one's endurance is not ready to bear the double strain on the nervous system and the muscles. On concluding, I stood totally spent, and Doris was silent for a long time. Then, she left her seat, came to me, and said in her quiet voice, "This is one of the most magnificent dances I have ever seen. It is that for a number of reasons, but chiefly because it is a man dancing." I memorized these words, for I was to need them.

Pauline had seen this preview also. I have learned over the decades that in dance matters she is almost unbelievably difficult to please. "It's a good dance," she told me. But, she added, "It's much too long. It can stand cutting." She designed a most handsome costume that made me look like one of the somberly elegant Spanish grandees in the El Greco painting, "The Burial of the Count of Orgaz."

The all-Bach program met with a resounding success, beyond our most cheerful expectations. It was expected to run for three consecutive Sunday evenings. Instead, it ran for eleven Sundays to packed houses. Doris was quite pleased. She was fond of saying that if she had her way she would compose and dance solely to the music of Bach. The trouble was that audiences wouldn't go along with this, finding it too much of one thing.

But the success of the program gave her the satisfaction of knowing that it ought to be tried again in the future. In the meantime we were planning another program, one completely different from the Bach evening. It was to consist of works based on indigenous American sources, both in this country and Mexico. *Song of the West*, to music of Lionel Nowak ("The Green Land") and Roy Harris ("Desert Gods"),[141] *Danzas Mexicanas*, which also had music by Nowak, and *El Salón México*, to music by Aaron Copland.[142]

In *Song of the West* Doris would present only the section "Desert Gods." This work, composed and presented during my absence in San Francisco, was a rhapsodic salute to the vast occident of the North American continent. I have often reflected on the infinite and irresistible allure this part of the world holds for many of us who were born there and have at one time or another lived there. The deserts of New Mexico, Arizona, and Utah...

[*Here the manuscript breaks off.*]

The abrupt ending of José Limón's memoir leaves us on the verge of discovering what he had to say about the most productive and celebrated period of his career. It is those missing thirty years, spanning the period from his first surviving choreographic work, the 1942 *Chaconne*, until his death as a world-renowned cultural figure in 1972, that are most responsible for Limón's legacy. The manuscript's premature end is also a sad reminder that his own life ended only a month before his sixty-fifth birthday.

What might he have written about if he had completed this autobiography? Some clues may be found in a folder of miscellaneous longhand notes with his manuscript in the Limón Papers at the Dance Collection.[1] One page has as a proposed title, "The Story of a Dancer's Career, 1930–1968." Among the notes in this folder that came to fruition in the manuscript was "The two births and places of birth," which became the author's point of departure. The quotation from Bertolt Brecht that follows—"Let none of us exult too soon: the womb is fertile still from which this monster crawled"—must have had deep resonance for an artist who had remade himself both as a dancer and as a choreographer. Limón then adds his own interpretation of Brecht's statement: "One is born, and reborn—just as one dies and dies again."

A rough outline sketched out several years before he actually began work on the manuscript is helpful in interpreting Limón's views of his different births. The outline has four principal sections, corresponding not so much to the periods of his life as to his position in the larger progression of modern dance. The first is devoted to "The Precursors," namely Isadora Duncan and Ruth St. Denis. Doris Humphrey was originally penciled in here, but then erased. Evidently, Limón decided that she deserved her own category, that of "Innovator." Notably missing from these first two sections are the male counterparts of St. Denis and Humphrey, Ted Shawn and Charles Weidman. Among Humphrey's contributions, Limón cites "A new concept of movement and gesture." Limón waits until the third section to introduce himself into the timeline, tellingly referring to his role as that of a "Perpetuator." All the proposed entries under this category have been touched upon in his manuscript, including what he calls his "apprenticeship with Humphrey-Weidman," from 1930 to 1940, and his first serious efforts at choreographic composition, notably *Danzas Mexicanas* and *Chaconne*.

It is with the last division of Limón's outline, entitled "The Limón Company," that the manuscript breaks off. Here he intended to focus on the works of both Humphrey (again mentioned first) and himself. He defines this period by listing his most notable dances, a roster that comprises his greatest legacy. Using these dances and fragments of his writings as guideposts, it is possible to complete the arc of his artistic life.

The first dance mentioned by Limón is *Concerto Grosso*, an important transitional work. It was originally a vehicle for Beatrice Seckler, Dorothy Bird, and Limón, who toured together as forerunners of the first Limón company in 1945–1946. This period could well have been thought of as another birth, as Limón was returning to civilian life after two years of army service. A member of the Special Services division, he had worked with composers such as Alex North and Frank Loesser in producing shows for his fellow soldiers. While his military duty required the making of entertainment, not war, it was nevertheless an adjustment when he left the service. He wrote: "On my return to civilian existence I was faced with a serious problem. I was thirty-seven years old. The years in the Army had meant for me an inevitable retrogression as a dancer. I could accept this and turn to something else, or I could work harder than ever and get myself back. I chose the latter course, and went to Nenette Charisse [then a prominent New York ballet teacher] for my rehabilitation."[2]

The Limón-Bird-Seckler trio led directly to the founding of the Limón company in the summer of 1946, with initial performances at Bennington College and a New York debut in January 1947 at the Belasco Theatre. In fact, *Concerto Grosso* (with Pauline Koner and Miriam Pandor) and *Chaconne* were the only Limón works on a program whose centerpiece was Humphrey's *Lament for Ignacio Sánchez Mejías* and also included her satiric *Story of Mankind*. Limón remembered the New York debut, his first postwar concert there, as "a huge success. The audience gave us a reception I shall never forget."[3]

The year 1949 was an auspicious one for Limón, as it witnessed the creation not only of a dance rooted in his native Mexico, *La Malinche*, but also one that would become an undisputed masterpiece, *The Moor's Pavane*. Of *La Malinche*, Limón wrote: "My father and mother and my grandmother in Mexico were fond of telling us stories, and I have made effective use of some of them."[4] The idea had been brewing since before the war, when he had approached Martha Graham about playing the title role, with Erick Hawkins as the Conquistador and himself as the Indian. They had several meetings to discuss the work, but as Limón noted, "the draft board had other choreography planned for me."[5] When he resurrected the idea in 1949, he enlisted two members of his own company, Pauline Koner and Lucas Hoving, to join him in the dance.

It was these two artists, along with Betty Jones, who formed the nucleus of Limón's company for many years and who also made up the original cast of *The Moor's Pavane*. A long letter he wrote to his fellow cast members on the tenth anniversary of the premiere tells something about the work's genesis:

> I was more than usually shaken and insecure. This dance might prove, in the eyes of the public, to be an impertinence, an almost sacrilegious presumption. I know how hard I had tried not to make a "dance version" of Shakespeare's "Othello." I had worked with all will and conscience to find a form which might prove valid and pertinent in terms of dance. I did not wish to infringe, nor paraphrase. From the moment when Mrs. Louis (Betts) Dooley, a few years previous to this evening in August 1949, had first put the idea into my very receptive mind, I had sought not a "retelling" of Shakespeare's "Othello," but a dance based on the old Italian legend. "Betts" had given me not only the impetus, but the form. She suggested using the four principal characters: Othello, Desdemona, Iago and Emilia, and unfold the tragedy in dances suggestive of those of the High Renaissance. As is my custom when some kind and well-meaning friend comes to me with "just the idea for a dance for you and your company," I listened courteously, meaning to give it consideration, and then go on to my own ideas. But this one hung on. "Othello" had always had a profound and powerful attraction for me, but I had no idea how to proceed other than to resort to a "choreographic version," and this I had no desire to do. Movement, gesture and pantomime were not enough—a form was needed, a form strong and distinct enough to justify the whole effort. It took about three years of brooding. The four principal protagonists, yes. That drastic removal from the play was an important step. But how to bring forth all the passion, grandeur, beauty, all the tragedy with only four dancers? The three years were an intense and incessant search for the answers. They came slowly. There was the usual turmoil and ferment. There were periods of great exaltation, when the solution seemed imminent, or even accomplished. This, as you might know, was almost surely followed by the disappointment of knowing that what had seemed resolved the day before was a mere delusion, and I had to begin all over again.[6]

Limón was aided in his struggles with this and all his other dances of the period by Doris Humphrey, who was the company's artistic director. Theirs was a professional relationship unparalleled in modern dance. Limón speaks of her crucial role in finding the music for *The Moor's Pavane*, the choreography of which had been created independently of the Purcell score we now think of being so inextricably connected to it:

> When we had the dance almost completely composed, I despaired at finding the right music for it. I searched for weeks. I listened, hoping to find suitable music in Monteverdi, in Bartok, in Schoenberg, and many others. No success. Again our Doris came to the rescue. She found us "The Gordian Knot Untied" and "Abdelazar Suite." These being music written for the theatre, it was a relatively simple matter to select sections which fitted our dance, and in turn, to adjust that dance to the music.[7]

Whatever uncertainties Limón might have experienced in creating *The Moor's Pavane*, he was clearly pleased by its success. "Audiences have liked it very much," he wrote, adding that in the eyes of its dancers, "it never stales, but seems fresh and challenging and exciting."[8] Another notable footnote about *Pavane* is that it marked the first of many Limón dances to be commissioned by the Connecticut College American Dance Festival, where Limón taught every summer from 1948 until the end of his life.

The next four works listed in Limón's outline, created between 1950 and 1956, all have biblical roots. Three of them—*The Exiles*, *The Traitor* and *There is a Time*—are well documented on film and continue to be part of the contemporary repertory. *The Visitation*, however, exists today only in the minds of its surviving dancers and the audiences who saw it in the years just after its 1952 premiere. A shared characteristic of all four works is the manner in which Limón distills the familiar biblical characters to express a broader idea. Adam and Eve become the exiles and Judas the traitor, while *The Visitation* represents Joseph, Mary, and an angel as "The Man," "His Wife," and "The Stranger." Limón described his creative process in a 1955 article, "Composing a Dance":

> My first requisite is an idea. I cannot function with abstractions, or with what is called absolute dance. I work out of the emotions, out of human experience, mine or those about which I have read or heard. Certainly there has to be a deeply felt motive or subject. There is usually a period of about two years during which I live with the idea. I think about it and read all I can find about it, usually during the long train rides across the continent on our concert tours. I sleep with it, and eat with it. I become obsessed and possessed. I try all sorts of movements and gestures which occur spontaneously, in the studio, or when I fancy that I am alone and unobserved, waiting for a subway, or an elevator, or in a room by myself....This goes on for weeks, then months, and then the time comes when I must begin or burst.[9]

The idea for *The Exiles* must have touched a deep chord in Limón, who had left his native Mexico some thirty-five years before. His original program note hints at some of the personal associations evoked by this story of banishment from Eden. "According to Dante, there is no greater anguish than past joys remembered in the midst of adversity. This dance was inspired by and dedicated to those desolate ones who remember some lost paradise, or serenity, or innocence, or homeland." Ironically, just after *The Exiles* was created, Limón was invited to Mexico as a distinguished native son. The Limón company took up residence at Mexico City's Instituto Nacional de Bellas Artes, whose dance department was then under the direction of the artist Miguel Covarrubias. Covarrubias became an important ally, and the association allowed Limón to explore various aspects of Mexico in six new works. Interestingly, while this was a notable chapter in Limón's career, none of the six Mexican creations was included on his list of significant dances.

Another biblically-inspired dance, *The Traitor*, serves as a case study in how Limón put his own twist on a familiar story. Here the title character refers not only to Judas but also to those who "named names" before the House Un-American Activities Committee, in full swing when the dance was created in 1954. Limón's original program note spells out the dual inspirations. "The arch-betrayer, Judas Iscariot, is used in this work to symbolize all those tormented men who, loving too much, must hate; these men who, to our own day, must turn against their loyalties, friends and fatherlands, and in some fearful cataclysm of the spirit, betray them to the enemy. This work, in its treatment, costuming and decor suggests our present era."

In *There is a Time*, Limón sought to evoke not merely the present, but eternity itself. Here was the ultimate expression of universality, dramatizing the familiar verses from Ecclesiastes that begin, "To every thing there is a season, and a time to every purpose under heaven." Limón's original program note explains the motif that he decided upon to express the concept of time. "A circle, endless, with no beginning and no end, appears as symbol of time and timelessness. That is the theme from which emerge other circles, like variations on the initial theme. These are in turn joyful, lyrical, somber, violent, but ever recur to the circular time motif, to remind the spectator that the great opposites, birth-death, love-hate, etc., are contained, and endured, in time."

Commissioned in 1956 by the Juilliard School of Music, *There is a Time* is a testament to its generous support of Limón throughout the 1950s and 1960s. Aside from commissioning the choreography, Juilliard commissioned the Norman Dello Joio score (which would later receive a Pulitzer Prize), provided the Juilliard Orchestra for the first performances (which took place in the Juilliard Theater), built the costumes in its costume shop, and offered free rehearsal space.

Another 1956 commission, this one from the Empire State Music Festival, allowed Limón to create *The Emperor Jones* to a commissioned score by Heitor Villa-Lobos. As with *The Moor's Pavane*, the work was based on a literary source, in this case Eugene O'Neill's celebrated play about an escaped murderer who sets himself up as emperor of a primitive tribe. Again, this was not to be a literal interpretation of the play but "a symbolic synthesis of a man's disintegration through terror."[10] *The Emperor Jones* was one of several works of this period that Limón created for an all-male cast.

In 1954, an important chapter of Limón's artistic life began when he led his company abroad on the first State Department tour by any American dance company. This first tour, a three-week expedition to South America, was followed by an even more extensive European tour in 1957. Traveling to the "Iron Curtain" countries of Poland and Czechoslovakia as well as to more familiar Western European nations, Limón experienced a profound emotional reaction that would lead to one of his most deeply felt works, *Missa Brevis*. "Poland is an experience which I will not fully grasp, I think, for quite some time," he wrote in a report on the European tour.

> The bare facts are simple—17 days of hard trouping, four cities, Poznan, Wroclaw, Katowice and Warsaw. Hard work—performances every night plus a good many matinees—marvelous opera houses, packed with a warm, perceptive public. But what I saw and felt as an artist and as a human being is probably the most complex and devastating experience of my life. Against a background of cities still lying eviscerated by the savagery of war, I met human beings of courage, serenity, nobility. There was no rancor, no bitterness. Only a tremendous resolution, a sense of the future. Poland had to be rebuilt. I am in awe of these brave people, of their passionate love for their identity, their tradition, their beautiful survival—but above all, their unspeakable courage. I am very humble and very proud to have performed for them.[11]

Limón poured his feelings into *Missa Brevis*, casting himself as the central figure who watches the faithful with anguish and inspiration, trying in vain to allow himself to join them. Limón was able to utilize the expanded forces of the Juilliard Dance Theater to represent the Polish people, and this became a turning point in his use of a large ensemble. The group would become even more important in later works, but here it first came into its own. John Martin commented on this development in his review in *The New York Times*:

> His use of the group as a group is a natural outgrowth of the subject and the material; when the individual emerges he is nonetheless an individual, and when he takes his personal flashes of emotional realization back into the group he is no less a part of the group. There is a remarkable awareness of the solitude of the individual, and yet also of the group as something more than a mere aggregation of solitudes.[12]

The most grandly-scaled work of Limón's career was *A Choreographic Offering*, which he created in 1964 as a tribute to Doris Humphrey. Not only was the dance lengthy (fifty-eight minutes) and densely populated (twenty-two dancers), but it also had a large concept, interweaving movement motifs from fourteen of Humphrey's dances. In a preliminary dedication, Limón referred to the dance as "a memorial bouquet," in which he had "taken all the flowers which are her movements and put them together as a *memento vitae*." The New York premiere of the work took place at the New York State Theater as part of a short-lived venture known as the American Dance Theatre, directed by Limón.

Limón's last works, produced in the early 1970s, were the culmination of lifelong passions and concerns. In *The Unsung* (1970), he created one of his finest celebrations of the male dancer, dedicating the New York premiere to Ted Shawn in recognition of his pioneering efforts for men in dance. A random note Limón scribbled concerning the god-like Indian chiefs of *The Unsung* read, "They were miraculous because they were beautiful, and beauty is always a miracle.[13] In 1971, Limón returned to one of his earliest inspirations—Isadora Duncan. *Dances for Isadora* expressed Limón's deep affection for the dancer, whom he never saw, but who nevertheless had a deep effect on his life. In an interview, he spoke of the emotions propelling the work: "I read Isadora's *My Life* and I became incandescent with the desire to dance. She was my dance mother, the Dionysian, the drunken spirit of the soul. And today, when I compose, I try to capture that Dionysian ecstasy of Isadora's."[14]

Orfeo and *Carlota*, which premiered during the ANTA Theater season just two months before Limón's death, are both deeply personal. *Orfeo*, a "lyrical lament of love and loss," was a spiritual tribute to his wife, Pauline Lawrence, who had recently died after thirty years of marriage. *Carlota* may also have been prompted by Lawrence's death, as it concerns the Empress Carlota's fragile state of mind following the death of her husband, Maximilian. Whether or not this connection was relevant for Limón, *Carlota* was one last revisiting of the Mexican theme, a final journey to the homeland Limón could never wholly forget.

Now, a generation after Limón's death, it is still possible to witness his dances and to experience firsthand some of the artistic statements he made through movement. Because his autobiography was never finished, these dances are his most lasting utterances. Among his notes is a scribbled phrase that could serve as his motto: "Transcend our day and become timeless." Limón's dances have done just that.

Covarrubias

JOSÉ LIMÓN

Some people are born with a rare gift. It is an endowment given to few mortals. They are persons of many talents and accomplishments. But their greatest achievement is the manner, the style, the grace with which they live their lives. Their presence transforms and literally electrifies the *ambiente* in which they move. They stimulate others; they heighten experience and perception; they inspire and challenge; they create delight and magic.

Two such beings were Miguel Covarrubias and his wife Rose.

It was my good fortune to encounter them in New York at an after-theater party halfway through the decade of the Thirties. They were both at that zenith that in most humans is ephemeral but in their case would endure for decades to come. Miguel was of distinguished and handsome appearance, a brilliant artist; Rose was a woman of great beauty and charm. They were much sought after by the denizens of the great world.

Prestigious journals seemed incomplete without Miguel's cartoons and drawings. The idiosyncracies and foibles of the rich, powerful, and famous were distilled through his uncanny insight into cartoons as revealing as they were hilarious. One of his great loves was the theater, and he would lovingly satirize its tragedians and buffoons. Rose had been a dancer on Broadway and had abandoned a successful career to marry Miguel and follow his destiny. On this evening, at this penthouse party, they were young, beautiful, and infinitely appealing.

I did not see them again until 1950. With all the predictability of a stroke of lightning, a letter arrived from Mexico City signed by Carlos Chávez. It explained that he was now director of the National Institute of Fine Arts and had appointed Miguel Covarrubias as head of its Department of Dance. He was aware of my accomplishments as a dancer and was anxious to discuss the possibility of my company being invited to perform in Mexico City. Miguel Covarrubias would be in New York shortly and would be happy to meet with me and discuss the idea.

I was enchanted of course at the prospect, and when Miguel made himself known I hurried to his hotel, and again saw him and Rose, this time not by the glamour of candlelight but in hot, broad daylight. My first impression held. Here were two supremely attractive people. I met them and was conquered.

I arranged to have them come to the studio where my dancers and I held our rehearsals. I wanted them to see some of our works.

Pauline Koner, Lucas Hoving, Betty Jones, and I were in our tights sweating at the barre when they arrived. I presented the dancers and Simon Sadoff, our accompanist and musical director. We began with *La Malinche*. Our visitors were quite impressed, I could see. After a pause to catch our breath, we danced *The Moor's Pavane*. At its conclusion, where I, as Othello, lay over the prostrate Betty Jones as the murdered Desdemona, I looked at our audience. Miguel was pale and speechless. Rose was weeping. It was moments before they could thank us.

Miguel suggested lunch. We hurried into our civilian attire and went across the street to the Carnegie Tavern. It was a gay and excited party. Both Miguel and Rose were in high spirits. He insisted on drinks to toast the occasion and on ordering the most elaborate steaks on the menu. Dancers worked hard and must partake of the best. He and Rose were full of plans and ideas.

When I asked the waiter for the check Miguel was outraged. It was his party. He had invited us and would take care of everything.

This was my first lesson with Miguel. He was the most generous of men. He lived to give to others.

Our next meeting was at the railroad station in Mexico City early that September. Miguel and Rose had brought along an entourage to welcome us. There were Institute officials, artists, and dancers. There was much excitement. It was a beautiful evening, and I was in a state of almost unbearable expectation. As a born Mexican who had left the country at seven years of age, I was in turmoil on seeing for the first time the fabled capital of my native land. In fact, I was close to tears.

We were driven to the hotel.

Miguel and Rose sensed the significance to me of the occasion. They did not put us up at a modern hotel, indistinguishable from any other in Detroit or Los Angeles. Instead, they selected the Hotel de Córtez, which is a building dating to 1753, a former convent, a beautiful old edifice in the best colonial Mexican style.

Pauline and I had a suite with balconied windows facing the Alameda. The interior and the furnishings were in superb taste, and there were flowers everywhere—roses, carnations, gladioli, and those most Mexican of flowers, tuberoses.

After the rest of the welcoming delegation had left, Miguel suggested supper. He took us to a *fonda* and ordered a magnificent repast.

Muy mexicano.

Miguel and Rose were determined that my first impressions on returning to my native land should be the right ones, indelible and above all beautiful.

Next morning we had breakfast in the sunlit patio of the hotel. Miguel's sense of artistic proportion called for a switch in languages. We spoke in Spanish. Rose, *norteamericana*, born in Los Angeles, was by now quite at home in her husband's native tongue, and we got along very well.

Then began the day's activities. Miguel took me down the Alameda to the Palace of Fine Arts. This monstrous and fascinating building was the first and possibly the ugliest thing I was to see in Mexico.

We had a busy and exciting morning. First we paid our respects to the *jefe*, Carlos Chávez. This charming and urbane man welcomed me like a long lost son or, at any rate, a long lost nephew. We had a most agreeable conversation during which he suggested that I consider the possibility of joining the Institute, to teach and direct the dancers.

There followed introductions to the other officials of the Institute, who greeted me with all cordiality and kindness.

Miguel showed me the great stage, where we were to perform. He took me to visit the studios of the Academy of Dance and introduced me to the dancers; then he showed me the studios where my company was to rehearse. We arrived at his office. The place was replete with books on art and archaeology. There were painting by famous artists on the walls and papers and magazines from foreign countries.

I was to spend many hours here with Miguel, planning and discussing our activities. I was to discover in him a man of towering erudition, an astounding mind full of restless energy and endless capacity.

Our performances at the Palace of Fine Arts were a huge success. Miguel took a very personal, almost proprietary interest in the entire project. He and Rose threw the weight of their considerable social and artistic prestige behind it. They gave luncheons and cocktail parties, presided at press conferences, and saw that we met, at charmingly appointed dinners, the right people.

Miguel wanted to design a poster to advertise the event. It was to have a figure of myself on it. However, the photographs I had brought from New York wouldn't do. He wanted something entirely original. In his office, for hours on end, I performed fragments of various dances, while he made preliminary sketches. Finally, he settled on a movement from the Bach *Chaconne in D Minor*. Wearing the appropriate costume, I froze in the movement he had chosen. It was an agonizing chore, but the result was a stunning drawing in the best Covarrubias style. Enlarged and accompanied by suitable lettering, it soon appeared on billboards and fences throughout the city and adjacent localities.

Carlos Chávez as well as Miguel and Rose were gratified by the public and critical response, which in every respect went beyond even the most sanguine of expectations.

The result was that I was invited officially to return and work with the Academy for a period of some months. We arrived, eager to start work, in January 1952. Without much ado I began auditioning and selecting dancers and rehearsing the works that Miguel and I had discussed and planned during my first visit. The main "opus" would be a choreographic setting to Carlos Chávez's *Los cuatro soles*, a massive symphonic work based on Aztec myths of the creation of the world. There would be another work by Maestro Chávez, *Antígona*, and, finally, to music by Silvestre Revueltas, a piece called *El Grito*.

The miraculous Miguel was working literally night and day. He was lecturing on archaeology at the National Museum and at the University, attending to his chores at the office as head of the Academy of Dance, and painting a mural of heroic proportions in the nave of a lovely colonial church on the Avenida Madero that the National Institute of Fine Arts had acquired and was to transform into a museum of Mexican folk art.

We would meet for lunch every day and discuss the decor, sets, and costumes he was designing for the productions. The waiters at the restaurant were accustomed to the Señor Covarrubias's luncheons. The table would be covered with manuscripts, books, sketches, pencils, and brushes. Miguel had a passion for historical and artistic authenticity. These conferences were for me a liberal education in the mythology of the pre-Colombian world, its history, architecture, costuming, and artifacts. Miguel had a habit, when discussing something, of drawing it for you. His mind and his pencil were equally at ease with the myths of the ancient Mayas, Toltecs, and Aztecs as with those of the archaic Hellenes.

After these luncheons I would return to my rehearsals and he to his multifarious activities. During evening rehearsals Rose would drop in to watch, and around midnight we would stroll across the Alameda to the chapel and watch Miguel, perched high on a scaffold, painting. The entire nave was a luminous vision, a gigantic map of Mexico, with figures dressed in the incredibly varied and colorful attire of its Indian tribes, and displaying a dazzling variety of toys, potteries, and textiles. The design of the whole was impeccable; the color was radiant. The total effect was breathtaking.

It would take all manner of persuasion, wheedling, coaxing, and sometimes even threats on Rose's part to get Miguel off the scaffolding. Without Rose's prodding he was likely to work the night through, forget to eat, get little or no sleep, and put in a heavy day's work on the morrow. His health was beginning to bother him, and Rose would worry. Grumbling at the interruption, he would adjust his tie, don his jacket, and be off with us to a restaurant.

I don't know whether Miguel was by nature indifferent to food or whether he was merely careless or defiant of Rose's constant solicitude and admonitions, but, when he had a menu before him, he would order the most outlandish and indigestible of foods. Mexican cuisine is famous for its delights. It is also notorious for concoctions that can corrode any stomach except one made of cast iron. To be reminded by Rose that all this was against the *médico*'s orders only ensured that Miguel would indulge himself.

After supper these two would drop me off at the Córtez and be off to Tizapán. Rose would tell me the next day that here he would retire to his study in pajamas and dressing gown and work on his new book until almost dawn, when he would snatch a few hours of rest and be up to do what would have laid low a lesser man.

The house at No. 5 Reforma in Tizapán was Rose's domain. It was a handsome place, designed in Mexican style by Miguel. It rambled in unexpected directions and with its unusual angles and levels offered a fascinating arrangement of walls, tiled roofs, patios, verandas, and passages. The courtyards were filled with a magnificent profusion of flowering plants, trees, and cacti. The spacious living room was dominated by a large portrait of Rose in the full flower of her beauty by Diego Rivera. The painter had managed to capture the compelling, almost majestic presence that was the essence of her being and seemed to be focused in the eyes. I would stand before the portrait and speculate on its singular perceptiveness, the work of art that was this woman.

She lived her life for one reason only, to be with Miguel and do for him. The house, full of rare artifacts, was a monument to his genius as a painter, writer, archaeologist, pedagogue, and humanist. Rose had accompanied him to the ends of the earth and gathered objects to delight his always exacting aesthetic sensibility. The rooms were replete with magnificent trophies from Bali, China, Africa, and the Americas.

Rose would give sumptuous luncheons. These occasions were in keeping with all that one associated with this extraordinary couple. For days the cooks and maids were occupied with the preparations of astonishing culinary miracles. It was *muy mexicano* in the best sense. Rose's table arrangements were no less spectacular. At these feasts one was likely to encounter world famous men and women. Miguel would literally have to be torn from his work and forced to attend his own parties. Yet once there, no one could surpass him in the grace and courtesy of a good host.

Rose, besides managing a household, would find time to devote to her painting and photography. She was very talented at both. She would paint exquisite portraits of children, and her flower pieces were things of great charm. On expeditions she was the official photographer and an assiduous one, and it is my hope that eventually her remarkable achievement as a photographer will become known to the public.

The conferences between Miguel and myself were always stimulating and productive. The rehearsals at the Academy continued at a furious pace. The dancers exerted themselves to the utmost. *Los cuatro soles, El grito,* and *Antígona* were making good progress. But we saw that other works would be needed to round out the season. A number of possibilities were discussed. Some were adopted, others rejected.

Miguel suggested a weekend expedition to Puebla. I had never visited this old city, and Miguel thought a short rest was in order. Presently, Miguel, his wife Rose, Pauline, and I were on our way in the official station wagon. Leaving the valley of Mexico and climbing to the heights above the city is always a heady experience, especially when one looks back at the panorama below. The mountainous road leading to Puebla is a historic one. Miguel was full of fascinating information not only about the history of the region, but also its anthropology, geology, botany, and zoology. We found his conversation totally engrossing.

We stayed at a charming old-style hotel and enjoyed a delightful supper full of the flavor of the old city. As always, an electrifying *ambiente* seemed to surround Miguel and his wife. The next morning we saw the town. We began with the shops and markets, which the ladies adored and where they bought innumerable trinkets. By slow stages we moved toward our objective, the great cathedral. Miguel knew my predilection for architecture, particularly Mexican colonial architecture. He had already shown me many treasures in the capital. I found the Puebla cathedral inspiring as could be. Then, Miguel guided me to a small chapel to the left of the main altar. I was totally unprepared for what I saw. Here was the fabled *El Dorado*, the half-dream, half-mirage that had maddened conquistadors with lust and frenzy for gold. The walls and ceiling were a mass of scrolls, convolutions, and sinuosities, all covered with gold leaf, each elaborate surface at once a source and mirror of golden radiance. Under an indescribably wrought canopy stood a sovereign Castilian lady, fair and blue-eyed, robed in a stiff, pearl-embroidered robe of sky-blue brocade and wearing a jewel-studded crown. In her arms rested a young prince, also in regal attire, also rosy, blond, and blue-eyed, and like her, crowned. This was a vision of the Queen of Heaven, Our Lady the Holy Mother of God, presenting the infant savior and redeemer, a vision worthy of the baroque ecstasies of St. Ignatius Loyola, Don Quixote, and perhaps Philip II himself.

Miguel knew the devastating effect this was having on me. Here was sublime theater. Both of us, renegade Catholics, rebels against our backgrounds, were enraptured, as artists, by the scene. We stood in silence for a long time. I examined the chapel minutely, drinking in the gorgeous extravagance.

At last Miguel suggested the resumption of our sight-seeing. The patient driver and the station wagon were waiting. We drove out of the city and after a while came to a small town. Again our objective was a church, this one called San Juan Ecatepec. The caretaker knew Covarrubias and was quite pleasant, unlocking the front portals and ushering us into the cool, cavernous interior.

This, I saw, was a replica of the golden chapel. But there was a difference. The baroque style had been subtly modified. It was just as grandiose and sumptuous, but the gold was not as dominant. The designs, covering the entire wall space and vaulted ceiling, were now radiant with green, blue, red, and yellow. The scrollwork did not have the elegance and sophistication of the Puebla chapel; rather there was a certain naiveté, a slightly provincial element to the total effect.

Miguel called my attention to the effigy of the Virgin and Child. They again occupied the place of honor under a canopy, but they were different. They were *mestizos*, mixed bloods—black-haired, black-eyed, and brunette-skinned. Their panoply, still celestial, was no longer entirely Castilian. It was part Indian.

Miguel, the historian, explained. The large cities in colonial Mexico were centers where the Spanish upper classes prevailed. The Virgin enshrined in the golden chapel in Puebla was one of them. As one moved away from the cities, the population tended to become *mestizo*. In the chapel at Ecatepec the Virgin was a *mestiza*.

After careful examination and discussion of the historic aspects of Ecatepec, we continued our journey. After much driving over roads increasingly primitive and neglected, we came to a remote, humble Indian village. Again, we headed for the church. We were admitted by a silent Indian caretaker. This was the climax of our expedition. The chapel of Santa María Tonantzintla was all that we had seen in Puebla and Ecatepec rendered in the language and from the imagination and sensibility of the Indian. His dark genius had transformed the high baroque into something with a primitive, crude splendor. The shapes, the forms, again in bold bas-relief, were no longer the sumptuously flowing curves of churrigueresque design. They were related to the sacred sculpture of the Toltecs and Aztecs. There were echoes of Teotihuacán. The angels and cherubs, covering the walls and ceiling as in the other chapels, were now strange, fantastic figures of the Indian imagination. There were archangels, angels, mermaids, and imaginary beasts. The color was violently beautiful, totally and triumphantly uninhibited—crimson, magenta, bright pink, cerulean and turquoise blue, yellow, chartreuse, purple. Only an occasional trace of gold reminded one of the prototype in Puebla.

The Virgin and Child were Indians. In this chapel, in this isolated and forlorn village, the Spanish conquest and centuries of Spanish domination seemed nullified. Miguel explained that the chapel had been built on the spot where a temple to the Mother Goddess Tonantzintla had once stood. This had been demolished and its stones used to erect the present chapel. The manner and style of representation—not only of the Virgin and Child but also of the angels and cherubs—had been taken over by the Indians, and they had created this barbaric splendor.

The Mother Goddess stood serene, holding her child. But she was surrounded by a joyous pandemonium. Every figure was playing some musical instrument, a viol, a trumpet, a guitar, cymbals, or drums. Heaven was a place for joy, for music, for celebration.

"Miguel," I exclaimed, "the entire place is dancing! Heaven is a huge party!"

"I was hoping you would see that," he replied. "Perhaps you will make us a dance based on what you have seen today. We need it for our season."

This was the Covarrubias method, manner, and style. Give people delight. And Beauty. Take them to it. Let them see it, feel it, eat it, drink it. Instruct. Charm. Then, see what happens. Both Miguel and Rose were assiduous and adept at this. They seemed to live for it.

The dance, a miniature ballet, was named *Tonantzintla*. Miguel and I composed a program note, "It was the birthday of the infant Mermaid, and the Archangel and the angels were having a celebration in honor of the occasion."[1]

Miguel designed the stupendous decor and costumes. The little Mermaid, danced with ingenuous charm by Valentina Castro, a very young and talented dancer, was dressed, like her prototype in the ceiling at Tonantzintla, in bright pink and gold, and she held a crimson toy guitar. The angels, again from the chapel, were decked out in regal Aztec panoply, complete with feather headdresses. The Archangel, danced by myself, was a concession to Spanish influence. Miguel dressed me like a Roman centurion, with a simulated breastplate and leggings.

Because the chapel was architecturally a replica of the golden one at Puebla, and therefore of Spanish design, Miguel and I searched for Spanish music of the baroque era. We were lucky. The keyboard sonatas of Antonio Soler, brilliant, joyous music of the eighteenth century, gave us the right accompaniment. Four sonatas were selected and sensitively orchestrated by Rodolfo Halffter, the Spanish émigré composer then living in Mexico.

In composing this little ballet I kept in mind the style and import of what I had seen at Tonantzintla. The movement was ingenuous, full of childlike wonder and delight. There were motifs derived from Spanish jotas and fandangos. There was the formality and ornateness of the baroque. Above all, there was an evocation of holy, pagan joy.

The ballet was a stunning success, and was danced at every performance during the season. Miguel and Rose Covarrubias were like the proud parents of a wondrous child. *Tonantzintla* was truly theirs.

Works Choreographed by José Limón

LYNN GARAFOLA

Since Limón's early works were first shown at studio performances or group concerts for which few programs survive, it is next to impossible to establish accurate premiere dates. It is likely that several of the pre-1935 works listed below actually premiered before the dates given for them.

Etude in D-flat Major
Music: Alexander Scriabin
Premiere: Humphrey-Weidman Studio, New York, December 1930
Dancers: José Limón, Letitia Ide

Bacchanale (with Eleanor King and Ernestine Henoch*)
Music: percussion accompaniment
Premiere: Humphrey-Weidman Studio, New York, December 1930
Dancers: José Limón, Eleanor King, Ernestine Henoch
NOTE: This may have been the trio identified by Eleanor King as *Danse,* which was performed without music. If so, it was probably choreographed the following spring. See Eleanor King, *Transformations* (New York: Dance Horizons, 1978), pp. 95–96.

Petite Suite (with Eleanor King and Ernestine Henoch)
Music: Claude Debussy
Premiere: Humphrey-Weidman Studio, New York, spring 1931
Dancers: José Limón, Eleanor King, Ernestine Henoch
NOTE: This may have been the trio identified by Eleanor King in *Transformations* (p. 95) as *Cortège.*

Tango (also called *Tango Rhythms*)
Music: percussion score by José Limón
Costumes: Charles Weidman

Premiere: Humphrey-Weidman Studio, New York, spring 1931
Dancers: José Limón, Ernestine Henoch

B Minor Suite (also called *Polonaise, Rondeau, Badinerie* and *Suite in B Minor*)
Music: Johann Sebastian Bach
Premiere: St. Bartholomew Community House, New York, spring 1931
Dancers: Eleanor King, José Limón

Mazurka (with Eleanor King)
Music: Alexander Scriabin
Premiere: St. Bartholomew Community House, New York, spring 1931
Dancers: José Limón, Eleanor King

Two Preludes (solo)
Music: Reginald de Koven
Company: Little Group
Premiere: Westport Barn Theatre, Westport, Conn., 7 August 1931
Dancer: José Limón
NOTE: This was the first solo that Limón choreographed for himself. The Westport performance, sponsored by the Contemporary Arts Studio, was the official debut of the Little Group.

Danza (solo)
Music: Sergei Prokofiev
Company: Little Group
Premiere: Sharon, Conn., 18 Oct. 1931
Dancer: José Limón
NOTE: This was a private performance at the country home of the sculptor Emily Winthrop Miles.

*Later known as Ernestine Stodelle.

133

Roberta
Musical comedy in two acts.
Book and lyrics: Otto Harbach (after Alice Duer
    Miller's novel *Gowns by Roberta*)
Music: Jerome Kern
Producer: Max Gordon
Sets: Clark Robinson
Costumes: Kiviette
Premiere: New Amsterdam Theatre, New York, 18
    November 1933
Principal players: George Murphy (Billy Boyden,
    the Hoofer), Raymond Middleton (John Kent,
    the Fullback), Helen Gray (Sophie Teale, the
    Debutante), Bob Hope (Huckleberry Haines, the
    Crooner), Fay Templeton (Aunt Minnie—Trade
    Name, Roberta—the Modiste), Tamara
    (Stephanie, the Manager at Roberta's), Sydney
    Greenstreet (Lord Henry Delves, the Friend of
    Roberta), Lydia Roberti (Mme. Nunez,
    Clementina Scharwenka, the Star Customer)
NOTE: Limón, who did not receive a general credit,
choreographed "Blue Shadows," a group number
that came near the end of the first act.

Canción y Danza (also called *Dance*) (solo)
Music: Federico Mompou
Presenting organization: Experimental Dance
    Laboratory
Premiere: Studio 61, Carnegie Hall, New York, 30
    April 1933
Dancer: José Limón
NOTE: According to John Martin ("The Little
Group in Dance Debut," The *New York Times*, 26
May 1932, p. 31), *Canción* was performed in New
York prior to the Little Group's local debut at the
Provincetown Playhouse (25 May 1932). The
Experimental Dance Laboratory was a cooperative
organization sponsored by Sybil Bruner Fisk and
Winslow C. Beatty. Limón shared this concert with
Fe Alf (John Martin, "The Dance: Trying Out New
Talent," *The New York Times*, 30 Apr. 1933, sec. 9,
p. 6).

Pièces Froides (solo) (also called *Trois Pièces Froides*)
Music: Erik Satie
Presenting organization: Experimental Dance
    Laboratory
Premiere: Studio 61, Carnegie Hall, New York, 30
    April 1933
Dancer: José Limón

1935 (dance-drama)
Premiere: Perry-Mansfield Camp, Steamboat
    Springs, Colorado, summer 1935

Three Studies (solo)
Music: Carl Engel
Company: Charles Weidman and Group
Premiere: Washington Irving High School, New
    York, 12 October 1935
Dancer: José Limón
NOTE: This concert was in the Students Dance
Recitals series.

Nostalgic Fragments
Music: Igor Stravinsky (Suite pour petit orchestre,
    no. 2)
Costumes: Charles Weidman
Presenting organization: New Dance League
Premiere: Adelphi Theatre, New York, 22
    December 1935
Dancers: José Limón, Letitia Ide
NOTE: In addition to Limón and Ide, the other
participants in this concert were Anna Sokolow,
Merle Hirsh, Jane Dudley, Lily Mehlman, Sophie
Maslow, Rose Crystal, Marie Marchowsky, and
William Matons.

Prelude
Music: Francis Poulenc (from *Aubade*)
Costumes: Charles Weidman
Premiere: Adelphi Theatre, New York, 22
    December 1935
Dancers: José Limón, Letitia Ide
NOTE: In his review of this concert ("New Dance
League in First Recital," *The New York Times*, 23
December 1935, p. 15), John Martin does not
mention this duet being performed. However, he
does refer to it in his review of a concert given at the
New School for Social Research on 26 February
1936.

Satiric Lament
Music: Francis Poulenc (from *Aubade*)
Premiere: New School for Social Research, New
    York, 26 February 1936
Dancers: José Limón, Letitia Ide
NOTE: The other participants in this concert, which
was in the New School's Modern Dance Recital
series, were Letitia Ide, Hilda Hoppe, William
Matons and his Experimental Dance Group, and the
Rebel Arts Dance Group.

Hymn (solo)
Music: percussion
Costume: José Limón
Presenting organization: New Dance League
Premiere: Majestic Theatre, New York, 15 March
    1936
Dancer: José Limón
NOTE: In addition to Limón, the participants in this

"Men's Recital" were Charles Weidman, William Matons, Roger Pryor Dodge, John Bovingdon, Vladimir Valentinoff, Saki (a Japanese dancer), and John Adele, Momo du Johnson, and Abraham Cissi, who performed a series of African dances.

Danza de la Muerte (Dance of Death)
Music: Henry Clark ("Sarabande for the Dead," "Sarabande for the Living"), Norman Lloyd ("Interlude")
Scenery: Gerard Gentile
Costumes: Betty Joiner
Premiere: Vermont State Armory, Bennington, 12 August 1937
Dancers: José Limón, Pauline Chellis, Gertrude Green, Molly Hecht, Emily White, Mary Elizabeth Whitney, Mildred Wile, James Lyons, Alwin Nikolais, Peter Terry, James Welch
NOTE: The program note describes this suite of dances as "motivated by the present Civil War in Spain. The opening dance by the Group is a tragic ritual celebrating the dead. The Interlude contains three solos which deal with the personified causes of the destruction in Spain. The closing dance by the Group is one of defiance and dedication." Limón sometimes performed the three sections ("Hoch," "Viva," and "Ave") of the middle "Interlude" as a recital item with the title *Three Dances of Death.*

Opus for Three and Props
Music: Dmitri Shostakovitch
Scenery: Gerard Gentile
Costumes: Betty Joiner
Premiere: Vermont State Armory, Bennington, 12 August 1937
Dancers: José Limón, Esther Junger, Anna Sokolow

Danzas Mexicanas (also called *Suite of Dances About Mexico*)
Music: Lionel Nowak
Costumes: Pauline Lawrence
Premiere: Lisser Hall, Mills College, Oakland, 4 August 1939
Dancer: José Limón
NOTE: The five solos—"Indio," "Conquistador," "Peón," "Caballero," and "Revolucionario"—were based on symbolic figures from Mexican history. After the Second World War, the work was sometimes performed with only three sections: "Peón," "Caballero," and "Revolucionario."

Three Preludes (solo)
Music: Frédéric Chopin
Premiere: Genevieve Jones Studio, Pittsburgh, 11 February 1940
Dancer: José Limón

War Lyrics
Music: Esther Williamson
Text: William Archibald
Scenery: Gyorgy and Juliet Kepes
Costumes: José Limón
Company: José Limón and Group
Premiere: Lisser Hall, Mills College, Oakland, 27 July 1940
Dancers: José Limón (The Soldier), May O'Donnell (The Three Women), Lee Sherman, Bettye Gehring, Martha Ann Picton (Leaders of the Chorus), Delia Hussey, Marian Lacey, Oeloel Quitzow, Dixie Randall, Julia Sanford, Korah Louise Smith (Members of the Chorus)
Voice: Wyman Spalding
NOTE: This work, with costumes by Claire Falkenstein, was later performed without the chorus and narrator. A further revision, entitled *Three Women*, appears to have eliminated the Soldier as well.

Curtain Raiser (with May O'Donnell)
Music: Ray Green
Scenery: Claire Falkenstein
Premiere: Fresno State College Auditorium, 25 February 1941
Dancers: José Limón, May O'Donnell
Program note: "The characters in this dance present themselves in a gay, brilliant, and witty opening piece, each performer 'doing a turn.' This 'curtain raiser' is composed of five short sections; first, an introductory 'how d'you do' followed by a 'show off' march and then the opening prelude 'in between' followed by an 'oh so slow' adagio leading on to a finale that is a 'bang up finish.'"

This Story is Legend (with May O'Donnell)
Music: Ray Green
Spoken text: William Carlos Williams ("In the American Grain")
Scenery and costumes: Claire Falkenstein
Premiere: Fresno State College Auditorium, 25 February 1941
Dancers: José Limón, May O'Donnell
Narrator: Muriel Andrews
Program note: "This is a retelling of the story of Hernando de Soto and his discovery of the Mississippi...this dance drama recounts De Soto's search and countersearch for fabulous treasure in the vast unknown continent...the river is here symbolized as an alluring woman who beckons De Soto on through ordeal and hardship...at last he finds not gold but the river, and thus his failure becomes his triumph...his destiny is the discovery and final entombment in the waters of the

Mississippi...opening up a new continent...a new world."

Praeludium: Theme and Variations (with May O'Donnell)
Music: Ray Green
Premiere: Fresno State College Auditorium, 25 February 1941
Dancers: José Limón, May O'Donnell
Program note: "This theme and its variations have been conceived in a modern classic style of movement...the theme is stated and a set of nine variations follow...the theme is restated in conclusion."

Three Inventories on Casey Jones (with May O'Donnell)
A Fantasy.
Music: Ray Green
Decor: Claire Falkenstein
Premiere: Fresno State College Auditorium, 25 February 1941
Dancers: May O'Donnell (Engine), José Limón (Engineer)
Epigraph: "'Headaches and heartaches and all kinds of pain, / They ain't apart from a railroad train, / Stories of brave men, noble and grand, / Belong to the life of a railroad man.'
Program note: "These 'inventories' are based on the well-known American folk ballad and are intended as a humorous child's fantasy."

Alley Tune (with Helen Ellis)
Music: David Guion
Premiere: Gunter Hall, Colorado Collage, Colorado Springs, 30 July 1942
Dancers: José Limón, Helen Ellis
NOTE: One of several "elaborations and variations on...authentic forms" (see *Turkey in the Straw* and *Mazurka*, below, for others), this was presented at the Modern Dance Concert for Colorado College summer session students under the direction of Limón and Helen Ellis.

Turkey in the Straw (solo)
Music: traditional (arranged by David Guion)
Premiere: Gunter Hall, Colorado Collage, Colorado Springs, 30 July 1942
Dancer: José Limón

Mazurka
Music: Frédéric Chopin
Premiere: Gunter Hall, Colorado Collage, Colorado Springs, 30 July 1942
Dancers: José Limón, Helen Ellis

Chaconne (also called *Chaconne in D Minor*) (solo)
Music: Johann Sebastian Bach (from Sonata in D Minor for Unaccompanied Violin)
Costume: Pauline Lawrence
Company: Doris Humphrey and the Humphrey-Weidman Repertory
Premiere: Humphrey-Weidman Studio Theatre, New York, 27 December 1942
Dancer: José Limón
NOTE: In 1947 the music credit was changed to "Bach-Busoni" and the title to *Chaconne in D Minor*. According to a note in a 1947 program the piano arrangement was by Ferruccio Busoni.

Western Folk Suite
Music: Norman Cazden ("Reel," after a song by Woody Guthrie), Charles Ives ("Ballad of Charlie Rutlage"), traditional ("Pop Goes the Weasel," arranged by Esther Williamson)
Costumes: Pauline Lawrence
Company: José Limón and the Humphrey-Weidman Repertory Company
Premiere: Humphrey-Weidman Studio Theatre, New York, 11 March 1943
Dancers: José Limón, Maria Maginnis
Program note: "Ballad from Western Folk Suite—Charlie Rutlage:
    Another good cow puncher
    Has gone to meet his fate.
    I hope he'll find a resting place
    Within the golden gate.
    Another place is vacant
    In the ranch of the X I T.
    'Twill be hard to find another
    That's liked as well as he.
The ballad proceeds to tell how 'poor Charlie' was killed by falling from his horse during the spring round-up and how he will meet his loved ones 'beyond eternity, at the shining throne of grace.'"
NOTE: In 1945, Limón presented a revised version of this work, retitled *Western Dances*. It consisted of "Reel," "Two Ballads" ("Charlie Rutlage" and "Ef I Had a Ribbon Bow"), and "Pop Goes the Weasel." "Ef I Had a Ribbon Bow" and "Charlie Rutlage" were later performed as part of *Three Ballads* (1945).

Fun for the Birds
Lyrics: Brace Conning, John Shubert, William Galbraith
Music: Arthur Schwartz, Wadsworth Douglas
Stage director: Don Stevens
Premiere: Mosque Theatre, Richmond, Va., 5 September 1943

NOTE: Limón shared dance direction credit for this U.S. Army show with Thomas Knox. Limón's principal contribution was the number "We Speak for Ourselves," which was set to a poem by Lynn Riggs, had "original mood music" by Limón, and featured him as a soloist with Diane Roberts. The show was produced at Camp Lee, Virginia, where Limón was stationed for several months in 1943–1944.

Spanish Dance
Music: Manuel de Falla
Costumes: Pauline Lawrence
Company: Camp Lee Concert Dance Group
Premiere: Mosque Theatre, Richmond, Va., 13 February 1944
Dancers: José Limón, Audre Howell, William Howell
Program note (from a later program): "This is a dramatic fragment. In the passionate, yet formal, style of Spanish dances, it depicts the struggle of two cavaliers for the favor of a lady."

[Interlude Dances]
Music: Roy Harris (Folk Symphony)
Company: Camp Lee Concert Dance Group
Premiere: Mosque Theatre, Richmond, Va., 13 February 1944
NOTE: This was in square dance style.

Rosenkavalier Waltz
Music: Richard Strauss
Costumes: Pauline Lawrence
Company: Camp Lee Concert Dance Group
Premiere: Mosque Theatre, Richmond, Va., 13 February 1944
Dancers: José Limón, Diane Roberts, William Howell, Betty Carpenter
Program note (from a later program): "The perfumed elegance of the last century is evoked in these waltzes. Some are formal, some gay and light-hearted, but all speak with nostalgia of the romance and charm of a post era."

Mexilinda
Music: Sergei Rachmaninoff, Nikolai Rimsky-Korsakov, Norman Cazden, Manuel Infante, Darius Milhaud, Manuel de Falla, Johann Brahms, Johann Strauss
Costumes: Pauline Lawrence
Premiere: Service Club 1, Camp Lee, Va., 20 February 1944
Dancers: José Limón, Diane Roberts, William Howell, Betty Carpenter, William Duttenhofer, Libby Morano, Pat Pully, Richard Morgan, Audre Howell

NOTE: Limón "created and directed" all the dances of this "colorful dance and music presentation" (as announced in the flyer), which included, in addition to *Spanish Dance* and *Rosenkavalier Waltz*, a piece called *Western Dances* (to Norman Cazden). The program note for this item, which was performed by the entire company, read: "Old-time square dances as performed in the old West form the basis of this composition. For purposes of theater, variations and embellishments have been added in the form of solos, duets, and trios." Various numbers by the piano duo of Vronsky and Babin completed the program.

Deliver the Goods (A Quartermaster Corps Musical Revue)
Producer: Don Stevens
Book: Sidney Abel, John Thompson, Barry Farnol, Don Stevens
Music: Frank Hundertmark
Sets: Albert Rubens, Barry Farnol
Stage direction: Ray Hinkley, William Howell
Musical direction: Henry Aaron
Premiere: Camp Lee, Va., 27 April 1944
NOTE: In addition to creating the show's "original dances and routines," Limón appeared in Scene VIII, "Machete Eddy."

Song of the Medics
Book, music, and lyrics: Philip Freedman, Charles Broffman
Sets: Perry Watkins
Stage direction: Walter Armitage
Musical direction: George Kleinsinger
Costumes: Rowena Fairchild
Premiere: Fort Dix, N.J., 2 July 1944
NOTE: Limón's credit was for the "dance direction." The show, which was presented by the Reconditioning Service—Tilton General Hospital, was performed by enlisted men as well as "veteran patients."

Hi, Yank!
Music and lyrics: Frank Loesser, Alex North, Jack Hill, Jesse Berkman
Sets and costumes: Robert T. Stevenson, Al Hamilton
Choreography: José Limón
Premiere: Fort Dix, N.J., [August?] 1944
NOTE: Among Limón's contributions was the choreography and dance direction for the "Caribbean number."

Concerto (later called *Concerto Grosso*)
Music: Antonio Vivaldi (sometimes "Vivaldi-Bach")
Costumes: Pauline Lawrence

Premiere: Clifford Scott High School, East Orange, N.J., 11 April 1945

Dancers: José Limón, Beatrice Seckler, Dorothy Bird

Program note (added in 1950s): "The dignified fugue, the ravishing largo and the brisk finale of this concerto provide an opportunity for diversified yet sustained dance action for the Limón group, since the fugue gives an opportunity for the heroic and dramatic, while the largo forms the framework of an adagio movement of great beauty."

NOTE: In 1963 this was arranged for a larger cast, given a different musical setting, and retitled *Concerto in D Minor After Vivaldi*. The 1945 performance marked the debut of the group that was the immediate forerunner of the José Limón Dance Company.

Eden Tree

Music: Carl Engel, José Limón

Costumes: Pauline Lawrence

Premiere: Clifford Scott High School, East Orange, N.J., 11 April 1945

Dancers: José Limón (The Man), Beatrice Seckler (The Wife), Dorothy Bird (Lilith)

NOTE: This work consisted of five parts: "Idyll," "Discord," "Invocation," "Enchantment," and "The Return." Limón arranged the accompaniment for "Invocation" and the duet in "Enchantment." Later programs identify the accompaniment as "an arrangement of a score by Carl Engel, with additional themes by Merton Brown." Limón is not mentioned.

Three Ballads

Music: traditional (Kentucky mountain ballad), Charles Ives ("Ballad of Charlie Rutlage"), traditional (arranged by Elie Siegmeister)

Costumes: Pauline Lawrence

Premiere: Studio Theatre, New York, 19 May 1945

Dancers: Beatrice Seckler ("Ef I Had a Ribbon Bow"), José Limón ("Charlie Rutlage"), Dorothy Bird ("True Love")

NOTE: "Charlie Rutlage" was originally part of *Western Folk Suite* (1943) and, like "Ef I Had a Ribbon Bow," was performed in the revised version of the work, *Western Dances*, presented earlier in 1945.

Danza (solo)

Music: J. Arcadio

Costume: Pauline Lawrence

Premiere: Jacob's Pillow, Becket, Mass., 6 September 1946

Dancer: José Limón

NOTE: J. Arcadio was probably a pseudonym for Limón, whose middle name was Arcadio.

Masquerade (solo)

Music: Sergei Prokofiev (Sonata no. 5 in C Major, op. 38)

Costume: Pauline Lawrence

Premiere: Howard Hall, St. Louis, Mo., 29 November 1946

Dancer: José Limón

NOTE: This consisted of three parts: "Carte Blanche," "Secret Formula," and "Gordian Knot."

Song of Songs

Music: Lukas Foss

Costumes: Pauline Lawrence

Premiere: Hatch Memorial Shell, Charles River Esplanade, Boston, 19 August 1947

Dancers: José Limón and Miriam Pandor, with Ginka Vogel, Parian Temple, Annette Conrad, Ruth Wheeler, Anne Greene, Judith Haskell, Dianne Boyden, Mary Joann Hoyt, Elinor Goldsmith, Ruth Alexander, Sudie Bond, Marianne Sewall, William Barnum

Singer: Ruth Ellison

NOTE: The ensemble consisted of members of the Student Workshop of the Dance Department of the Duncanbury School of the Arts. The singer, a soprano, was a student in the Duncanbury voice department.

Sonata Opus 4

Music: Johann Sebastian Bach

Premiere: Hatch Memorial Shell, Charles River Esplanade, Boston, 19 August 1947

Dancers: José Limón, Miriam Pandor

La Malinche

Music: Norman Lloyd

Costumes: Pauline Lawrence

Company: José Limón and Company

Premiere: Jordan Hall, Boston, Mass., 24 March 1949

Company: José Limón and Company

Dancers: Pauline Koner (La Malinche), José Limón (El Indio), Lucas Hoving (El Conquistador)

Singer: Betty Jones

Program note: "Malintzin, an Indian princess, was given to Cortez on his arrival in Mexico. She became his interpreter and mouthpiece. Her astuteness and complete devotion served his cause so well that he conquered Mexico. She became a great lady and was baptized Dona Marina. After her death popular legend made her repentant spirit return to lament her treachery. For her there was no peace while her people were not free. During their struggles for liberation she returned as the wild Malinche to expiate her ancient betrayal."

NOTE: This was the first work that Limón choreographed for his own company.

The Moor's Pavane
Variations on the Theme of Othello.
Music: Henry Purcell, arranged by Simon Sadoff
Costumes: Pauline Lawrence
Company: José Limón and Company
Premiere: Palmer Auditorium, Connecticut College (2nd American Dance Festival), New London, 17 August 1949
Dancers: José Limón (The Moor), Lucas Hoving (His Friend), Pauline Koner (His Friend's Wife), Betty Jones (The Moor's Wife)
Program note (added in 1952): "This ballet with choreography by José Limón won the *Dance Magazine* award for outstanding creation in the field of American modern dance. The dance takes its theme from the basic plot of *Othello,* which is told completely within the form of the dance. The four characters are on the stage at the rise of the curtain and they never leave it. Here is portrayed the tragedy of Everyman when he is caught in the pattern of tragic living. The ballet is therefore timeless in its implication."
NOTE: Simon Sadoff was the company's pianist and musical director.

The Exiles
Music: Arnold Schoenberg (Chamber Symphony no. 2, op. 38)
Scenery: Anita Weschler
Costumes: Pauline Lawrence
Company: José Limón and Company
Premiere: Palmer Auditorium, Connecticut College (3rd American Dance Festival), New London, 11 August 1950
Dancers: José Limón, Letitia Ide
Epigraph (added later): "'They, looking back, all the eastern side beheld / Of Paradise, so late their happy seat.' *Paradise Lost,* John Milton."
Program note (added later): "According to Dante, there is no greater anguish than past joys remembered in the midst of adversity. This piece of choreography was inspired by and dedicated to those desolate ones who remember some lost paradise, or serenity, of innocence, or homeland. The work is, like the symphony, in two parts:
"The first describes the man and the woman lamenting their expulsion from a paradise. In the second movement they remember the ecstatic and innocent joy which was theirs, and how they came to forfeit it.
"The choreographic style reflects the neo-romanticism of the Schoenberg score—the poignant, voluptuous beauty of the first movement, and the corrascating joyousness of the second—the somber coda marks the return of the protagonists to the cruel reality of their exile."

Concert
Music: Johann Sebastian Bach (preludes and fugues, arranged by Simon Sadoff)
Costumes: Pauline Lawrence
Company: José Limón and Company
Premiere: Palmer Auditorium, Connecticcut College (3rd American Dance Festival), New London, 19 August 1950
Dancers: Simon Sadoff, José Limón, Pauline Koner, Lucas Hoving, Betty Jones, Ruth Currier

Los cuatro soles (The Four Suns)
Music: Carlos Chávez
Libretto: Carlos Chávez, Miguel Covarrubias
Sets and costumes: Miguel Covarrubias
Company: Academia de la Danza Mexicana (augmented by members of the Ballet Nacional and students from the Academia's regional dance department and from the Escuela de Educación Física)
Premiere: Palacio de Bellas Artes, Mexico City, 31 March 1951
Principal dancers: Xavier Francis (Father Heaven), Evelia Beristain (Mother Earth), José Limón (Plumed Serpent), Lucas Hoving (Espejo Humeante [Steaming Mirror])
Program note (excerpt): "A ballet in four scenes based on an ancient legend explaining the pre-Hispanic concept of the universe. According to the ancient Mexicans, the world was created four times and as many times destroyed by each of the four elements—water, air, fire, and earth—in terrible catastrophes—floods, hurricanes, volcanic eruptions, and long droughts—caused by the cosmic struggle of the Plumed Serpent (Quetzalcoatl), the god of civilized peoples, symbol of good, light, peace, and wisdom, and his ferocious antagonist, the Steaming Mirror (Tezcatlipoca), the god of barbaric tribes, evil, shadows, and war."

Tonantzintla
Music: Antonio Soler (orchestrated by Rodolfo Halffter)
Scenery and costumes: Miguel Covarrubias

Company: Academia de la Danza Mexicana
Premiere: Palacio de Bellas Artes, Mexico City, 31 March 1951
Dancers: José Limón (The Archangel), Valentina Castro (The Mermaid), Marta Castro, Rocío Sagaon, Beatriz Flores (The Angels)
Program note: "This dance was inspired by the sumptuous and ingenuous spirit of Mexican baroque art as represented by the decoration of the name of the Indian church of Santa María Tonanzintla near Cholula. A little mermaid is feted on her birthday by the angels and archangels who are her architectural companions. The character of peasant simplicity and primitive splendor of the Tonanzintla decoration has determined the choreographic style."

Diálogos (also called *Dialogues*)
Music: Norman Lloyd
Scenery and costumes: Julio Prieto
Premiere: Palacio de Bellas Artes, Mexico City, April 1951
Dancers: José Limón (The Emperor/The President), Lucas Hoving (The Captain/The Archduke)
Program note: "A dramatic dance based on two fundamental episodes in the history of Mexico—the clash of two distinct races that resulted in the Mexican nation. In the first episode—1520—the European captain seizes by force from the Indian emperor his crown, his throne, and his empire, while the emperor, overcome with superstition, surrenders without struggle to the enterprising conquistador. In the second episode—1867—the conflict between two historical figures of different race ends the other way around: the Austrian archduke, an instrument of imperialism, is the victim of his lack of understanding toward a people that refuses to be his vassal. His adversary, the Indian president, has the strength and nobility of his race and a new political weapon, republican democracy, which smashes the imperialist attempt. In the first episode the two protagonists confront one another personally; in the second, they never meet. The characters—The Emperor, The Captain, The President, The Archduke—are merely symbols here, not historical personages."[1]
NOTE: Limón returned to this subject in *Carlota* (1972), one of his last works.

Antígona (Antigone)
Music: Carlos Chávez
Sets and costumes: Miguel Covarrubias
Prologue: Salvador Novo
Company: Academia de la Danza Mexicana
Premiere: Palacio de Bellas Artes, Mexico City, 24 November 1951
Dancers: José Limón (Creon), Rosa Reyna (Antigone), Guillermo Arriaga, Jesús Iñiguez, Guillermo Keys Arenas, Antonio de la Torre, Rosalio Ortega, Juan Casados
Speaker: Raúl Dantes
Program note: "A dramatic dance, *Antigone* relates the final scene of the Greek tragedy of Sophocles. Its subject is the rebellion against the tyranny represented by Antigone and the usurper Creon, the brother of Oedipus and tutor of his children. The dance begins when Creon orders the body of one of his nephews, in rebellion against the usurper of his father's throne, to be left unburied for the vultures and dogs to devour. Antigone reveals her opposition to the abominable decree and tries to bury her brother, ignoring the order of the King. But the guards surprise her and lead her to Creon, who tries by all means possible to dissuade her and yield to his authority. His efforts are in vain, and she is condemned to be buried alive in a dungeon. As always, heroic resistence against tyranny is, in the end, a greater triumph than the immediate victory of injustice. The dance ends with the emptiness of proud Creon's triumph."

Redes (Nets)
Music: Silvestre Revueltas (from the film *The Wave*)
Libretto: José Revueltas
Sets and costumes: Department of Theatrical Production
Company: Academia de la Danza Mexicana
Premiere: Palacio de Bellas Artes, Mexico City, 8 December 1951
Dancers: José Limón (El "Grito"), Rosa Reyna, Raquel Gutiérrez, Marta Bracho, Rocío Sagaon, Beatriz Flores, Marta Castro, Valentina Castro, Nellie Happee, Elena Jordan, Olga Cardona, Guillermina Peñaloza (The Women), Xavier Francis, Guillermo Keys Arenas, Guillermo Arriaga, César Bordes, Antonio de la Torre, Juan Casados, Rosalio Ortega, Farnesio Bernal (The Men), Ricardo Demarest, Jesús Iñiguez, Edmundo Mendoza, Victor Díaz, Juan Keys, Benjamín Gutiérrez (The Enemies)
Program note (excerpt): *The Black Scream* symbolizes chaos, negation, anguish, oppression. *El "Grito"* (The "Scream") is the awakening of consciousness, creative force, freedom. *The Nets* represent collective work and unity."
NOTE: *El Grito* (1952) was a revised version of this work.

The Queen's Epicedium

Music: Henry Purcell ("Elegy on the Death of Queen Mary")
Costumes: Pauline Lawrence
Company: José Limón and Dance Company
Premiere: Palmer Auditorium, Connecticut College (5th American Dance Festival), New London, 21 August 1952
Dancers: Letitia Ide, Ruth Currier, Lavina Nielsen
Singer: Betty Jones
Program note: "This Epicedium, or Funeral Ode, refers to the dead sovereign as Queen of Arcadia, and tells of the grief of the nymphs and shepherds. The sonorous Latin verses speak of the broken lyre, and a world filled with tears, and how the lambs no longer frolic, but are lost and dying. It ends on a note of consolation for the unhappy Arcadians, pointing to the Queen's star, shining brightly in the distant heavens."

The Visitation

Music: Arnold Schoenburg (Piano Pieces, op. 11)
Costumes: Pauline Lawrence
Company: José Limón and Dance Company
Premiere: Palmer Auditorium, Connecticut College (5th American Dance Festival), New London, 23 August 1952
Dancers: José Limón (The Man), Pauline Koner (His Wife), Lucas Hoving (The Stranger)
Program note: "This dance is based on the legend of the Annunciation, in which the lives of two lowly human beings were transfigured utterly after a visit by a celestial messenger. It tells of omnipotence, and the great mystery of faith. 'He hath put down the mighty from their seat, and hath exalted the humble and the meek.'"

El Grito (The Shout)

Music: Silvestre Revueltas (from the film The Wave)
Libretto: José Revueltas
Costumes: Consuelo Gana
Company: José Limón and Dance Company
Premiere: Juilliard Concert Hall, New York, 5 December 1952
Dancers: José Limón, Beatriz Flores, Betty Jones, Ruth Currier, Lavina Nielsen, Lucy Venable, Stuart Hodes, David Wood, Dick Fitz-Gerald, Michael Hollander, Richard Englund, June Dunbar, Pepi Hamilton, Ellen van der Hoeven, Sandra Pecker, Russell Sohlberg, Ernesto Gonzales, Philip Capy, Jeff Duncan, Edward Green, Juan Valenzuela
Program note: "El Grito is the Shout of Cry, the Awakener. In his hands are the strands that are woven into a net. The making of the net gives joy to those making it and, seeing that it is good, they celebrate the accomplishment. Then come the Silencers and their dark triumph. But the Shout resurges and is brought back to life by those he awakened.

"El Grito was first performed in Mexico City under the title of Redes. It was commissioned by Miguel Covarrubias, the head of the Academía Nacional de la Danza. The music by Silvestre Revueltas was originally composed as a score for the film The Wave and was subsequently arranged into a symphonic suite. The script for the ballet is by the composer's brother, José Revueltas.

"The original title of the work, Redes, means 'the nets,' and alludes to the gigantic nets woven by the Mexican fishermen."
NOTE: The work was in five parts: "The Awakening," "The Net," "The Festival," "The Silencers," and "The March." In addition to members of the Limón company, the cast included dancers from other companies and students from Limón's classes at the Dance Players Studio.

Don Juan Fantasia

Music: Franz Liszt
Costumes: Pauline Lawrence
Company: José Limón and Dance Company
Premiere: Palmer Auditorium, Connecticut College (6th American Dance Festival), New London, 22 August 1953
Dancers: José Limón (Don Juan), Lucas Hoving (Don Gonzalo), Betty Jones, Ruth Currier, Lavina Nielsen (The Ladies)

Ode to the Dance

Music: Samuel Barber (Capricorn Concerto, op. 21)
Scenery: Paul Trautvetter
Costumes: Pauline Lawrence
Company: José Limón and Dance Company
Premiere: Juilliard Concert Hall, New York, 29 January 1954
Dancers: José Limón (Dedication of the Place), Betty Jones, Ruth Currier (Celebrants), Lucy Venable, Melisa Nicolaides, Michael Hollander (Dance of Inheritance)

The Traitor

Music: Gunther Schuller (Symphony for Brasses)
Scenery: Paul Trautvetter
Costumes: Pauline Lawrence
Company: José Limón and Dance Company
Premiere: Palmer Auditorium, Connecticut College (7th American Dance Festival), New London, 19 August 1954

Dancers: José Limón (The Traitor), Lucas Hoving (The Leader), Charles Czarny, Richard Fitz-Gerald, Michael Hollander, Alvin Schulman, Otis Bigelow, John Coyle (His Followers)
Epigraph: "'See, I go down into the nethermost pit, in order that you may rise in the highest to God.' *The Nazarene* by Sholem Asch."

Scherzo
Music: John Barracuda, Stoddard Lincoln, Lucy Venable (percussion improvisation)
Premiere: Juilliard School of Music, New York, 11 May 1955
Dancers: Richard Fitz-Gerald, Michael Hollander, Harlan McCallum, Charles Nicoll, Sheldon Ossosky, Chester Wolenski, Patricia Christopher, Jemima Ben-Gal, Patricia Christopher, Lola Huth, Melissa Nicolaides
NOTE: This was a study of the work presented in the summer at the American Dance Festival.

Scherzo
Music: Hazel Johnson (percussion score)
Costumes: Pauline Lawrence
Company: José Limón and Dance Company
Premiere: Palmer Auditorium, Connecticut College (8th American Dance Festival), New London, 19 August 1955
Dancers: Richard Fitz-Gerald, Michael Hollander, Harlan McCallum, John Barber
NOTE: This was based on a study presented earlier in the year at the Juilliard School of Music.

Symphony for Strings
Music: William Schuman
Costumes: Pauline Lawrence
Company: José Limón and Company
Premiere: American Dance Festival, Connecticut College (8th American Dance Festival), New London, 19 August 1955
Dancers: José Limón, Pauline Koner, Lucas Hoving, Betty Jones, Ruth Currier, Lavina Nielsen

Variations on a Theme (later called *"There is a Time"*)
Music: Norman Dello Joio ("Meditations on Ecclesiastes")
Costumes: Pauline Lawrence
Company: José Limón and Dance Company
Premiere: Juilliard Concert Hall, New York, 20 April 1956
Dancers: José Limón, Pauline Koner, Betty Jones, Ruth Currier, Lucas Hoving, Lavina Nielsen, Richard Fitz-Gerald, Michael Hollander, Harlan McCallum, John Barker, Chester Wolenski, Martin Morginsky

Program note (added later): "A circle, endless, with no beginning and no end, appears as symbol of time and timelessness. This is the theme, from which emerge other circles, like variations on the initial theme. These are in turn, joyful, lyrical, somber, violent, but ever recur to the circular time-motif, to remind the spectator that the great opposites, birth-death, love-hate, etc., are contained, and endured, in time."

King's Heart
Music: Stanley Wolfe
Scenery: Durevol Quitzow
Costumes: Pauline Lawrence
Company: Juilliard Dance Theater
Premiere: Juilliard Concert Hall, New York, 27 April 1956
Dancers: Melisa Nicolaides (Queen), Anna Friedland, Patricia Christopher (Queen's Attendants), John Barker, Kevin Carlisle, Harlan McCallum, Durevol Quitzow, Chester Wolenski, David Wynne (Her Warriors)
Program note: "A queen, exhorting her captains to valor in the face of the approaching enemy, reminds them that although her body is that of a weak woman, her heart is that of a king."

The Emperor Jones
Dance-drama after the play of Eugene O'Neill.
Music: Heitor Villa-Lobos
Scenery: Kim Edgar Swados
Costumes: Pauline Lawrence
Company: José Limón and Company
Premiere: Empire State Music Festival, Ellenville, N.Y., 12 July 1956
Dancers: José Limón (The Emperor Jones), Lucas Hoving (The White Man), Richard Fitz-Gerald, Michael Hollander, Harlan McCallum, Chester Wolenski, Martin Morginsky, Jose Gutierrez (The Emperor's Subjects)
Program note (added later): "In the play by O'Neill, Jones, a fugitive from a chain gang, sets himself up as emperor of an island domain. He becomes a tyrant, and his mistreatment of his subjects causes them to rebel, hunt him down and bring him to an ignominious end.
"This dance version elaborates on the central theme, that of the superstitious terror of the hunted emperor. In the style of a free fantasy, the dance makes no attempt to adhere to the play's sequence, but rather seeks to give it another dimension. There are a series of episodes which concern Jones' visions and hallucinations of his earlier life. There is a prisoner chain-gang, a slave ship, Jones' first murder, an atavistic African

ritual, and his desperate hoax that only his own silver bullet could destroy him. The reduction of a swaggering tyrant to a groveling pitiful figure is one of the great American playwright's most penetrating and terrifyingly human portrayals."

Rhythmic Study
Music: self-accompanied
Premiere: Juilliard School of Music, New York, 12 December 1956
Dancers: Richard Fitz-Gerald, Michael Hollander, Harlan McCallum

Blue Roses
A choreographic fantasy based on *The Glass Menagerie*, by Tenessee Williams.
Music: William Lorin (based on themes of Paul Bowles)
Costumes: Pauline Lawrence
Company: José Limón and Dance Company
Premiere: Palmer Auditorium, Connecticut College (10th American Dance Festival), New London, 16 August 1957
Dancers: Lucas Hoving (The Son), Lavina Nielsen (The Mother), Betty Jones (The Daughter), José Limón (A Friend of the Son), Michael Hollander, Harlan McCallum, Chester Wolenski, Ronald Chase, Vol Quitzow, Kenneth Bartness (Gentleman Callers [and figures symbolic of the son's wanderlust])
Program note: "Three Dreamers—A mother whose children must be what they are not, a son for whom some escape must exist, and a daughter with a secret magic world peopled with glass toys.
"A Friend of the Son—invited as a possible suitor for the young girl who is already another's financée."

Missa Brevis
Music: Zoltán Kodály ("Missa Brevis in Tempore Belli")
Projection and costumes: Ming Cho Lee
Company: Juilliard Dance Theater (with members of the José Limón Company)
Premiere: Juilliard Concert Hall, New York, 11 April 1958
Dancers: José Limón, Betty Jones, Lola Huth, Lucy Venable, Michael Hollander, Harlan McCallum, Chester Wolenski, Ruth Currier, and Vol Quitzow (of the José Limón Company), with Juilliard students Diane Adler, Roberta Ampel, Jemima Ben-Gal, Patricia Christopher, Deborah Jowitt, Diane Quitzow, Martha Wittman; John Blanchard, James Payton, Baird Searles, Ronald Tassone, John Wilson, David Wynne

Singers: Juilliard Chorus
Program note: "Zoltán Kodály wrote the *Missa Brevis in Tempore Belli* at the end of World War II. The first performance was given in the cellar of a bombed-out church in Budapest."

Serenata
Music: Paul Bowles
Scenery: Thomas Watson
Costumes: Pauline Lawrence
Company: José Limón and Dance Company
Premiere: Palmer Auditorium, Connecticut College (11th American Dance Festival), New London, 14 August 1958
Dancers: José Limón (The Lover), Pauline Koner (His Lady), Betty Jones (The Lady's Voice), Chester Wolenski (The Lover's Voice)
Epigraph:
"How the night sings,
  How the dawn sings....
  Where are you going, my love,
  With the air in a goblet
  And the sea in a glass?....
  I will carry you, naked,
  Opened flower, limpid form,
  To where the silks are trembling with cold....
  Come quickly, now,
  Before yellow nightingales
  Weep among the branches."
    —Federico García Lorca

Dances (in Honor of Poznan, Wroclaw, Katowice, and Warszawa)
Music: Frédéric Chopin
Costumes: Lavina Nielsen
Company: José Limón and Dance Company
Premiere: Palmer Auditorium, Connecticut College (11th American Dance Festival), New London, 15 August 1958
Dancers: Lola Huth, Chester Wolenski, Betty Jones, Harlan McCallum, Michael Hollander, Ruth Currier, Lucy Venable
NOTE: Limón later presented a shortened version of this work under the title *Mazurkas*. It was accompanied by the following program note: "These dances were composed after a visit to Poland in 1957, as a tribute to the heroic spirit of its people."

Tenebrae, 1914
Episodes in the life of Edith Cavell.
Music: John Wilson
Scenery: Ming Cho Lee
Costumes: Pauline Lawrence
Company: José Limón and Dance Company

Premiere: Palmer Auditorium, Connecticut College
(12th American Dance Festival), New London, 13
August 1959
Dancers: Ruth Currier, Harlan McCallum, Chester
Wolenski, Robert Powell, James Payton, Stephen
Paxton
Singer: Betty Jones
Epigraph: "'Patriotism is not enough. I must have
no hatred nor bitterness towards anyone.'—*Edith
Cavell*, in a letter written before her execution."

The Apostate
Music: Ernst Krenek (Elegy for Strings)
Scenery: Ming Cho Lee
Costumes: Pauline Lawrence
Company: José Limón and Dance Company
Premiere: Palmer Auditorium, Connecticut College
(12th American Dance Festival), New London, 15
August 1959
Dancers: José Limón (The Apostate), Lucas Hoving
(The Galilean), Betty Jones (The Olympian)
Epigraph: "'Take not away my mad love for that
which is no more, for that which has been is more
glorious and beautiful than all that is.'—*Julian,
Emperor of Rome.*"
Program note: "Julian the Apostate, he has been
named. A monk, he was destined to become
Imperator. The last puissant champion of pagan
Hellas, he sought to restore the worship of the
Hellenic gods. To him Christianity was a dark
and barbarous affront to the human spirit. His
was a struggle of Olympus against Golgotha.
Mortally wounded in battle, his last words were:
'Galilean, Thou hast conquered.'"

Barren Sceptre (with Pauline Koner)
Music: Gunther Schuller (Music for Violin, Piano,
and Percussion)
Costumes: Pauline Lawrence
Company: José Limón and Dance Company
Premiere: Juilliard Concert Hall, New York, 8 April
1960
Dancers: José Limón (The Thane), Pauline Koner
(His Consort)
Epigraph:
"Stars, hide your fires,
Let not light see my black and deep desires."
—*Macbeth*, Shakespeare

Performance (Over the Footlights and Back)
Variations on a theme of William Schuman.
Music: Hugh Aitken, William Bergsma, Jacob
Druckman, Vittorio Giannini, Norman Lloyd,
Vincent Persichetti, Robert Starer, and Hugo
Weisgall

Company: Juilliard Dance Ensemble
Premiere: Juilliard Concert Hall, New York, 14
April 1961
Dancers: Julia Alessandroni, Carlotte Bailis, Nurit
Cohen, Alice Condodina, Ilene Goldberg, Kathy
Gosschalk, Jane Higgins, Judith Hogan, Marcia
Kurtz, Beatrice Lamb, Marcia Lerner, Nancy
Lewis, Carol Miller, Joan Miller, Marianne
Monnikendam, Francia Roxin, Shirley Scheer,
Janet Mansfield Soares, Ann Vachon, Eugenia
Volz, Joyce Wheeler, Micheline Wilkinson, Judith
Willis, Constance Zander, Bruce Becker, Richard
Browne, James Flowers, Elbert Morris, Myron
Howard Nadel, James Payton, Don Price, Koert
Stuyf, Robert Weber, Carl Wolz, Carl Woods,
David Wynne

The Moirai (The Fates)
Music: Hugh Aitken
Costumes: Pauline Lawrence
Company: José Limón and Dance Company
Premiere: Palmer Auditorium, Connecticut College
(14th American Dance Festival), New London, 18
August 1961
Dancers: Betty Jones (Klotho), Lola Huth
(Lachesis), Ruth Currier (Atropos), Chester
Wolenski (Man)
Program note: "Klotho of the distaff holds raw
wool, incipient man; Lachesis spins and measures
a thread, his allotted destiny; Atropos, the
implacable, with her shears severs it. Man,
creature, vehicle, adversary of destiny, perpetually
confronts the Fates."

I, Odysseus
Music: Hugh Aitken
Costumes: Nellie Hatfield, Elizabeth Parsons
Properties: Thomas Watson, William McIver
Company: José Limón and Company
Premiere: Palmer Auditorium, Connecticut College
(15th American Dance Festival), New London, 18
August 1962
Dancers: Simon Sadoff (Zeus), Betty Jones
(Athena), Ruth Currier (Circe), Harlan
McCallum (Poseidon), Lola Huth (Calypso),
Louis Falco (Hermes), José Limón (Odysseus),
Lucy Venable (Penelope), David Wynne, Joseph
Schlichter, Donato Capozzoli, Chase Robinson
(Companions of Odysseus), Betty Jones, Ruth
Currier, Lola Huth, Sally Stackhouse, Lenore
Latimer (Sirens)
Singer: Francis Bull

Sonata for Two Cellos (solo)
Music: Meyer Kupferman

Costumes: Pauline Lawrence
Premiere: Palmer Auditorium, Connecticut College
(14th American Dance Festival), New London, 19
August 1961
Dancer: José Limón

The Demon
Music: Paul Hindemith
Scenery and costumes: Malcolm McCormick
Company: José Limón Company
Premiere: Juilliard Concert Hall, New York, 13
March 1963
Dancers: José Limón (The Demon who may not be
a Demon but is a Demon); Votaries of Lucifer:
Betty Jones (Priestess), Ruth Currier (Martyr),
Lola Huth (Witch), Harlan McCallum
(Philosopher), Louis Falco (Poet); Lucas Hoving
(Archangel who may not be an Archangel but is
an Archangel), Betty Jones, Ruth Currier, Lola
Huth, Harlan McCallum, Louis Falco (Angels
who may not be Angels but are Angels)
Program note: "If, as is sometimes maintained, it
was rebellious Lucifer and his cohorts who were
victorious in the celestial war of long ago, and he
usurped the highest throne, then there is some
question as to the true identity of The Demon,
and still graver question as to who and what is
good or evil."
NOTE: Consisting of six parts ("Fallen Monarch,"
"Black Mass," "Archangel," "Parade of Sins,"
"Confrontation," and "Finale"), Hindemith's work
premiered in Germany in 1924. The Juilliard
program described the style of Limón's "original
presentation" as being "highly typical of the
German theatre in the 1920s. [His] new choreographic treatment of the score is a free fantasy,
emerging directly from the spirit and quality of the
music." The Juilliard performances were conducted
by the composer.

Concerto in D Minor After Vivaldi
Music: Johann Sebastian Bach
Costumes: Pauline Lawrence
Company: Juilliard Dance Ensemble
Premiere: Juilliard Concert Hall, New York, 10
May 1963
Dancers: Carmen Biascoechea, Marcia Kurtz,
Beatrice Lamb, Libby Nye, Francia Roxin, Judith
Willis, Raymond Cook, Morris [later Morse]
Donaldson
NOTE: This was a restaging by Limón and Betty
Jones of his 1945 *Concerto Grosso* for a larger cast.

Two Essays for Large Ensemble
Music: Johann Sebastian Bach (excerpts from *A
Musical Offering*)
Company: Juilliard Dance Ensemble
Premiere: Juilliard Concert Hall, New York, 17
April 1964
Dancers: Pamela Anderson, Rhoda Antman, Joan
Ashpitz, Roberta Brawer, Margaret Cicierska,
Carol Conte, Laura Glenn, Susan Hess, Judith
Hogan, Kelly Hogan, Dana Holby, Jeannette
Jensen, Michele Larsson, Karen MacKay, Jennifer
Muller, Libby Nye, Dorothy Putnam, Carol
Miller Reynolds, Julie Schimmel, Tamara
Woshakiwsky, Peter DeNicola, Edward DeSoto,
Daniel Lewis, Fritz Ludin, John Parks, Ramon
Rivera, David Taylor, Michael Uthoff, Lance
Westergard
Program note: "These two sections are part of a
projected work to be set to 'A Musical Offering'
in its entirety. The finished work will be "a
choreographic offering" in memory of Doris
Humphrey. It will be based on movement themes
from her dances. The present 'Essays' contain
quotations and variations on motifs from 'New
Dance,' 'Passacaglia and Fugue in C Minor' and
'Pleasures of Counterpoint.'"

A Choreographic Offering
Music: Johann Sebastian Bach (*A Musical Offering*)
Costumes: Pauline Lawrence
Company: José Limón and Dance Company
(augmented by American Dance Festival
students)
Premiere: Palmer Auditorium, Connecticut College
(17th American Dance Festival), New London, 15
August 1964
Dancers: Betty Jones, Libby Nye, Michael Uthoff,
Jennifer Muller, Fritz Ludin, Alice Condodina,
Daniel Lewis, Sally Stackhouse, John Parks, Kelly
Hogan, Laura Glenn, Louis Falco
Students: Margaret Beals, Karen Craig, Selina Croll,
Brenda Dixon, Edward Effron, Laurie Freedman,
Mary Ellen Freese, Margaret Gottelmann, Michal
Ann Goldman, Vija Martinsons, Mimi Mason,
Judith Offard, Lynn Ramsbottom, Jacqueline
Rice, Dora Sanders, Nancy Topf, Kay Uemura,
Jody Zirul
Program note: "This work, set to *A Musical
Offering*, is in memory of Doris Humphrey. It is
based on movements from her dances, and
contains variations, paraphrases, and motifs from
*Gigue, Sarabande, Water Study, Dionysiacques,
Pleasures of Counterpoint, Circular Descent,
Handel Variations, Air for Ground Bass,*

Rudepoema, New Dance, With My Red Fires, Passacaglia and Fugue in C Minor, Ruins and Visions, and *Invention.*

"The two sections 'Dance for Twenty-eight' were premiered at Juilliard School of Music on April 17, 1964 under the title *Two Essays for Large Ensemble.*"

Variations on a Theme of Paganini
Music: Johannes Brahms (excerpts from Variations on a Theme of Paganini, op. 35)
Costumes: Charles D. Tomlinson
Company: Juilliard Dance Ensemble
Premiere: Juilliard Concert Hall, New York, 12 February 1965
Dancers: Martha Clarke, Ze'eva Cohen, Carla Maxwell, Lourdes Puertollano, Tamara Woshakiwsky, Clifford Allen, Edward Effron, Dennis Nahat, Ramon Rivera, David Taylor

Dance Suite
Music: Serge Prokofiev
Costumes: Linda Zaslow
Company: Brooklyn College Modern Dance Club
Premiere: George Gershwin Theatre, Brooklyn College, 7 May 1965
Dancers: Eunice Banowitch, Anne Fisher, Leone Fligman, Joanne Frank, Stefanie Kaplan, Isabel Mandelbaum, Gerri-Ellen Musicant, Laura Singer, Tina Zuckerman

My Son, My Enemy
Music: Vivian Fine
Costumes: Pauline Lawrence, Charles D. Tomlinson
Company: José Limón and Company
Premiere: Palmer Auditorium, Connecticut College (18th American Dance Festival), New London, 14 August 1965
Dancers: José Limón (Father), Louis Falco (Son), Jennifer Muller (Venus), Alice Condodina, Ann Vachon, Lenore Latimer, Daniel Lewis, Jennifer Scalon, Kelly Hogan, Laura Glenn, Fritz Ludin, John Parks, Peter Randazzo, Clyde Morgan, David Krohn, Sarah Ford, Tamara Woshakiwsky, Carla Maxwell, Avner Vered, David Earle
Program note: "'If you obey me, I assure you and I promise, in the name of God, that I will not punish you, and if you return I will love you more than ever. But if you do not, I give you as your father my eternal curse; and as your sovereign, I assure you that I shall find the means of punishing you.' Letter from Peter, Czar of Russia, to his son Alexis."

The Winged
Music: Hank Johnson (incidental music)
Costumes: Pauline Lawrence
Company: José Limón and Company
Premiere: Palmer Auditorium, Connecticut College (19th American Dance Festival), New London, 20 August 1966
Dancers: José Limón, Louis Falco, Betty Jones, Sally Stackhouse, Jennifer Muller, Lenore Latimer, Jennifer Scanlon, Laura Glenn, Carla Maxwell, Sarah Ford, Tamara Woshakiwsky, Diane Mohrmann, Daniel Lewis, Fritz Ludin, John Parks, Clyde Morgan, Avner Vered, Jim May, Edward De Soto
Epigraph: "Wings seen and unseen bear us aloft."
Program note: "These dances were composed without music and are designed to be performed in silence, with few exceptions, where music is used to relieve the silence."
NOTE: Limón was dissatisfied with the incidental music for this work, and a new score was commissioned from the composer Jon Magnussen for a production at the Juilliard School in 1995 under the supervision of Carla Maxwell, the Limón Dance Company's artistic director. The company now performs the work with the new score.

MacAber's Dance
Music: Jacob Druckman (Animus I for Trombone and Electronic Tape)
Company: Juilliard Dance Ensemble
Premiere: Juilliard Concert Hall, New York, 20 April 1967
Dancers: Anthony Salatino (Major Domo), Carla Maxwell, Laura Glenn, Linda Rabin, Lynne Wimmer, Maxine Goodman, Marla Metzner, Robyn Cutler, Elaine Crevier, Michele Friesen, James Murphy, Edward DeSoto, Stephen Reinhardt, Robert Iscove, John Griffin, Thomas Rawe, with Maria Barrios, Sandra Brown, Leslie Butler, Amy Gale, Jane Honor, Kathleen McClintock, Sue Roberta Melworth, Carole Schweid, Erroll Booker, Alan Gering (Celebrants)
Program note: "The tradition of the Dance Macabre has its origins in the frenzied rituals of the Middle Ages when Europe was devastated by the Black Death. These rites of penitence and exorcism were celebrated in the city of Paris at the instigation of a legendary figure, a Scot by the name of MacAber, an officer in the king's guard. Dances of Death are endemic among us to this day."
NOTE: According to the program, thematic motifs were contributed by Edward DeSoto, Maxine

Goodman, Marla Metzner, and James Murphy.

Psalm

Music: Eugene Lester
Costumes: Pauline Lawrence
Company: José Limón and Company
Premiere: Palmer Auditorium, Connecticut College (20th American Dance Festival), New London, 19 August 1967
Dancers: Louis Falco (The Burden Bearer), Sally Stackhouse, Jennifer Muller (Expiatory Figures), Lenore Latimer, Jennifer Scanlon, Laura Glenn, Carla Maxwell, Tamara Woshakiwsky, Diane Mohrmann, Alice Condodina, Daniel Lewis, Fritz Ludin, Clyde Morgan, Avner Vered, Jim May, Edward DeSoto (Expiatory Figures)
Singer: Tom Love
Epigraph: "'And praised. *Auschwitz.* Be. *Maidanek.* The Lord. *Treblinka.* And Praised. *Buchenwald.* Be. *Mauthausen.* The Lord. *Belzec.* And Praised. *Bobibor.* Be. *Chalmno.* The Lord. *Ponary.* And Praised. *Theresienstadt.* Be. *Warsaw.* The Lord. *Vilna.* And Praised. *Skrzysko.* Be. *Bergen-Belsen.* The Lord. *Janow.* And praised. *Dora.* Be. *Neuengamme.* The Lord. *Pustkow.* And praised...' From *The Last of the Just* by Andre Schwarz-Bart."

Comedy

Music: Josef Wittman
Company: José Limón and Company
Premiere: Palmer Auditorium, Connecticut College (21st American Dance Festival), New London, 10 August 1968
Principal dancers: Sarah Stackhouse, Louis Falco, Jennifer Muller
Program note: "Over two thousand years ago Aristophanes posed a challenge to women that they have had neither the courage nor wit to accept. A present-day Lysistrata, in this dance, attempts to convince her sisters that they are in possession of a most potent, if not secret, weapon."
NOTE: Interestingly, Limón returned here to the theme of the work in which he had made his professional debut as a member of the Humphrey-Weidman company—Norman Bel Geddes's lavish production of *Lysistrata*, which opened at the Walnut Street Theatre, Philadelphia, on 28 April 1930.

Legend

Music: music for tape selected by Simon Sadoff
Company: José Limón and Company
Premiere: Palmer Auditorium, Connecticut College

(21st American Dance Festival), New London, 17 August 1968
Dancers: Clyde Morgan (Slave), Daniel Lewis (Master), Louis Falco (Dark Angel)
Program note: "This work is dedicated to the memory of black patriots and martyrs."

La Piñata

Music: Burrill Phillips
Scenery: Douglas Schmidt
Costumes: Pauline Lawrence, Betty Williams
Company: Juilliard Dance Ensemble
Premiere: Juilliard Concert Hall, New York, 20 March 1969
Dancers: Francis Patrelle, Larry Grenier, Gary Masters, Aaron Osborne, Maria Barrios, Robyn Cutler, Risa Steinberg, Eugene Harris, Marc Stevens, Gene Stulgaitis; Elizabeth Bickel, Ilze Dreimanis, Gretchen Eisenberg, Randall Faxon, Mary Margaret Giannone, Kathleen Harty, Hannah Kahn, Pamela Knisel, Linda Levy, Jane Lowe, Dalienne Majors, Nancy Paris, Margaret Randi, Carole Schweid, Suzanne Smith, Evelyn Thomas, Evan Williams, Kim Luke, Richard Ornellas, Godfrey Sackeyfio, Timothy Young
Singer: Judith Hubbell
Program note: "This is a birthday, celebrated with the songs and games and toys of infancy, far away and long ago, with something beautiful which was shattered, and a kind saint, who rocked you to sleep at the end."

The Unsung (Work in Progress)

"Pantheon: Metacomet, Pontiac, Tecumseh, Red Eagle, Black Hawk, Osceola, Sitting Bull, Geronimo."
Music: danced in silence
Costumes: Charles D. Tomlinson
Company: Juilliard School Dance Division
Premiere: Juilliard Theater, New York, 26 May 1970
Dancers: Daniel Lewis, Clyde Morgan, Edward DeSoto, Louis Solino, Charles Hayward, Aaron Osborne, Jerome Weiss, Gary Masters
NOTE: The finished work premiered the following year.

And David Wept

Music: Ezra Laderman
Lyrics: Joe Darion
Scenery: Neil DeLuca
Producer: Pamela Ilott
Director: Jerry Schnur
Musical director: Alfredo Antonini
Premiere: WCBS-TV News Special, 11 April 1971

Singers: Sherrill Milnes (David), Rosalind Elias (Bathsheba), Ara Berberian (Uriah)
Dancers: Daniel Lewis (David), Jennifer Muller (Bathsheba), Aaron Osborne (Uriah)
NOTE: This original cantata based on the Old Testament story of David and Bathsheba was Limón's first work choreographed for network television.

Revel
Music: Elizabeth Sawyer (Woodwind Quintet)
Costumes: Charles D. Tomlinson
Company: Juilliard Dance Ensemble
Premiere: Juilliard Theater, New York, 5 May 1971
Dancers: Ann DeGange, Jennifer Douglas, Janet Eilber, Judy Endacott, Barbara Feldman, Hannah Kahn, Susan McGlorthin, Buenaventura Negron-Rivera, Risa Steinberg, Debra Zalkind, Ryland Jordan, Gregory Mitchell, Peter Sparling

Yerma
An Opera in Three Acts.
Music: Heitor Villa-Lobos
Libretto: Federico García Lorca
Stage direction: Basil Langton
Scenery and costumes: Allen Charles Klein
Original paintings: Giorgio de Chirico
Conductor: Christopher Keene
Company: Santa Fe Opera
Premiere: Santa Fe, New Mexico, 12 August 1971
Principal singers: Mirna Lacambra (Yerma), John Wakefield (Juan, Her Husband), Theodor Uppman (Victor, A Shepherd), Frederica von Stade (Maria)

The Unsung
"Pantheon: Metacomet, Pontiac, Tecumseh, Red Eagle, Black Hawk, Osceola, Sitting Bull, Geronimo."
Music: danced in silence
Costumes: Charles D. Tomlinson
Company: Juilliard Dance Ensemble
Premiere: Walnut Street Theatre, Philadelphia, 5 November 1971
Dancers: Edward De Soto, Ryland Jordan, Daniel Lewis, Aaron Osborne, Martial Roumain, Louis Solino, Peter Sparling, Marc Stevens
Program note (added later): "This is is a paean to the heroic defenders of the American patrimony."

Isadora (Five Visions of Isadora Duncan) (also called *Dance for Isadora* [Five Evocations—in Homage] or *Dances for Isadora* [Five Evocations of Isadora Duncan])
Music: Frédéric Chopin

Costumes: Charles D. Tomlinson
Company: José Limón Dance Company
Premiere: Cleveland Museum of Art, Cleveland, 10 December 1971
Dancers: Ann Vachon (Primavera), Carla Maxwell (Maenad), Jennifer Scanlon (Niobe), Laura Glenn (La Patrie), Libby Nye (Scarf Dance)
Program note (added later): "Isadora Duncan (1878–1927), an American interpretive dancer, was one of the forerunners of the modern dance. Her dancing was largely improvisational. Her greatest contribution to the dance, apart from her own magnetic and eccentric personality, consisted of establishing a precedent for breaking existing taboos in the dance so that subsequent dancers might develop their talents regardless of tradition. She met a bizarre death when her scarf caught in a rear wheel of her automobile and strangled her."

The Wind (new work in progress)
Music: Joseph Castaldo ("Kaleidoscope")
Company: Philadelphia Dance Theatre
Premiere: Philadelphia Musical Academy, 17 December 1971
Dancers: Marilyn Bennett, Tom Brown, Carolyn Coles, Sharon Pinsley, Brigitta Trommler, and Nina Auth, Nancy Brandenburg, Maureen Devine, Alice Forner, Ellen Forman, Hara Gelber, Shelia Kurmatz, Gail Lashman, Ines Reisin, Joan Sloss, Victoria Solomon, Lovice Weller, Van Williams, Robin Yanow

Orfeo
Music: Ludwig von Beethoven (op. 95, no. 11 in F Minor)
Costumes: Charles D. Tomlinson
Company: José Limón Dance Company
Premiere: ANTA Theater (City Center American Dance Marathon), New York, 2 October 1972
Dancers: Aaron Osborne (Orfeo), Laura Glenn (Eurydice), Robyn Cutler, Risa Steinberg, Nina Watt (Guardians of the Dead)
Program note (added later): "Orfeo, dancing his lyrical lament of love and loss, calls his beloved Eurydice from the dead. She comes in, swathed in veils and protected by her Guardians, and their duet of the love of the soul ensues. The reality of death arrives, and Eurydice returns to Hades leaving Orfeo once again with his tortuous doubts and hopes."

Carlota
Music: danced in silence
Costumes: Charles D. Tomlinson
Company: José Limón Dance Company

Premiere: ANTA Theater (City Center American Dance Marathon), New York, 5 October 1972

Dancers: Carla Maxwell (Carlota, Empress), Peter Sparling or Gary Masters (Maximilian, Emperor), Edward DeSoto (Benito Juarez, President), Robyn Cutler, Risa Steinberg, Nina Watt (Court Ladies), Louis Solino, Marc Stevens, Aaron Osborne (Guerillas)

Program note: "The crazed Carlota survived the death of her husband and the catastrophic fall of the ill-fated Mexican Empire for fifty years. Before her, nightly, were re-enacted past glories and disasters. Her beloved Max would return to confound his enemies and lead his forces to an ultimate triumph, and crown her once more with the glittering imperial crown of Mexico." Later program note: "A danced drama recalling the despair and tragedy of the Austrian Archduke, Maximilian, and his Belgian wife, Carlota, during their days of exile in Mexico. Through Carlota's crazed mind she dreams of the return of her husband and the glories that once were theirs in the Mexican court. She remembers also the later days when the scheming Republican leader, Juarez, fought his bitter battle which resulted in the tragic death of Maximilian—an innocent man caught in the conspiracy of history. *Carlota* is danced in silence."

Waldstein Sonata (with Daniel Lewis)

Music: Ludwig von Beethoven (Piano Sonata no. 21 [*Waldstein*])

Costumes: Robert Yodice

Company: Juilliard Dance Ensemble

Premiere: Juilliard Theater, New York, 26 April 1975

Dancers: Roxolana Babiuk, Dian Dong, Virginia Edmands, Dianne Hulburt, Pierre Barreau, William Belle, Robert Swinston, Leigh Warren

Program note: "José Limón worked with his company on 'The Waldstein Sonata' in the winter of 1971. The work has been reconstructed and completed by Daniel Lewis."

Luther

Music: Ezra Laderman

Scenery: Tom John

Costumes: Charles D. Tomlinson

Producer: Pamela Ilott

Director: Jerome Schnur

Premiere: WCBS-TV, *For Our Times* series, 26 October 1986

Host: Ted Gill

Dancer: José Limón

NOTE: Recorded in 1972, the film was set aside after Limón's death later that year and lost for more than a decade. In 1986 the footage was edited for broadcast.

Introduction

1. Dorothy Bird and Joyce Greenberg, *Bird's Eye View: Dancing with Martha Graham and on Broadway* (Pittsburgh: University of Pittsburgh Press, 1977), p. 179.
2. Selma Jeanne Cohen, ed., *Seven Statements of Belief* (Middletown, Conn.: Wesleyan University Press, 1969), p. 23.
3. Eleanor King, *Transformations: The Humphrey-Weidman Era* (Brooklyn, N.Y.: Dance Horizons, 1978), p. 18.
4. *Ibid.*, p. 96.
5. Wylie Sypher, *Four Stages of Renaissance Style: Transformations in Art and Literature 1400–1700* (Garden City, N.Y.: Doubleday, 1956), p. 113.
6. Doris Humphrey, "What Shall We Dance About?" *Trend: A Quarterly of the Seven Arts*, June–August 1932. In Cohen, *Seven Statements*, pp. 252–254.
7. José Limón, Scrapbook: Programs and Clippings, 1943–1944, Dance Collection, New York Public Library for the Performing Arts (hereafter DC-NYPL).
8. José Limón, "The Virile Dance," *Dance Magazine*, Dec. 1948. In Walter Sorell, *The Dance Has Many Faces* (Cleveland: World Publishing Co. [1951]), pp. 192–196.
9. The script, taken from various English translations of García Lorca's poem, may be found among Doris Humphrey's papers [1946] at the Dance Collection, and is reproduced in Cohen, *Seven Statements*, pp. 243–247.
10. Norma Stahl, "Concerning José Limón," *The Saturday Review of Literature*, 16 January 1955, p. 33.
11. Ann Vachon, "Limón in Mexico: Mexico in Limón," in *José Limón: The Artist Re-viewed*, ed. June Dunbar (Amsterdam: Harewood Academic Publishers, 1999).
12. Barthel, Joan. "Dancers are Chosen People," *The New York Times*, 31 July 1966, sec. 2, p. 12.

Autobiography

1. In the original manuscript Limón dates his encounter with Kreutzberg to late 1928. In fact, after a single concert with Tilly Losch at the Cosmopolitan Theatre, on 8 January 1928, Kreutzberg did not perform in New York until 20 January 1929, when he and Yvonne Georgi gave a joint recital at the Hudson Theatre. In subsequent weeks, the two performed at the Fulton Theatre (January 29–February 2) and the Gallo Theatre (February 10), concluding their visit with a concert at the Craig Theatre (March 1). The Gallo

concert, which took place on a Sunday afternoon and opened with a Chopin *Polonaise*, most closely agrees with the description that Limón gives of his "birth" later in the manuscript.

2. Save for a four-year-period in the 1880s, Porfirio Díaz ruled Mexico uninterruptedly from 1876 to 1911.

3. The Battle of Cananea occurred early in the Revolution, which began in 1911.

4. "'Mamá grande' Flavia was a yearly visitor. She would come and preside at my mother's confinements" (author's note).

5. *Porfiristas* were supporters of Porfirio Díaz. *Maderistas* supported his opponent, the liberal Francisco Madero, who was elected president in 1911 during the initial phase of the Mexican Revolution. *Revolucionarios* supported the Revolution; *federales* supported the Federal or central government.

6. Richard Halliburton was the author of popular adventure books, including *The Royal Road to Romance* (1925), *The Glorious Adventure* (1927), *The Flying Carpet* (1932), and *Seven League Boots* (1935).

7. Kreutzberg seems to have given only one performance at the Gallo Theatre, a Sunday matinee on February 10. The program, which had piano accompaniment by Louis Horst, opened with *Polonaise* (to Chopin), and included thirteen other numbers: *Preludes* (Scriabin), *Variations* (Mozart), *Révolte* (Wilckens), *Mechanical Dance* (Prokofiev), *Mazurka* (Scriabin), *Romantic Dance Scenes* (Debussy), *Tango* (folk music), *Mexican Dance Song* (folk music), *The Angel of the Last Judgement* (Wilckens), *Persian Song* (Satie), *The Spirit of Evil* (no composer given), *Comical Waltz* (Schulhoff), and *Russian Dance* (Wieniawski). Unfortunately, the playbill did not identify the performers of the individual dances. For a review of the concert, see "Joint Dance Recital," *The New York Times*, 11 Feb. 1929, p. 27. This unsigned review was presumably by John Martin, who wrote two bylined Sunday essays about the German visitors ("The Dance: German Art," *The New York Times*, 20 Jan. 1929, sec. 8, p. 8; and "The Dance: Kreutzberg," *The New York Times*, 27 Jan. 1929, sec. 9, p. 8).

8. Helen Tamiris (1902–1966) studied dance at the Neighborhood Playhouse with Irene Lewisohn, at the Metropolitan Opera School, and with Michel Fokine. She performed at the Metropolitan and did commercial work, and in 1927 gave her first concert, consisting of solo works. In 1930, she organized the Dance Repertory Theatre, in which Martha Graham, Doris Humphrey, and Charles Weidman also participated, and, when this failed, she formed her own group: it was in this period that she choreographed the cycle of *Negro Spirituals* that is her most enduring work. Like Senia Gluck-Sandor, Felicia Sorel, and Lasar Galpern, she taught movement classes at the Group Theatre and choreographed dances for its productions. An activist, she sat on the executive committee (with Humphrey, Sorel, Gluck-Sandor, and Weidman) of the WPA's New York Dance Project, for which she produced *Salut au Monde* in 1936, and the following year, for the Federal Dance Theatre, the immensely successful *How Long, Brethren?*. In the 1940s and 1950s, she choreographed numerous musicals, including *Up in Central Park* (1945), *Annie Get Your Gun* (1946), *Fanny* (1954), and the 1946 revival of *Show Boat*.

9. Senia Gluck-Sandor (1899–1978) was born in Harlem of Jewish parents and studied dance at the Neighborhood Playhouse. He made his professional

debut in 1918 as a dancer and mime in the Metropolitan Opera's production of *Le Coq d'Or* staged by Adolph Bolm, left to go on tour with Bolm's Ballet Intime (performing under the name Senia Gluckoff), and danced with Michel Fokine's company at the Hippodrome (probably in the ballet *Thunderbird*). In the 1920s he worked in vaudeville and on Broadway, becoming in 1927 overture and prolog producer at the Paramount Theatre, a job he held for four years. In 1931, with his wife Felicia Sorel, he founded the Dance Center, and produced during the 1931–1932 season his own versions of the modern ballet classics *Salomé*, *Prodigal Son*, *El Amor Brujo*, and *Petrouchka* (with designs by Vincente Minnelli), in addition to presenting Weidman's *The Happy Hypocrite* and Edna Guy in recital with her group. In 1936 he staged scenes for the Group Theatre and choreographed *The Eternal Prodigal*, a dance drama that was the first production of the WPA Federal Dance Theatre. The following year, when the Dance Center reopened after a brief hiatus, he invited José Limón to play the role of John the Baptist in *Salomé*. Around this time, Jerome Robbins began to work with him as well. In the late 1930s, his personal and professional partnership with Sorel ended. Although he continued to choreograph and perform (in 1964 Robbins cast him as the Rabbi in *Fiddler on the Roof*), painting became the all-consuming interest of his later decades.

Felicia Sorel (ca. 1906–1972) studied at the Neighborhood Playhouse as well as with Louis Chalif, Fokine, and Michio Ito. Beginning in the late 1920s, she worked closely with Gluck-Sandor, both as a choreographer and as a dancer. She starred in most Dance Center productions and worked with him on various dramatic productions as well as with the Group Theatre. In addition, she directed the dances in the opera productions of the WPA Music Project. After severing their longstanding partnership, she embarked upon a career as a "dramatic choreographer," in the words of John Martin, designing dances for dramatic productions, including *Everywhere I Roam* (1938) and *Lysistrata* (1946), which was performed by an all-black cast. In 1938, she developed a program of jazz dances, some to musical settings of poems by Langston Hughes, and, the following year, worked on a revue for the Labor Stage Theatre with Limón, Weidman, Helen Tamiris, and Pauline Koner. In the early 1940s, Wilson Williams, founder of the Negro Dance Company, invited her to become its codirector; for its first performance, in 1943, she choreographed *Dance Calinda*. (Gluck-Sandor's contribution was *St. James Infirmary*.) She also choreographed the dances for a revival in the 1940s of *Run, Little Chillun!*. After the Second World War she taught at the American Theatre Wing and the American Academy of Dramatic Arts.

10. Michio Ito (1892–1961) left his native Japan in 1911 and the following year enrolled at the Dalcroze institute in Hellerau. The First World War brought him to England, where he collaborated with W.B. Yeats on *At the Hawk's Well*, the first of the poet's "plays for dancers." He moved to New York in 1916, and was quickly absorbed into the city's dance and theater life. He taught extensively (among his students were Pauline Koner, Angna Enters, and Felicia Sorel), choreographed many solos and group works (including one in 1928 for the Neighborhood Playhouse group that featured Martha Graham and Benjamin Zemach), and directed and created movement for plays, pantomimes, and revues. In 1929, he settled in Los Angeles, where he created a number of "symphonic choreographies," as he called the large-

scale works he produced for outdoor theaters such as the Hollywood Bowl. In 1941, following the outbreak of hostilities between the United States and Japan, Ito was deported from Los Angeles as an enemy alien.

11. Benjamin Zemach (1901–1997) was born in Bialystock, in the heart of the Jewish Pale. In 1917, he went to Moscow, where he became an early member of the Hebrew-language Habima Theater, which his brother had founded in the wake of the Russian Revolution. He worked closely with the director Evgeny Vakhtangov, who staged the Habima's celebrated production of *The Dybbuk*, and studied as well with Konstantin Stanislavsky and Vsevolod Meyerhold, who gave classes and also worked with the group. In addition, he studied dance with Inna Chernetskaia, one of the most prominent of the era's "free" dancers, and with Vera Moslova, a former Bolshoi dancer. In 1925, the Habima left the Soviet Union on a tour that ended with half the group settling in what was then Palestine and the other half, including Zemach, in New York. In the late 1920s, he became active in the dance group based at the Neighborhood Playhouse. It was here that he performed with Humphrey, Weidman, Martha Graham, and Michio Ito, and created solo concert works, which, like his group pieces, were typically grounded in Judaic history and ritual. He left New York for the West Coast in 1932, but returned in 1936, at the invitation of Max Reinhardt, and the following year choreographed *Pins and Needles* for the International Ladies' Garment Workers' Union. In 1942, he returned to Los Angeles, where he lived until 1971, when he settled in Israel.

12. Elsa Findlay was the daughter of Joseph John Findlay, a professor of education who instituted the first Dalcroze courses at Manchester University. With her father's encouragement she studied eurhythmics with the master at Hellerau, and in 1914 was engaged by Ruth St. Denis and Ted Shawn to teach the subject as part of the curriculum at their American Academy of Dance. She later taught at the New York Dalcroze School. In 1929, she formed the Elsa Findlay Dance Ensemble, which gave concerts in and around New York City during the 1930s. In 1956, Findlay became chairman of the eurhythmics department at the Cleveland Institute of Music. Her book, *Rhythm and Movement: Applications of Dalcroze Eurhythmics*, was published in 1971.

13. Charles Laskey danced with the Humphrey-Weidman company and in Senia Gluck-Sandor's production of *Salomé* for the Dance Center before joining the American Ballet in 1935. In the next several years he created roles in a number of Balanchine ballets, including *Serenade* (1935), *Orpheus and Eurydice* (1936), and *The Card Game* (1937). He partnered Vera Zorina in the Broadway production of *I Married an Angel* (1938) and the Hollywood version of *On Your Toes* (1939) and played the Evil One in the film *I Was an Adventuress* (1940), all choreographed by Balanchine. After the Second World War, he appeared in the Ballet Society productions of *Punch and the Child* and *The Triumph of Bacchus and Ariadne* (1948).

14. The Guild concert took place on 31 March 1929. Limón, listed on the program as Jose Lemon, was one of four male dancers in Weidman's *Rhythmic Dances of Java*. The Guild Theatre, which later became the ANTA Theatre, was where the José Limón Dance Company gave its last New York season before Limón's death in 1972.

15. Norman Bel Geddes (1893–1958) was one of the most innovative American

designers of the 1920s and 1930s as well as a major theater director. Among his most outstanding achievements were his productions of Max Reinhardt's *The Miracle* (1924), *Hamlet* (1931), and *Dead End* (1935). *Lysistrata* opened on 28 April 1930 at the Walnut Street Theatre, Philadelphia. The incidental dances and concluding bacchanale were choreographed by Humphrey.

16. This was *Concerto in A Minor*, which premiered at the Guild Theatre, New York City, on 31 March 1929.

17. *Water Study* premiered at the Civic Repertory Theatre, New York City, on 28 October 1928.

18. *Color Harmony* premiered at the Little Theatre, Brooklyn, on 24 March 1928.

19. *Drama of Motion* premiered at Maxine Elliott's Theatre, New York City, on 6 January 1930.

20. *Life of the Bee* premiered at the Guild Theatre, New York City, on 31 March 1929. The work is described in greater detail below (see pp. 29–30).

21. *The Happy Hypocrite* premiered at the Craig Theatre, New York City, on 7 February 1931. It had music by Herbert Elwell and a libretto after Max Beerbohm's "Fairy Tale for Tired Men."

22. *Ringside* premiered at the Civic Repertory Theatre, New York City, on 28 October 1928. Weidman was the Referee. In this 1931 revival, Laskey and Limón played the two Boxers.

23. *Steel and Stone* premiered at the Craig Theatre, New York City, on 4 February 1931. In 1932, it was retitled *Dance of Work* and often performed as a companion piece to *Dance of Sport*.

24. *The Shakers* premiered at the Craig Theatre, New York City, on 1 February 1931.

25. William (Bill) Bales (1910–1990) received his early dance training in Pittsburgh. He danced with the Humphrey-Weidman company from 1936 to 1940, when he joined the faculty of Bennington College. He taught at Bennington until 1966, leaving to organize the dance program at SUNY-Purchase, where he served as dean of the performing arts division until 1975. In 1943, he formed a trio with Sophie Maslow and Jane Dudley that toured the United States until the early 1950s; among his contributions to the repertory were *Peon Portraits* and *Haunted Ones*. In the 1950s he also contributed dances to New York City Opera productions.

26. Lee Sherman (d. 1998) joined the Humphrey-Weidman company in 1938, dancing in both the Humphrey and Weidman repertories and assuming most of Limón's roles when the latter left the company. In the 1950s, Sherman worked on Broadway, choreographing musical comedies such as *Catch a Star* (1955).

27. Kenneth Bostock danced in the Humphrey-Weidman company from 1934 to 1936. In 1938 he teamed up with Sybil Shearer, Eleanor King, William Bales, and George Bockman, all Humphrey-Weidman veterans, and other concert dancers to form the Theatre Dance Company.

28. William (Bill) Matons danced with the Humphrey-Weidman company from 1933 to 1936 and again in 1940. He appeared in a number of Weidman works, including *Ringside*, *Studies in Conflict*, *Candide* (1933), *Traditions* (1935), and *American Saga* (1936).

29. The duet from *La Valse* premiered at Maxine Elliott's Theatre, New York City, on 6 January 1930; the full work received its first performance at

Robin Hood Dell, Philadelphia, on 19 August 1930.

30. Eleanor King (1906–1991) danced with the Humphrey-Weidman company from 1928 to 1935, and was a member—with Limón, Letitia Ide, and Ernestine Henoch (later Stodelle)—of the Little Group, for which she created her first choreography. Her 1937 dance drama *Icaro*, which incorporated poetry and had music by David Diamond and Franziska Boas, led to a Bennington fellowship in 1938, the year she banded together with Sybil Shearer, William Bales, George Bockman, and Kenneth Bostock, all Humphrey-Weidman veterans, and other concert dancers to form the Theatre Dance Company. In 1942, she settled in Seattle, where she opened a studio and began to incorporate Native American material into her choreography. In the next several decades a fascination with Asian dance forms and traditions led her to research classical dance and drama in Japan, shaman dance in Korea, and trance dance in Bali, Sri Lanka, and Burma. Her memoir, *Transformations: The Humphrey-Weidman Era*, was published in 1978.

31. Cleo Atheneos danced with the Humphrey-Weidman company from 1928 to 1934. She appeared in many Humphrey works, including *Air for the G String* (1928), *Color Harmony*, *Life of the Bee*, *Concerto in A Minor*, *La Valse*, *Burlesca* (1931), and *Dionysiaques* (1932).

32. Sylvia Manning danced with the Humphrey-Weidman company from 1928 to 1932. She appeared in Humphrey's *Air for the G String*, *Color Harmony*, *Concerto in A Minor*, and *Burlesca*, as well as in Weidman's *The Happy Hypocrite*.

33. Celia Rauch danced with the Humphrey-Weidman company from 1928 to 1932.

34. Katherine Manning (d. 1974) danced with the Humphrey-Weidman company from 1928 to 1938. She created roles in numerous Humphrey works, both earlier ones and later ones, including *New Dance* (1935), *Theatre Piece* (1936), and *Passacaglia* (1938), and also appeared in Weidman's *The Happy Hypocrite* and *This Passion* (1938). A frequent teaching assistant to Humphrey, she taught at the Bennington School of the Dance at Mills College in 1939.

35. Virginia Landreth danced with the Humphrey-Weidman company from 1928 to 1931.

36. Dorothy Lathrop danced with the Humphrey-Weidman company from 1928 to 1934, appearing in many Humphrey works, including *Air for a G String*, *Color Harmony*, *Concerto in A Minor*, *La Valse*, and *Dances for Women*.

37. Rose Crystal danced with the Humphrey-Weidman company from 1929 to 1931.

38. Rose Yasgour danced with the Humphrey-Weidman company from 1928 to 1933.

39. Letitia Ide (d. 1993) danced with the Humphrey-Weidman company from 1930 to 1937, with the Little Group founded in 1931, and with José Limón's company from 1946 to 1958. She appeared in many Humphrey and Weidman works as well as in the shows *Lysistrata*, *Americana*, *As Thousands Cheer*, and *Life Begins at 8:40*. During her tenure with the Limón company, she created roles in Limón's *The Exiles* and in Humphrey's *Lament for Ignacio Sánchez Mejías* (1946), *Day on Earth* (1947), and *Corybantic* (1948). She later supervised revivals of both *Lament* and *Day*.

40. Ernestine Henoch (later Stodelle, b. 1912) danced with the Humphrey-Weidman company from 1930 to 1934, appearing in many works, including *Dances of Women, Dionysiaques, Orestes, Air for the G String,* and *Candide.* She also appeared in the productions of *Lysistrata, Americana,* and *School for Husbands,* and was a member of the Little Group, founded in 1931. After leaving the Humphrey-Weidman company, she founded a studio with her husband, the Russian theater director Theodore Komisarjevsky (see note 83), and at his urging created *Homage to Isadora* (1939). The author of *The First Frontier: The Story of Louis Horst and the American Modern Dance* (1964), *The Dance Technique of Doris Humphrey and its Creative Potential* (1978), and *Deep Song: The Dance Story of Martha Graham* (1984), Stodelle supervised many Humphrey revivals, including *Air for the G String, Pleasures of Counterpoint,* and *Two Ecstatic Themes.*

41. *Descent into a Dangerous Place* premiered at Maxine Elliott's Theatre, New York City, on 9 January 1930.

42. The Dance Repertory Theatre was formed in 1930 and gave seasons in 1930 and 1931.

43. Irene Lewisohn (d. 1944) and her sister Alice Lewisohn Crowley (d. 1972) were born in New York City to wealthy Jewish parents. Through their father, Leonard Lewisohn, they met Lillian Wald, the director of the Henry Street Settlement on the Lower East Side, and became involved with its activities. In 1907, they began teaching local children and organizing pageants, festivals, dance dramas, and plays. To expand the scale of their productions, they founded the Neighborhood Playhouse on Grand Street in 1915. During the twelve years of its operation—from its inaugural performance of the choral dance drama *Jeppthal's Daughter* to its final performance of *The Grand Street Follies of 1927*—the Lewisohn Sisters spent a half-million dollars of their inheritance on Playhouse programs. Their most successful productions of this period included *The Dybbuk,* the Hindu play *The Little Clay Cart,* and *Salut Au Monde,* based on the poem by Walt Whitman. In 1928, Irene, with Rita Wallach Morgenthau, founded the Neighborhood Playhouse School of the Theatre. Irene continued to produce work for the stage, choreographing a series of orchestral dramas. Her collaborations with the Cleveland Orchestra, under the direction of Nikolai Sokoloff, included Ernest Bloch's *Israel* (1928) and Richard Strauss's *Ein Heldenleben* (1929). In 1937, Irene founded the Costume Institute, chiefly with costumes from her and Alice's many theater productions. After Irene's death, this became part of the Metropolitan Museum of Art. In the 1930s Alice moved to Switzerland, where she lived until her death. Her book *The Neighborhood Playhouse: Leaves From a Theatre Scrapbook* (1959) provides an account of the Lewisohns' many productions.

44. Irene Lewisohn's production of Richard Strauss's symphonic tone poem *Ein Heldenleben* premiered at the Manhattan Opera House, New York City, on 26 April 1929. The cast included Martha Graham, Doris Humphrey, and Charles Weidman.

45. *Die Glückliche Hand* was not a Lewisohn production, but was produced by the League of Composers and the Philadelphia Orchestra Association. A highly prestigious commission, it teamed Humphrey with stage director Rouben Mamoulian, designer Robert Edmond Jones, and conductor Leopold Stokowski. The first performance took place in Philadelphia on 11

April 1930, on the same program as the American premiere of Léonide Massine's *Rite of Spring*, with Martha Graham as the Chosen Maiden.

46. *Dances for Women* premiered at the Craig Theatre, New York City, on 1 February 1931. Dane Rudhyar (1895–1985) was born in France and studied briefly at the Paris Conservatory before settling in the United States in 1916. Deeply interested in theosophy, he abandoned his real name, Daniel Chennevière, for the Hindu name that he used professionally. His compositions, which reflected his appreciation of Asian music, were used by a number of modern dancers, including Ruth St. Denis (*Dancer from the Court of King Ahasuerus*), Humphrey (*The Call, A Salutation, Breath of Fire*, in addition to *Dances for Women*), Weidman (*Studies in Conflict*), Tina Flade (*Paeans*), Lester Horton (*Flight from Reality*), and Sybil Shearer (*Prologue*). In 1937, Rudhyar spent the summer session in residence at Bennington.

47. For a list of Limón's works, see above (pp. 133–149).

48. J. Alden Weir (1852–1919) studied with Jean Léon Gérôme in Paris and was strongly influenced by James A.M. Whistler, especially the latter's lightened color palette and compositional devices derived from Japanese prints. Sometimes called an American impressionist, Weir was one of the first Americans to admire Edouard Manet and to introduce his work into the United States. He served as president of the National Academy of Design in 1915–1917.

49. Blanche Talmud was a core member of the company of actor/dancers at the Neighborhood Playhouse, where she taught dance and served as Irene Lewisohn's assistant. She played leading roles in Lewisohn's *White Peacock, A Burmese Pwe*, and *Music of the Troubadors*. In her book *The Neighborhood Playhouse*, Alice Lewisohn Crowley refers to Talmud as one of the theater's "well-loved stars."

50. The *Bloch String Quartet* was commissioned by the Elizabeth Sprague Coolidge Foundation and had its premiere at the Library of Congress, Washington, D.C., on 23 April 1931. The scenario was conceived as an "action interpretation" by Irene Lewisohn; the actual staging was by Humphrey and Weidman.

51. *Dionysiaques*, for Humphrey and an ensemble of seventeen, premiered at the Guild Theatre, New York City, on 13 March 1932.

52. Gene Martel danced with the Humphrey-Weidman company from 1932 to 1934, appearing in Humphrey's *Water Study* and Weidman's *Studies in Conflict*.

53. *The Little Soldiers* was presented at the Robin Hood Dell at Fairmont Park, Philadelphia, on 18 August 1931, with the Italian title *Piccoli Soldati*. When the work was revived at the Palais Royale, New York City, in 1933, the title was changed to *L'Amour à la Militaire*.

54. *Nocturne* was presented at the Robin Hood Dell at Fairmont Park, Philadelphia, on 18 August 1931, with the Italian title *Notturno*.

55. *Americana* opened at the Shubert Theatre, New York City, on 7 October 1932.

56. *Candide*, with music composed and arranged by Genevieve Pitot and John Coleman, opened at the Booth Theatre, New York City, on 5 May 1933. A revised version was presented in 1936 under the sponsorship of the Federal Dance Project.

57. Pauline Koner (b. 1912) studied with Michel Fokine, Michio Ito, and Angel Cansino among others. She performed with Fokine's company in 1928, Ito's

in the 1929–1930 season, and with Yeichi Nimura in 1930, the same year she presented her first solo concert, which took place at the Guild Theatre, New York City. During the 1930s and 1940s, she developed a varied repertory of solo works that she toured internationally. From 1946 to 1960, Koner was associated with the Limón company, creating roles in many works, including Limón's *La Malinche*, *The Moor's Pavane*, and *There is a Time* and Humphrey's *Ruins and Visions*. For her own company, founded in 1949 with Humphrey as artistic advisor, she choreographed many solo and group works, including *The Shining Dark* (1956), *The Farewell* (1962), and *Solitary Songs* (1963). A well-known teacher and lecturer, Koner has taught at the Juilliard School since 1986.

58. Born in New York City, Esther Junger (Klempner) studied at the Neighborhood Playhouse with Bird Larson, whose sudden death inspired Junger's 1929 solo *Go Down to Death*. In the 1930s, she gave a number of solo recitals in New York City and appeared as a featured dancer in Gluck-Sandor's *El Amor Brujo* and *Petrouchka* as well as a number of other productions. Her show credits included *Life Begins at 8:40*, *Parade*, and *Dark of the Moon*. Awarded a Bennington fellowship in 1937, Junger was the only recipient of this award not associated with a "Big Four" choreographer. In later decades, she choreographed numbers for Ringling Brothers, Barnum, and Bailey Circus, Billy Rose's Diamond Horseshoe Show, and television.

59. Anita Weschler, a sculptor and painter born in New York City, has shown her work at numerous venues, including the Metropolitan Museum of Art, Museum of Modern Art, and Art Institute of Chicago. Her life-sized sculpture of José Limón, entitled "Prologue," has been exhibited at the Whitney Museum.

60. The house mentioned in this passage, near Blairstown, New Jersey, was purchased jointly by Charles Weidman and José Limón around 1932. Limón later bought another farm in the same area with his wife, Pauline.

61. *Suite in E* premiered at Lewisohn Stadium, New York City, on 8 August 1933. Humphrey choreographed the Sarabande and the Gigue; the opening Prelude, however, was choreographed by Weidman.

62. Charles Humphrey Woodford was born on 8 July 1933 at the Lying-In Hospital.

63. Kurt Graff studied with Rudolf von Laban and danced with Laban's Kammertanz group in Berlin. After helping to found the Paris branch of the Laban school, Graff toured for one season with Kurt Jooss, then resigned to fill Harald Kreutzberg's post as lead dancer at the Berlin Staatsoper, where he had earlier appeared as a soloist. Graff then left Berlin to partner Grace Cornell on her European and American tours, during the course of which they were married.

Grace Cornell (later Graff) studied ballet in Chicago (with Adolph Bolm) and in Italy (with Enrico Cecchetti), and modern dance in Germany (with Laban). She presented her first solo concert at the Théâtre des Champs-Elysées, Paris, and made her American debut shortly thereafter at the Booth Theatre in New York City, later dancing with the Philadelphia Orchestra, under the direction of Leopold Stokowski. She returned to Europe and, with Kurt Graff as her partner, embarked on an extensive international tour. The two returned to the United States to appear together in the touring production of Irving Berlin's *As Thousands Cheer*. After the show closed, they founded a successful school and company based in Chicago. They later established Fieldstone, a summer training camp in Newfane, Vermont.

64. Eleanor Frampton studied with Portia Mansfield prior to attending the University of Nebraska with her lifelong collaborator, Helen Hewett. After graduating in 1918, Frampton taught in Lincoln, Nebraska, where the young Charles Weidman was one of her pupils. Frampton, Hewett, and Weidman soon moved to Los Angeles to study at the Denishawn school. Using Ted Shawn's connections, the two women began touring in vaudeville, making their debut at the Hoyt's Theatre in Long Beach, California, on 22 November 1920 in an act billed as "Frampton and Hewitt [sic] in Bizarre and Exotic Dances." In 1931, upon the recommendation of Doris Humphrey, Frampton became head of the dance department at the Cleveland Institute of Music. After the department was dissolved, she worked with young people at a settlement house in Cleveland.

65. A Denishawn student and dancer, Robert Gorham created the role of the Emperor in Ted Shawn's *Xochitl* (1921). When an injury prevented him from performing, he was replaced by Charles Weidman, then a newcomer to the company. Gorham attended the University of Virginia before returning to Denishawn for the 1923–1924 season, when he appeared in such works as Shawn's *Cuadro Flamenco* and Ruth St. Denis's *Ishtar of the Seven Gates*.

66. *Xochitl* premiered in Long Beach, California, in June 1921. The choreography was by Ted Shawn and the music by Homer Grunn.

67. See note 9 above.

68. Harry Losee began his career as a Denishawn dancer, appearing in such works as *Algerian Rifle Dance*. He later pursued a successful career in New York, appearing in Gluck-Sandor's *Salomé*, dancing at the Metropolitan Opera House, and presenting his own concerts. In the 1930s, he became Sonja Henie's chief choreographer, staging her lavish ice revues and the numbers in her films. His screen choreography credits include *Thin Ice* (1937), *My Lucky Star* (1938), *Happy Landing* (1938), and *Second Fiddle* (1939), all vehicles for Henie, as well as *Shall We Dance* (1937), starring Fred Astaire and Ginger Rogers.

69. Robbins recalled Gluck-Sandor and the Dance Center in a 1995 interview conducted by Ellen Sorrin and now at the New York Public Library's Dance Collection.

70. Hassard Short (1877–1956) directed more than forty musicals, including *Roberta*, *The Great Waltz*, *Lady in the Dark*, and various editions of the *Music Box Revue*. He made innovative use of moving stages and was among the first to replace footlights with lights hung from the auditorium.

71. This "super panorama of entertainment," as *The New York Times* critic Brooks Atkinson called it, opened at the Music Box Theatre on 30 September 1933 and ran for 400 performances. The revue was cleverly tied together by the device of pretending that each song and sketch was derived from a newspaper headline. Thus, the first-act finale, "Easter Parade," seemed to come to life from a turn-of-the-century rotogravure section.

72. Born in Wales, Lawrence Langner (1890–1962) emigrated to the United States in the years before World War I. In 1914, he was one of the founders of the Washington Square Players, and subsequently an organizer of the Theatre Guild, the most exciting producing organization of the 1920s and

1930s, which he was to run during its greatest years, supervising more than 200 productions. He built the Westport (Connecticut) Country Playhouse and was founder and president of the American Shakespeare Festival in Stratford, Connecticut.

The School for Husbands opened at the Empire Theatre, New York City, on 16 October 1933. The play was directed by Langner and designed by Lee Simonson. Humphrey and Weidman choreographed the ballet interlude, "The Dream of Sganarelle."

73. *Rudepoema* and *Alcina Suite* premiered at the Guild Theatre on 15 April 1934, *Duo-Drama* on 6 January 1935. *Alcina Suite* was choreographed jointly by Humphrey and Weidman. In an unusual lapse of memory, Limón seems to have conflated the two Guild concerts.

74. Beatrice Seckler danced with the Humphrey-Weidman company from 1935 to 1942. She created leading roles in many Doris Humphrey and Charles Weidman works and, as time went on, assumed some of Humphrey's original roles in repertory works such as *The Shakers*. With José Limón and Dorothy Bird, she formed the trio that immediately preceded the formation of the Limón company, dancing in the premieres of his *Concerto Grosso*, *Eden Tree*, and *Three Ballads* and in Humphrey's duet *The Story of Mankind* (1946). Later, Seckler danced as a guest artist with the companies of Sophie Maslow and Anna Sokolow, performed as soloist in the short-lived New York City Dance Theatre of 1949, and served as artistic director of the Dancers' Theatre Company, a repertory group founded in 1964.

75. Eva Desca danced with the Humphrey-Weidman company from 1938 to 1940, appearing in such works as *The Happy Hypocrite*, *New Dance*, *To the Dance*, and *Theatre Piece*. She later presented shared recitals of her work with Lee Sherman (1940) and Jessica Flemming (1947).

76. Edith Orcutt danced with the Humphrey-Weidman company from 1935 to 1938.

77. Born in Denver, Katherine Litz (1918–1978) was a leading dancer with the Humphrey-Weidman company from 1934 to 1942. Sybil Shearer, a friend and fellow-company member, introduced Litz to Agnes de Mille in the early 1940s. Litz worked with de Mille, first touring with her company, then appearing, for two years, in the Chicago production of de Mille's *Oklahoma!* and later, from 1945 to 1947, on Broadway in *Carousel*. In the late 1940s and 1950s, Litz became known for her solo creations, including *Daughter of Virtue* (1949), *Blood of the Lamb* (1950), and *Super Duper Jet Girl* (1953). Her most successful group work, *Dracula* (1959), featured Charles Weidman, Buzz Miller, Gemze de Lappe, and Aileen Passloff as soloists. Litz also performed in many plays and, in the 1960s, appeared regularly in productions of the Judson Poets' Theater.

78. Sybil Shearer was a leading dancer with the Humphrey-Weidman company from 1935 to 1938 and one of the ten Humphrey-Weidman veterans who formed the Theatre Dance Company in 1938. In 1941, she briefly served as Agnes de Mille's assistant. Shortly thereafter, she launched a highly successful solo career, initially centered in New York City, then, after 1943, in Chicago. During the 1940s and 1950s she produced numerous solo works, including *Let the Heavens Open That the Earth May Shine*, *In a Vacuum*, *In the Cool Garden*, *As the Twig is Bent*, and *Shade Before Mars*. In the late 1950s, Shearer began working with groups, producing *This Thicket* (1959),

In Place of Opinions (1964), and *Spells and Rituals* (1971). In 1976, with the filmmaker Helen Morrison, she created *A Sheaf of Dreams*, an hour-long motion picture containing several dance segments. The Morrison-Shearer Charitable Foundation was established in 1990 by Shearer to award grants to artists and to maintain the Morrison-Shearer Museum and Archives in Northbrook, Illinois. A critic and writer, she is at work on a multivolume memoir.

79. *Iphigenia in Aulis* premiered at the Academy of Music, Philadelphia, on 23 February 1935. The work was produced by the Philadelphia Orchestra Association, directed by Herbert Graf, and designed by Norman Bel Geddes. The nine dances were jointly choreographed by Humphrey and Weidman.

80. *New Dance* premiered at the College Theatre, Bennington College, on 3 August 1935. The score was by Wallingford Riegger. During Limón's lifetime, the "Variations and Conclusion" from *New Dance* was the only Humphrey piece from the 1930s represented in the Limón company repertory, a measure of Limón's high regard for the choreography.

   Wallingford Riegger (1885–1961) received his first formal training in music at the Institute of Musical Art in New York, where he studied composition with Percy Goetschius. He continued his studies in Germany, returning to the United States in 1917 to teach cello at Drake University in Iowa. Active in the 1920s in the Pan-American Association of Composers, which included Edgard Varèse, Charles Ives, Henry Cowell, and Carl Ruggles, he focused his compositional energies in the 1930s, when he spent several summers as a composer in residence at Bennington, on writing music for modern dance. Among his choreographic collaborators were Martha Graham (*Frenetic Rhythms*, *Chronicle*), Charles Weidman (*Candide*, revival), Doris Humphrey (*New Dance*, *Theatre Piece*, *With My Red Fires*), Hanya Holm (*Dance in Two Parts*, *City Nocturne*, *Trend*), Anna Sokolow (*Case History No. —*), and Erick Hawkins (*Chaconne: The Pilgrim's Progress*).

81. George Bockman began dancing while studying design at the Pratt Institute of Fine Arts. He made his debut as a dancer in the 1933 production of Molière's *School for Husbands*, with choreography by Humphrey and Weidman. From 1934 to 1938 he danced with the Humphrey-Weidman company. In addition to performing in many repertory works, he appeared as Joseph, opposite Lillian Gish as Mary, in Delos Chappell's staging of Bach's *Christmas Oratorio*, choreographed by Humphrey. He was involved, as a choreographer, dancer, and designer, in the Theatre Dance Company, founded in 1938 by former Humphrey-Weidman dancers. Around this time, Bockman joined the faculty of the Adelphi Institute and became a design consultant for Eugene Loring's Dance Players, costuming Loring's *Duke of Sacramento* (1942). In later years, he costumed works by other choreographers, including Hanya Holm's *Parable* (1943) and Eleanor King's *American Folk Suite* (1950).

82. *Theatre Piece* premiered at the Guild Theatre, New York City, on 19 January 1936; *With My Red Fires*, at the Vermont State Armory, Bennington, Vermont, on 13 August 1936.

83. Theodore Komisarjevsky (1882–1954) was born in Venice, Italy, the son of the first tenor of the Russian Imperial Opera and brother of the great actress Vera Kommissarzhevskaya. He studied architecture at the Imperial Institute

in Moscow before embarking on a distinguished career as theater director, producer, designer, translator and adaptor of plays, as well as a designer of cinema interiors. From 1906 to 1910 he served as managing director of his sister's theater in St. Petersburg; thereafter, he worked extensively in Moscow, developing his idea of "synthetic theater." After serving as managing director of the Bolshoi Ballet and Opera (1918–1919), he made his Covent Garden debut with a production of *Prince Igor* (1919) and subsequently mounted all of Chekhov's plays in the British capital. From 1932 to 1939, he worked at Stratford-on-Avon, where he directed seven Shakespeare plays.

Komisarjevsky's American productions, prior to settling in the United States in 1939, included *Peer Gynt* and *The Tidings Brought to Mary* for the Theatre Guild's 1922–1923 season. With his third wife, Ernestine Stodelle, he founded a school of drama and dance. In New York he directed various plays, including *Russian Bank* (1940) and *Crime and Punishment* (1947), and also mounted a number of productions for the New York City Opera, including *Love for Three Oranges* (1949) and *Wozzeck* (1952). He was the author of several books, including *The Costume of the Theatre* (1932).

84. *Exhibition Piece* premiered at the Guild Theatre, New York City, on 15 April 1934. The choreography was by Humphrey.

85. Nicolas Slonimsky (1894–1995) studied piano and composition in his native St. Petersburg before emigrating to Paris. In 1923 he settled in the United States and became an accompanist and vocal coach at the newly founded Eastman School of Music. Moving to Boston, he conducted the Harvard University Orchestra (1927–1930) and the Boston Chamber Orchestra (1927–1934) and made guest appearances with other ensembles, conducting mainly modern music. Better known as a conductor than as a composer, he wrote several books on music and also edited a number of important reference works.

86. *Traditions* premiered at the New Dance League, New York City, on 12 October 1935.

87. *Studies in Conflict* premiered at the New School for Social Research, New York City, on 5 January 1932. The score was by Dane Rudhyar, arranged by Vivian Fine and Pauline Lawrence.

88. A. Lehman Engel (1910–1982) studied at Cincinnati Conservatory, Juilliard, and privately with Roger Sessions. He was active both as a conductor and a composer, and during the 1930s, worked closely with a number of modern dance choreographers, including Martha Graham (*Ekstasis, Transitions, Perspectives* ["Marching Song"], *Imperial Gesture, Salutation*), Charles Weidman (*Traditions, Atavisms, Lynchtown*), Gluck-Sandor (*Ballet in Six Parts*), and Erick Hawkins (*Insubstantial Pageant*). In the 1940s he collaborated with Ruth Page on a group of solos to poetry with the collective title *Dances with Words and Music*. A successful composer for Broadway, films, television, radio, and theater, he was the author of *This Bright Day* (1956), an autobiography.

89. May O'Donnell (b. 1906) was a member of Martha Graham's company from 1932 to 1938 and from 1944 to 1952, when she returned as a guest artist, creating roles in *Appalachian Spring* (1944), *Herodiade* (1944), *Dark Meadow* (1946), and *Cave of the Heart* (1946). O'Donnell created her first work, *Of Pioneer Women*, in 1937, and presented her first solo concert, *So Proudly We*

Hail, in San Francisco in 1940. In the early 1940s she collaborated with José Limón and her husband, the composer Ray Green, and in late 1949 she founded her first company. At the studio she ran for many years with Gertrude Shurr her students included Robert Joffrey, Gerald Arpino, and Dudley Williams.

90. Dorothy Bird (d. 1996) was born on Vancouver Island, British Columbia. In 1930, she attended the Cornish School of Fine and Applied Arts, where she studied with Martha Graham. Joining the Graham company in 1931, she appeared in *Primitive Mysteries, Panorama*, and *Chronicle*. Bird left the Graham company in 1937 and in the next decade appeared in ten Broadway musicals, including *Lady in the Dark*. In the mid-1940s, she formed a trio with José Limón and Beatrice Seckler and also taught modern dance at the School of American Ballet. Her autobiography, *Bird's Eye View: Dancing with Martha Graham and on Broadway* was published in 1997.

91. Anna Sokolow (b. 1910) grew up on New York's Lower East Side. She first studied dance with Elsa Pohl and then, from age fifteen, at the Neighborhood Playhouse with Blanche Talmud, Bird Larson, Martha Graham, and Louis Horst. She performed with Graham's company from 1930 to 1938, serving as Horst's assistant and also choreographing works such as *Anti-War Cycle* (ca. 1933), *Strange American Funeral* (1935), *Slaughter of the Innocents* (1937), and *Facade* (1937) that had a strong social content.

After she left Graham's company, Carlos Merida of the Mexican Ministry of Culture invited Sokolow and twelve dancers to teach and perform in Mexico. Thus began a decade-long involvement with the Mexican dance community. After an initial eight-month visit in 1939, Sokolow spent half of each of the next nine years in Mexico City, teaching, performing, and directing Mexico's first modern dance company. After the Second World War she became involved with modern dance in Israel, working with the Inbal Dance Theater and, in 1962, establishing the Lyric Theatre. The Players Project, the company founded by Sokolow in New York in 1971, remains active. Since 1959, Sokolow has maintained an association with the Juilliard School. Her works have been mounted on companies throughout the world, including the Limón Dance Company.

92. Sophie Maslow (b. 1911) studied with Blanche Talmud and Martha Graham at the Neighborhood Playhouse. She danced with the Graham company from 1931 to 1942, appearing in such works as *Primitive Mysteries, Letter to the World*, and *Deaths and Entrances*. She presented her first choreography in 1934 under the auspices of the New Dance League and continued to participate in its annual concerts for several years. Her early works, mostly political in theme, included *Two Songs about Lenin* (1935) and *Women of Spain* (1937). From 1942 to 1954 she performed with the Dudley-Maslow-Bales Trio, which toured extensively and had a close association with the New Dance Group. *Dust Bowl Ballads* (1941) and *Folksay* (1942) were two of Maslow's most successful early works. She founded her own company in 1956. In addition to choreographing for the concert stage, Maslow has choreographed several Broadway shows, organized the annual Hannukah Festival at Madison Square Garden, and staged dances for the New York City Opera.

93. Gertrude Shurr (1903–1992) was born in Riga, Latvia, and came to the United States as a child. She studied at the Neighborhood Playhouse with Bird

Larson and Martha Graham, the New York Denishawn school, and the Humphrey-Weidman studio. After dancing with the Denishawn company from 1925 to 1927, she briefly joined the Humphrey-Weidman group, appearing in such works as *Color Harmony* and *Concerto in A Minor*, but soon left to teach at the Graham studio. She joined the Graham company in 1930 and for the next eight years appeared in many works, including *Primitive Mysteries*, which she later helped revive. After the premiere of *American Document* (1938), Shurr left the company and moved to the West Coast where she worked with May O'Donnell, a longtime professional associate, and taught, from 1939 to 1940, at San Francisco State College. From 1957 to 1973 Shurr taught at the High School for Performing Arts in New York City. She is the author, with Rachael Dunaven Yocom, of *Modern Dance: Techniques and Teaching* (1980).

94. Ethel Butler (d. 1996) left high school to study with Martha Graham at the Neighborhood Playhouse in 1931, joining her company two years later. In the following decade, she created roles in works such as *Deaths and Entrances* and became one of Graham's principal teaching assistants. In 1946 she opened a studio in Bethesda, Maryland, where she taught until 1978, when she accepted a teaching post at the University of Maryland.

95. Lillian Shapero (later Rauch, d. 1988) studied with Michio Ito, Louis Horst, and Martha Graham. She danced with the Graham company from 1929 to 1935, appearing in such works as *Heretic* and *Primitive Mysteries*, for which she served as Graham's stand-in. From 1932 to 1952 she served as choreographer for the Maurice Schwartz Art Theater and was noted for successfully integrating modern dance into Yiddish plays. She directed the Lillian Shapero dance group from 1936 to 1939. Her last choreography was for the 1982 television production *Higher Than Heaven*, set to a folk cantata composed by her husband, Maurice Rauch.

96. Martha Hill (1900–1995) graduated in 1920 from the Kellogg School of Physical Education in Battle Creek, Michigan, where she taught gymnastics and ballet until 1923. For the next three years she served as director of dance at Kansas State Teachers College. She began studying with Martha Graham in the mid-1920s and danced with her company from 1929 to 1931. As a dance educator and administrator, Hill was influential in shaping the development of modern dance in educational institutions and on the concert stage. During her long teaching career, she served on the faculties of Bennington College (1932–1951), New York University School of Education (1930–1951), and the Juilliard School (1951–1985). Her most notable achievement may well have been the summer dance programs that she founded and directed at Bennington College (1934–1942), and then later at Mills College (1939), University of Southern California (1946), and Connecticut College (1948–1951).

97. Mary Josephine Shelly (1902–1976) pursued careers both in dance education and in the United States military. She taught at the University of Oregon (1924–1928), Teachers College (1929–1932) and New College (1932–1933) at Columbia University, and the University of Chicago (1935–1938). In 1934, with Martha Hill, she founded and served as administrative director of the Bennington School of the Dance. Her long association with Bennington College continued in various capacities (with interruptions for military service during the Second World War) until the early 1950s. In 1954, she

resigned as the college's director of personnel to head the Girl Scouts of America, which she directed until the mid-1960s.

98. The composer Norman Lloyd (1909–1980) studied at New York University, receiving his M.S. in 1936, and taught at Sarah Lawrence until 1945, spending summers at Bennington College, where he and his pianist wife Ruth were engaged as accompanists and where he taught the course "Music for Dancers." He conducted and played many of the premieres at Bennington and accompanied most of the classes and workshops. During the 1930s and 1940s he wrote music for a number of modern dance choreographers, including Martha Graham (*Panorama, Opening Dance*), Hanya Holm (*Dance of Work and Play*), Charles Weidman (*Quest, This Passion*), José Limón (*Danza de la Muerte, La Malinche*), Doris Humphrey (*Inquest, Invention, Lament for Ignacio Sánchez Mejías,* and *Invention*), Anna Sokolow (*Three Jazz Preludes*), and Merce Cunningham and Jean Erdman (*Seeds of Brightness*). From 1949 to 1963 he was a member of the faculty of the Juilliard School of Music. In the 1960s, he served as dean of the Oberlin College Conservatory, and in 1965 as director of arts programming for the Rockefeller Foundation.

99. The work, although Limón does not refer to it by this title, was *Orestes*. It was choreographed in 1933 and only performed at the Humphrey-Weidman Studio.

100. Ada Korvin danced with the Humphrey-Weidman company from 1931 to 1936.

101. *This Passion*, with music by Norman Lloyd, premiered at the Guild Theatre, New York City, on 23 January 1938.

102. *Race of Life* premiered at the Guild Theatre, New York City, 9 January 1938. The Chicago-born composer and pianist Vivian Fine (b. 1913) spent a number of summers at Bennington in the 1930s, while continuing her studies at the Dalcroze School and with Roger Sessions. In addition to *Race of Life*, she composed scores for Charles Weidman's *Opus 51*, Hanya Holm's *They Too are Exiles*, Martha Graham's *Alcestis*, and José Limón's *My Son, My Enemy*. A cofounder of the American Composers' Alliance, she taught at New York University, Juilliard, the Connecticut College School of Dance, Bennington, and other institutions.

103. Here Limón left space in the manuscript for a "Blake quotation."

104. *Quest: A Choreographic Pantomime* premiered at the Vermont State Armory on 13 August 1936. The music was by Norman Lloyd except for one section, "Transition," by Clair Leonard.

105. Ben Belitt (b. 1911) served as assistant literary editor of *The Nation* for two years before joining the literature faculty of Bennington College in 1938. A poet, translator, and literary critic, he became actively involved in the dance community at Bennington. He taught an interdisciplinary workshop at the 1939 summer festival at Mills College, wrote poems for dancers, and staged works to poetry. "Wilderness Stair," the original title of Martha Graham's *Diversion of Angels*, came from a line in one of Belitt's poems. In addition to publishing various books of his own poetry, he is a translator of Pablo Neruda.

106. Francis Fergusson (1904–1986), born in Alburquerque, New Mexico, was a director, theater critic, and professor of theater and literature. After graduating from Harvard in 1923, he received a Rhodes Scholarship to study at

Oxford. Returning to the United States, he served as associate director of the American Laboratory Theatre in New York City from 1926 to 1930, wrote criticism and lectured at the New School for Social Research, then joined the faculty of Bennington College in 1934. In 1947, he left Bennington to direct the seminars in literary criticism at the Institute for Advanced Study in Princeton. The author of *The Idea of a Theater* (1948), *Dante's Drama of the Mind* (1953), and *Trope and Allegory* (1976), Fergusson served as general editor of the Laurel Shakespeare series.

107. Gregory Tucker (b. 1908) was a pianist and composer on the Bennington College faculty and a member of the faculty of the Bennington School of the Dance. He collaborated with a number of modern dance choreographers, including Hanya Holm (*Metropolitan Daily*), Louise Kloepper (*Statement of Dissent*), Sophie Maslow (*The Village I Knew*), Marian Van Tuyl (*Clinic of Stumble*), Jean Erdman (*Four-Four Time*), Jane Dudley, Sophie Maslow, and William Bales and Martha Hill (*The People, Yes!*).

108. Julian de Gray was a pianist and composer who headed for a time the piano department at the University of Miami, Florida. In the early 1930s he gave at least two recitals at Town Hall in New York City.

109. Set and lighting designer Arch Lauterer (1904–1957) taught at Bennington College from 1933 to 1942, collaborating with the major figures of modern dance and developing his influential, spare aesthetic. He designed numerous modern dance productions including Martha Graham's *Panorama, American Document, El Penitente, Letter to the World, Punch and Judy*, and *Deaths and Entrances*, Doris Humphrey's *Passacaglia* and *Decade*, Hanya Holm's *Trend, Dances of Work and Play, The Golden Fleece*, and *Tragic Exodus*, in addition to works by Charles Weidman, Eleanor King, Louise Kloepper, and Merce Cunningham. From 1946 to 1957 Lauterer taught at Mills College.

110. A musicologist, composer, and choral director, Henry Leland Clarke was born in Dover, New Hampshire, in 1907. He studied piano and violin, attended Harvard University, where he received his Master's in 1929, then went to Paris to study composition with Nadia Boulanger at the Ecole Normale de Musique. He taught music at Bennington College from 1936 to 1938, Westminster Choir College (1938–1942), UCLA (1947–1958), and the University of Washington (1958–1977).

111. Robert Guyn McBride was born in Tuscon, Arizona, in 1911. A versatile musician and prolific composer, he studied composition with Otto Luening at the Univeristy of Arizona. From 1935 to 1936 McBride taught music at Bennington College. His scores for dances include Erick Hawkins's *Show Piece* (1937), produced by Ballet Caravan, and Martha Graham's *Punch and the Judy* (1941). From 1945 to 1957 he worked in New York, composing music for films such as *Farewell to Yesterday* and *The Man with My Face*. In 1957, he joined the faculty of the University of Arizona.

112. *Façade—Esposizione Italiana* premiered at the Vermont State Armory, Bennington, on 12 August 1937. The music was by Alex North.

113. Pauline Chellis studied with Margaret H'Doubler at the University of Wisconsin, the first academic institution to confer a degree in dance. A pioneer of modern dance in Boston, she opened a studio and school there in 1929, subsequently organizing a concert group and summer festival courses. Among the guest teachers and lecturers at her school in the 1930s and 1940s

were Martha Graham, Louis Horst, John Martin, Doris Humphrey, José Limón, and Dorothy Bird.

114. Reared in Southington, Connecticut, Alwin Nikolais (1910–1993) received his first theatrical experience at a local drama center that he had helped found. From 1935 to 1937, he directed the Park Marionette Theatre in Hartford, where he studied dance with Truda Kaschmann, a former student of Mary Wigman. Nikolais attended the Bennington summer dance festival from 1937 to 1939, appearing in José Limón's *Danza de la Muerte* (1937), studying percussion with Franziska Boas, and becoming deeply influenced by Hanya Holm. In the late 1930s, while still working with Kaschmann, he formed his own company, and their joint collaboration *Eight Column Line* (1939) was one of his early successes. In 1948, after serving in the army and dancing with Holm's workshop group, he began teaching and performing at the Henry Street Playhouse. He remained there until 1970, directing the Playhouse Dance Company, later renamed the Nikolais Dance Theatre, and creating a unique style of dance-theater, one that fully integrated movement, music, costume, lighting effects, and stage design. In the 1950s and 1960s, Nikolais choreographed his signature abstract works (*Kaleidoscope*, 1953, 1956; *Prism*, 1956; *Allegory*, 1959; *Totem*, 1960; *Imago*, 1963; *Vaudeville of the Elements*, 1963) and became known nationally and internationally. In 1978, he founded the Centre National de Danse Contemporaine in Angers, France, which he directed for three years. Eleven years later, he merged his company with that of Murray Louis, a longtime collaborator.

115. Actually, she performed only one section from *American Provincials*—"Act of Piety." Also on the program were *Opening Dance*, *Lamentation*, *Frontier*, *Satyric Festival Song*, *Immediate Tragedy*, *Spectre 1914* (from *Chronicle*), and *Harlequinade*.

116. *Immediate Tragedy—Dance of Dedication* premiered at the Vermont State Armory on 30 July 1937. Born in Menlo Park, California, Henry Cowell (1897–1965) became one of America's foremost composers of modern music. As a child, he studied first violin and then piano. By the time he made his formal debut in 1914, he had written over a hundred pieces and begun his compositional experiments with tone clusters. Enrolling at the University of California, Berkeley, he studied with Charles Seeger, E.G. Stricklen, and Wallace Sabin. In the 1920s, he made successful tours of the United States and Europe, becoming the first American composer to visit the Soviet Union (1928) and publish there. In 1927, he founded the *New Music Quarterly* and a few years later a record series. He suffered a period of imprisonment (1936–1940) on a charge of homosexuality, for which he was later pardoned. He subsequently married the ethnomusicologist Sidney Robertson. Throughout his career, his musical output remained prolific and diverse in style, a reflection in part of his interest in world music. He lectured at numerous conservatories and universities, and had close professional associations with the New School for Social Research (1928–1963), the Peabody Conservatory of Music (1951–1956), and Columbia University (1951–1965).

Cowell worked with many dancers and choreographers over the years, creating compositions that were flexible in duration and instrumentation and giving courses in music theory and percussion. As early as 1923, the Irish-born Paris Opéra dancer Yvonne Daunt presented a concert of dances to his music in the French capital. For Doris Humphrey, Cowell performed his innovative piano composition *The Banshee* live to her 1928 dance of the same title. He created original scores for Elsa Findlay (*Men and Machines*, 1930), Charles Weidman (*Steel and Stone*, 1931, and *Dance of Sports*, 1932), Hanya Holm (*Salutation*, 1936, and *Dance of Introduction*, 1940), Martha Graham (*Immediate Tragedy*, 1937, and *Deep Song*, 1937), Bonnie Bird (*Hilarious Curtain Opener*, 1939), Erick Hawkins (*Trickster Coyote*, 1941), and Jean Erdman (*Changingwoman*, 1954). For a list of his compositions for dance, see "Chronology of Dance Scores (1923–1960)," *Dance Scope*, no. 6 (Spring 1966), pp. 14–15.

117. *American Document* premiered at the Vermont State Armory, Bennington, on 6 August 1938.

118. *On My Mother's Side* seems to have premiered at Vassar College, Poughkeepsie, N.Y., on 20 January 1940. The first New York performance appears to have been the following March 31 at the Ninety-Second Street YM-YWHA.

119. Playwright William Archibald (d. 1953) danced with Humphrey-Weidman in 1938 and 1939. He wrote the text for a number of modern dance works, including Charles Weidman's *On My Mother's Side* and José Limón's *War Lyrics*. He was the author of the book for *Carib Song*, a 1945 musical, with dances by Katherine Dunham.

120. A pianist, composer, conductor, and teacher, Lional Nowak was born in Cleveland in 1911. He studied piano with Beryl Rubenstein and Edwin Fischer and composition with Herbert Elwell, Roger Sessions, and Quincy Porter at the Cleveland Institute of Music, where he also composed and played for Eleanor Frampton. From 1932 to 1938, he was director of music at Fenn College in Cleveland. From 1938 to 1942, he served as musical director of the Humphrey-Weidman company, contributing music to Humphrey's *The Green Land* and *The Story of Mankind*, Weidman's *Flickers*, *On My Mother's Side*, and *A House Divided*, and Limón's *Danzas Mexicanas*. Nowak joined the faculty of Bennington in 1948. After a stroke in 1980 prevented him from using his left hand, Nowak composed and commissioned several works for right-hand piano.

121. Portia Mansfield (also Swett, 1887–1979) was born in Chicago, studied dance with Louis Chalif and at the Cambridge Normal School with Luigi Albertieri, and attended Smith College where she met Charlotte Perry (1890–1983), a native of Denver. After graduating from Smith, Mansfield taught dance in Omaha, Nebraska, and then, from 1912 to 1914, she and Perry taught at a settlement house in Chicago. In 1913 or 1914 they bought land in Eldora, Colorado, where they founded the Perry-Mansfield School of the Theatre and Dance. The following year, the camp moved to its current site in Steamboat Springs. The two women directed the camp for more than fifty years, donating it to Stephens College in 1963. Mansfield, a one-time member of the Pavley-Oukrainsky Ballet, ran the dance programs at the camp while Perry directed the drama programs and wrote many original plays. Beginning in the late 1920s, the camp attracted major modern dance figures as teachers and guest artists, including Louis Horst (as musical director), José Limón, Doris Humphrey, Charles Weidman, Hanya Holm, Helen Tamiris, and Daniel Nagrin. Prominent Perry-Mansfield graduates in theater include Julie Harris, Dustin Hoffman, and Lee Remick. During the camp's off-season, Perry and Mansfield maintained various concert groups. In the

1960s, Mansfield earned a doctorate in anthropology from New York University, while also operating a mountain climbing school for boys. Perry also did graduate work at New York University as well as at the Bank Street Cooperative School in New York. She taught at Hunter College for eight years, before moving to Monterey, California, to teach at the Santa Catalina School.

122. *Opus 51* premiered at the Vermont State Armory, Bennington, on 6 August 1938.

123. Born in Joplin, Missouri, Harriette Ann Gray (ca. 1914–1987) attended the Perry-Mansfield School of the Theatre and Dance where she studied with José Limón during the summer 1935. From 1936 to 1940 she danced leading roles with the Humphrey-Weidman company and served as personal assistant to the directors. In 1941 she moved to Hollywood, where for the next ten years she assisted the choreographer Jack Cole, taught movement to actors, danced in films, and helped form the New Studio for Dancers and Actors. In 1955, she joined the faculty of Stephens College, where she taught until 1979. From 1946 to 1979 she directed the dance program at the Perry-Mansfield camp. It was because of Gray's long tenure at Stephens College that ownership of the camp passed to the college in 1963.

124. *Passacaglia in C Minor* premiered at the Vermont State Armory, Bennington, on 5 August 1938.

125. *Keep Off the Grass*, a revue in two acts, opened at the Broadhurst Theatre, New York City, on 23 May 1940. The music and book were by James McHugh, the lyrics by Al Dubin, the direction by Edward Duryea Dowling, the staging by Fred de Cordova, and the scenery and costumes by Nat Karson. Limón appeared in several numbers, including "This is Spring," "A Latin Tune, a Manhattan Moon, and You," "Clear Out of This World," "Look Out for My Heart," "I'm in the Mood," and "This is Winter."

126. *On Your Toes*, a musical comedy in two acts and thirteen scenes, opened at the Imperial Theatre, New York City, on 11 April 1936. The music was by Richard Rodgers, the lyrics by Lorenz Hart, the staging by Worthington Miner, the scenery by Jo Mielziner, and the costumes by Irene Sharaff. Balanchine choreographed the three big dance scenes—"La Princesse Zenobia Ballet," "On Your Toes," and "Slaughter on Tenth Avenue Ballet."

127. Born in Elmira, New York, pianist-composer Esther Williamson (later Ballou, 1915–1973) studied with Otto Leuning and Wallingford Riegger at Bennington College. She composed scores for many student dancers at the Bennington festivals and also worked with Limón and Louise Kloepper at Mills College. Her compositions for dance include Kloepper's *Earth Saga* (1938) and Limón's *War Lyrics* (1940). She received a Masters degree from Juilliard, where she taught from 1943 to 1950. From 1959 until the year of her death, she taught at American University.

128. Alfred Frankenstein was the art, music, and dance critic of *The San Francisco Chronicle*.

129. Durevol later danced with the Limón company under the name Vol Quitzow.

130. Betty Horst (*née* Bessie Cunningham) married Louis Horst in 1909. When he became musical director of Denishawn in 1915, she joined the company at his insistence. Although she had little formal training, she became a core

member of the group, remaining in the company for several years. She later taught dance at the School of Theatre of Golden Bough in Carmel, California.

131. *Choreartium* premiered at the Alhambra Theatre, London, on 24 October 1933; *Les Présages*, at the Théâtre de Monte-Carlo on 13 April 1933; *Symphonie Fantastique*, at Covent Garden, London, on 24 July 1936; *Seventh Symphony*, at the Théâtre de Monte-Carlo on 5 May 1938, and *Gaîté Parisienne*, at the Théâtre de Monte-Carlo on 5 April 1938. The music for *Gaîté* was by Jacques Offenbach.

132. *Rouge et Noir* premiered at the Théâtre de Monte-Carlo on 11 May 1939.

133. *Bacchanale* premiered at the Metropolitan Opera House, New York, on 9 November 1939. The music was from *Tannhauser*.

134. Casimir Kokitch, a Yugoslavian dancer, danced with the Ballet Russe de Monte Carlo from 1938 to 1943, when he was drafted into the U.S. Army, and again in 1946–1947. He was a fine character dancer and also excelled in dramatic roles. Among his most successful creations was the Head Wrangler in Agnes de Mille's *Rodeo* (1942). He was briefly married to the ballerina Alexandra Danilova.

135. *Partita in G Major* premiered at the Humphrey-Weidman Studio Theatre, New York City, on 27 December 1942.

136. *Four Chorale Preludes* premiered at the Humphrey-Weidman Studio Theatre, New York City, on 27 December 1942.

137. Maria Maginnis danced with the Humphrey-Weidman company from 1940 to 1943.

138. Gloria García danced with the Humphrey-Weidman company from 1940 to 1944.

139. Molly Davenport danced with the Humphrey-Weidman company from 1940 to 1944.

140. Nona Schurman danced with the Humphrey-Weidman company from 1940 to 1942. She later taught at Illinois State University. In 1972, she published *Modern Dance Fundamentals* with Sharon Leigh Clark.

141. The earliest version of *Song of the West* premiered at Madison College, Harrisonburg, Virginia, on 8 November 1940.

142. *El Salón México* premiered at the Humphrey-Weidman Studio Theatre, New York City, on 11 March 1943.

Afterword

1. All quotations from these notes are in Folder 464, José Limón Papers, DC-NYPL.

2. José Limón, "Letter to Pauline, Betty and Lucas on the occasion of the 10th Anniversary of *The Moor's Pavane*," 1 September 1959, pp. 4–5.

3. *Ibid.*

4. José Limón, "Composing a Dance," *The Juilliard Review*, 2, no. 1 (Winter 1955), p. 18.

5. Limón, "Letter," p. 5.

6. *Ibid.*, pp. 1–2.

7. *Ibid.*, p. 6.

8. *Ibid.*, pp. 6–7.

9. Limón, "Composing a Dance," p. 18.

10. José Limón, quoted by Robert Bagar in the program for the premiere of *The Emperor Jones*, August 1956.

11. José Limón, letter to various sponsors of the tour, 6 January 1958, p. 3, Folder 484, José Limón Papers.

12. John Martin, José Limón's Tribute to the Human Spirit," *The New York Times*, 18 May 1958, sec. 2, p. 14.

13. This is in Folder 464, José Limón Papers.

14. Quoted by Walter Terry in "The Legacy of Isadora Duncan and Ruth St. Denis," *Dance Perspectives*, 5 (Winter 1960), p. 47.

Covarrubias

1. This is a reworking of the original Spanish program note rather than an exact translation. For the latter, see the list of Limón works.

Works Choreographed by José Limón

1. When the work was performed the following August at the American Dance Festival, the program note read somewhat differently: "Two adversaries confront each other perpetually in the Mexican scene. Although separated by centuries, they are ever the same two: the foreign invader who seeks to dominate, and the Mexican who defends his soil and his integrity. Sometimes, as in the episode—1520, a Spanish conquistador assaults a weak and superstitious Indian Emperor and seizes his crown, his throne and his empire. In the episode—1867, the conflict is between an Austrian Archduke, instrument of imperialism, and an Indian President, armed with a potent weapon, a scroll symbolizing the concepts of Liberty and Democracy. In the first episode, the encounter is personal, intimate, face to face. In the second, the struggle is between two who never meet nor know each other until one has been eliminated."

MELINDA COPEL

Special Collections and Unpublished Material

American Dance Festival. Clippings files, scrapbooks, photograph files, video-recordings of performances dating from 1955, as well as press, performance, and faculty records. American Dance Festival Archives, Duke University.

Humphrey, Doris. Notated Theatrical Dances. Labanotation scores for several of Humphrey's dances that were choreographed for the Limón company. Films or videotapes are available for some items. Dance Notation Bureau, New York City.

———. Papers, 1925–1957. Includes 33 items of correspondence between Doris Humphrey and José Limón and/or Pauline Lawrence Limón. Dance Collection, New York Public Library for the Performing Arts (hereafter referred to as DC-NYPL).

José Limón Dance Company. Clippings. DC-NYPL.

Juilliard School. Production files of Limón works produced by the Juilliard Dance Ensemble as well as performances by the Limón company that took place at the Juilliard School. These files include correspondence, clippings, programs, rehearsal photographs, and production photographs. Biographical file on Limón including clippings and photographs. Faculty records. 1951–1972. Juilliard School Archives, New York City.

King, Eleanor. Papers, 1931–1991. DC-NYPL.

Lawrence, Pauline. Letters to Doris Humphrey, 1931–1951. 64 items. Doris Humphrey Collection. DC-NYPL.

———. Pauline Lawrence Limón Collection. Documents the early years of the Limón company. Personal correspondence, including 196 letters between Pauline and José Limón, 594 items of professional correspondence, choreographic notes, costume sketches, performance contracts, legal documents, bills, and financial records. DC-NYPL.

Limón, José. Clippings. Material divided chronologically into five folders: to 1949, 1950–1959, 1960–1967, 1968–1972, undated. DC-NYPL.

———. Collection of Printed Music Used by José Limón. 18 pieces with choreographic notes. DC-NYPL.

———. Correspondence. American Ballet Theatre. Records, 1936–ca. 1967. DC-NYPL.

———. Correspondence with Agnes de Mille. 14 items. Agnes de Mille Collection. DC-NYPL.

———. Letters to Doris Humphrey. Doris Humphrey Collection, 1940–1954. DC-NYPL.

———. Miscellaneous Manuscripts. Includes letters to Hans Hacker, Marian Horosko, and Regina Woody. DC-NYPL.

——. Notated Dances. Labanotation scores for six of Limón's dances. Pauline Lawrence Limón Collection. DC-NYPL.

——. Notated Theatrical Dances. Labanotation scores for fifteen of Limón's dances. Films or videotapes available for some. Dance Notation Bureau, New York City.

——. Papers, ca. 1927–1972. Personal and professional correspondence; Limón autobiography and other writings; choreographic and production notes; dance chronologies; legal documents; memorabilia; financial records. DC-NYPL.

——. Papers, Clippings, Correspondence, Programs, Contracts. José Limón Dance Foundation, New York City.

——. Programs, 1929–1972. Programs for most performances in which Limón danced and works that he choreographed or directed. DC-NYPL.

——. Scrapbook: Programs and Clippings, 1943–1944. Covers the period during which Limón served in the U.S. Army. DC-NYPL.

——. Scrapbook: Programs, Clippings, School Announcements, 1937–1945. Includes material on Limón's activities at Bennington and Mills Colleges, the musical comedy *Keep Off the Grass*, and Limón's appearances with May O'Donnell. DC-NYPL.

Page, Ruth. Scrapbooks: v. 13, 1949–1951. Programs and clippings from the 1950 Paris tour of Page's Les Ballets Américains in which Limón participated. DC-NYPL.

Schwartz, Sheldon. Supplement to *The Choreographic Works of José Limón* by Juliette Waung. 1973. DC-NYPL.

Books and Articles

Adler, Diane. "'To You I Hand the Torch': The Vital Continuity from Teacher to Student." *Dance Magazine*, July 1953, pp. 36–37.

Anderson, Jack. "José Limón: Obituary." *The Dancing Times*, Jan. 1973, p. 200.

Baril, Jacques. "Les fondateurs de la *modern dance* aux Etats-Unis—2e génération." In *La Danse Moderne*. Paris: Vigot, 1977.

Barnes, Clive. "José Limón Interprets Saga of Maximilian and Carlota, American Dance Marathon, New York, October 5, 1972." *The New York Times*, 6 Oct. 1972, p. 8.

Barthel, Joan. "'Dancers Are Chosen People.'" *The New York Times*, 31 July 1966, sec. 2, p. 12.

Becker, Svea. "From Humphrey to Limón: A Modern Dance Tradition." *Dance Notation Journal*, 2, no. 1 (Spring 1984), pp. 37–52.

Beiswanger, George. "New London: Residues and Reflections, Part V." *Dance Observer*, Mar. 1957, pp. 37–39.

Bird, Dorothy, with Joyce Greenberg. *Bird's Eye View: Dancing with Martha Graham and on Broadway*. Foreword by Marcia B. Siegel. Pittsburgh: University of Pittsburgh Press, 1997.

Burnside, Fiona. "Intellectuality Versus Emotionality: A Comparison of Modern Dance Techniques." *Ballett International*, Sept. 1991, pp. 20–23.

Burt, Ramsay. *The Male Dancer: Bodies, Spectacle, Sexualities*. London: Routledge, 1995, pp. 101–134.

Cohen, Selma Jeanne. *Doris Humphrey: An Artist First*. Middletown, Conn.: Wesleyan University Press, 1972.

Copel, Melinda. "The 1954 Limón Company Tour to South America: Goodwill

Tour or Cold War Cultural Propaganda?" In *José Limón: The Artist Re-viewed*, edited by June Dunbar. Amsterdam: Harewood Academic Publishers, 1999.

"Creative Togetherness. Louis Falco Talks to D and D." *Dance and Dancers*, Oct. 1973, pp. 22–26.

Cunningham, Katherine S. "A Legacy of José Limón." *Dance Scope*, 7, no. 2 (Spring/Summer 1973), pp. 6–13.

"Dance and Diplomacy." *Dance Magazine*, Mar. 1961, p. 13.

"*Dance Magazine*'s 1957 Awards: The Presentation." *Dance Magazine*, Mar. 1958, pp. 30–33, 65–71.

"*Dance Magazine*'s Awards." *Dance Magazine*, Feb. 1958, pp. 27, 34–35.

"D.C. Representative Presents Capezio Award to Limón." *Dance News*, Apr. 1964, p. 5.

De Mille, Agnes. *The Dance in America*. Washington, D.C.: United States Information Service, 1971.

Dunbar, June, ed. *José Limón: The Artist Re-viewed*. Amsterdam: Harewood Academic Publishers, 1999.

Duncan, Donald. "José Limón Reports on Asia Tour." *Dance Magazine*, Feb. 1964, pp. 31–32.

Dunham, Anne. "Modern Dance Evolution in Mexico." *Mexican-American Review*, Dec. 1951, pp. 30–32, 106, 108, 110.

Durán, Lin. "La creatividad de José Limón." *México en el Arte*, 25 (Spring 1990), pp. 73–77.

"The Four Suns: A Mexican Legend in Ballet." *Dance Magazine*, June 1951, pp. 18–19.

Gottlieb, Beatrice. "The Theatre of José Limón." *Theatre Arts*, Nov. 1951, pp. 27, 94–95.

Hering, Doris. "Dance Debuts at Lincoln Center." *Dance Magazine*, Feb. 1963, p. 23.

———. "José Limón: Midstream Vintage Years in Retrospect." *Dance Magazine*, Nov. 1973, pp. 42–47.

"L'Héritage Humphrey-Limón." *Nouvelles de Danse*, no. 24 (Summer 1995), pp. 9–102. Includes articles by Daniel Dobbels, Marilen Breuker, Marcia B. Siegel, Lawrence Louppe, Selma Jeanne Cohen, Doris Humphrey, and Marion Bastien.

Hill, Martha. "José Limón and His Biblical Works." *Choreography and Dance*, 2, pt. 3 (1992), pp. 57–61.

Hollander, Michael. "*Mazurkas*: Origins, Choreography, Significance." In *José Limón: The Artist Re-viewed*, edited by June Dunbar. Amsterdam: Harewood Academic Publishers, 1999.

Humphrey, Doris. "Doris Humphrey Answers the Critics." *Dance and Dancers*, Mar. 1959, pp. 21.

Jones, Betty. "Voices of the Body." In *José Limón: The Artist Re-viewed*, edited by June Dunbar. Amsterdam: Harewood Academic Publishers, 1999.

"José Limón." *Cuadernos del CID-Danza*, no. 3 (1985), pp. 1–16. Includes articles by Rosa Reyna, C. Delgado Martínez, and José Limón.

"José Limón." *Current Biography*. New York: H. W. Wilson, 1968.

"José Limón and Company to Tour Europe and Near East." *Dance Observer*, Feb. 1957, pp. 23.

Jouhet, Serge. "José Limón, ou le rêve humaniste." *Danser*, July–Sept. 1983, pp. 48–49.

Jowitt, Deborah. "Modern Movers." In *Time and the Dancing Image*. Berkeley: University of California Press, 1988, pp. 149–198.

Karstens, Lindley Crouch. *Dance Collage*. Urbana, Ill.: University of Illinois Press, 1974, pp. 96–99.

King, Eleanor. *Transformations: A Memoir by Eleanor King: The Humphrey-Weidman Era*. Brooklyn, N.Y.: Dance Horizons, 1978.

Kisselgoff, Anna. "'Lysistrata' in Limón's Eyes." *The New York Times*, 12 Aug. 1968, pp. 13, 19.

Koner, Pauline. *Solitary Song*. Durham: Duke University Press, 1986.

——. "The Truth About 'The Moor's Pavane.'" *Ballet Review*, 8, no. 4 (1980), pp. 387–396.

Kriegsman, Sali Ann. *Modern Dance in America: The Bennington Years*. Boston: G. K. Hall, 1981.

Kupferberg, Herbert. "José Limón, Modern Dance Pioneer, Dead at 64." *Dance News*, Jan. 1973, pp. 1, 4.

Lewis, Daniel. *The Illustrated Dance Technique of José Limón*. New York: Harper and Row, 1984.

Limón, José. "An American Accent." In *The Modern Dance: Seven Statements of Belief*, edited by Selma Jeanne Cohen. Middletown, Conn.: Wesleyan University Press, 1966, pp. 17–27.

——. "American Dance on Tour." *The Juilliard Review*, Spring 1958, pp. 8–11, 25–28.

——. "Composing a Dance." *The Juilliard Review*, 2, no. 1 (Winter 1955), pp. 17–23.

——. "Dance in Education—Four Statements: Jean Erdman, Alwin Nikolais, Patricia Wilde, José Limón." *Impulse* (1968), pp. 64–81.

——. "Dancers are Musicians are Dancers." *Juilliard Review Annual* (1966–1967), pp. 4–10.

——. "The Dancers' Status Here and Abroad: Comparisons and Observations." *Dance Observer*, Mar. 1958, pp. 37–39.

——. "Dialogues: Two Dramatic Dances by José Limón." *Dance Magazine*, Aug. 1951, pp. 14–15.

——. "El lenguaje de la danza." *El Universal*, Nov. 1960, sec. 4, p. 3. Reprinted in *Cuadernos del CID-Danza*, no. 3 (1985), pp. 1–16.

——. "'Tonanzintla' [sic]: A Ballet by José Limón." *Dance Magazine*, Aug. 1951, pp. 12–13, 28–29.

——. "Music is the Strongest Ally to a Dancer's Way of Life." In *The Dance Experience*, edited by Myron Howard Nadel and Constance Gwen Nadel. New York: Praeger, 1970, pp. 189–194.

——. "The Universities and the Arts." *Dance Scope*, 1, no. 2 (Spring 1965), pp. 23–27.

——. "The Virile Dance." In *The Dance Has Many Faces*, edited by Walter Sorell. 2d ed. New York: Columbia University Press, 1966, pp. 82–86.

Lloyd, Margaret. "José Limón." In *The Borzoi Book of Modern Dance*. New York: Knopf, 1949, pp. 198–213.

Lubell, Naomi. "José Limón—Interview." *Dance Observer*, Aug.–Sept. 1937, p. 78.

Mahler, Elfrida, Ramiro Guerra, and José Limón. *Fundamentos de la danza*. 2d ed. Havana: Editorial Pueblo y Educación, 1982.

Manasevit, Shirley D. "A Last Interview with Charles Weidman." *Dance Scope*, 10, no. 1 (Fall 1975–Winter 1976), pp. 32–50.

Manchester, Phyllis Winifred. "Seventh American Dance Festival." *Dance News*, Sept. 1954, p. 11.

Marks, J. "The Signature of Locality: José Limón in San Francisco." *Dance Digest*, May 1957, pp. 170–174.

Martin, John. "Auspicious Debut." *The New York Times*, 27 May 1945, sec. 2, p. 7.

———. "Diplomacy: Limón Makes Conquest in South America." *The New York Times*, 23 Jan. 1955, sec. 2, p. 11.

———. "José Limón Comes Into His Own—Helen Tamiris and 'It's Up to You.'" *The New York Times*, 4 Apr. 1943, sec. 2, p. 5.

———. "Limón: Artist Undertakes Mexican Government Project." *The New York Times*, 24 Dec. 1950, sec. 2, p. 6.

———. "A Major Force Enters the Field." *The New York Times*, 12 Jan. 1947, sec. 2, p. 3.

———. "'Missa': José Limón's Tribute to the Human Spirit." *The New York Times*, 18 May 1958, sec. 2, p. 14.

———. "A Tour: Limón to South America with Government Aid." *The New York Times*, 14 Nov. 1954, sec. 2, p. 13.

Maxwell, Carla. "Artistic Succession and Leadership in a Modern Dance Company." In *José Limón: The Artist Re-viewed*, edited by June Dunbar. Amsterdam: Harewood Academic Publishers, 1999.

McDonagh, Don. "José Limón." In *The Complete Guide to Modern Dance*. Garden City, N.Y.: Doubleday, 1976, pp. 203–210.

Mindlin, Naomi. "José Limón's *The Moor's Pavane*: An Interview with Lucas Hoving." *Dance Research Journal*, 24, no. 1 (Spring 1992), pp. 13–26.

Moore, Lillian. "José Limón." *The Dancing Times*, Sept. 1957, pp. 537–538.

Mueller, John E. "Dancefilms: Limón's Tormented Traitor." *Dance Magazine*, May 1981, pp. 26–30.

Murphy, Ann. "Lucas Hoving and José Limón: Radical Dancers." In *José Limón: The Artist Re-viewed*, edited by June Dunbar. Amsterdam: Harewood Academic Publishers, 1999.

"Obituary: José Limón." *Britannica Book of the Year*. Chicago: Encyclopedia Britannica, 1973.

Owen, Norton. "The Dance Heroes of José Limón." In *José Limón: The Artist Re-viewed*, edited by June Dunbar. Amsterdam: Harewood Academic Publishers, 1999.

Palmer, Winthrop. "José Limón." *Dance News Annual*, 1953, pp. 72–78.

Peralta, Delfor. "José Limón." *Danse et Rythmes*, Oct.–Nov. 1957, pp. 10–11.

Pollack, Barbara. "José Limón and Company in Europe." *Dance Magazine*, Apr. 1958, pp. 32–33, 75–79.

———, and Charles Humphrey Woodford. *Dance is a Moment: A Portrait of José Limón in Words and Pictures*. Pennington, N.J.: Princeton Book Company, 1993.

Prevots, Naima. *Dance for Export: Cultural Diplomacy and the Cold War*. Hanover, N.H.: Wesleyan University Press/University Press of New England, 1998.

———. "$410—Was That a Necessary Expense?" In *Proceedings of the Society of Dance History Scholars* (1992), pp. 1–10.

Schulman, Alvin. "The Modern Dance Goes to South America." *Dance Observer*, Mar. 1955, pp. 33–34.

"Season in Review." *Dance Magazine*, Feb. 1953, pp. 53–54, 56, 58.

Shearer, Sybil. "Chicago." *Ballet Review*, 23, no. 2 (Summer 1995), pp. 9–11.

Siegel, Marcia B. *Days on Earth: The Dance of Doris Humphrey*. New Haven: Yale University Press, 1987.

———. "José Limón (1908–1972)." *Ballet Review*, 4, no. 4 (1973), pp. 100–104.

———. *The Shapes of Change: Images of American Dance*. Berkeley: University of California Press, 1979.

Sorell, Walter. "Memorial for José Limón, The Juilliard School, Lincoln Center, December 14, 1972." *Dance News*, Jan. 1973, p. 4.

Stackhouse, Sarah. "The Essence of Humanity: José Limón After a Half-Century." In *José Limón: The Artist Re-viewed*, edited by June Dunbar. Amsterdam: Harewood Academic Publishers, 1999.

Tegeder, Ulrich. "Knowing the Common Roots: An Interview with Carla Maxwell and Anna Sokolow." *Ballett International*, Nov. 1984, pp. 8–13.

Terry, Walter. "Doris Humphrey's Dance Works and the Dancing of José Limón." *New York Herald Tribune*, 28 Dec. 1947, sec. 5, p. 2.

———. "Limón's 'The Traitor.'" *New York Herald Tribune*, 29 Aug. 1954, sec. 4, p. 2.

———. "Mexico Produces a New Triumvirate: Limón, Chávez, Covarrubias." *Dance Magazine*, June 1951, pp. 17, 40.

Tipton, Jennifer. "Thomas Skelton, Lighting Designer." In *José Limón: The Artist Re-viewed*, edited by June Dunbar. Amsterdam: Harewood Academic Publishers, 1999.

Todd, Arthur. "Mexico Responds to Modern Dance and José Limón." *Dance Observer*, Mar. 1951, pp. 39–40.

———. "Transatlantic Exchange: Limón for London." *Dance and Dancers*, Sept. 1957, pp. 11–14.

Tomlinson, Charles D. "Paulina Regina." In *José Limón: The Artist Re-viewed*, edited by June Dunbar. Amsterdam: Harewood Academic Publishers, 1999.

Umboldi, Oscar. "José Limón y el lenguaje más elocuente." *Buenos Aires Musical*, 15, no. 245 (19 Oct. 1960), p. 1.

Vachon, Ann. "Limón in Mexico: Mexico in Limón." In *José Limón: The Artist Re-viewed*, edited by June Dunbar. Amsterdam: Harewood Academic Publishers, 1999.

Warren, Larry. *Anna Sokolow: The Rebellious Spirit*. Pennington, N.J.: Princeton Book Company, 1991.

Waung, Juliette. *The Choreographic Works of José Limón*. New York: Juilliard School of Music, 1957.

Woodford, Charles H. "My Dance Family." In *José Limón: The Artist Re-viewed*, edited by June Dunbar. Amsterdam: Harewood Academic Publishers, 1999.

Unpublished Theses and Dissertations

Alpert, Carol Sue. "Doris Humphrey's Influence on José Limón." M.F.A. thesis, University of Oklahoma, 1972.

Burgering, Jacques J. "Lucas Hoving: The Circle That Goes Around." M.A. thesis, American University, 1995.

Friesen, Joanna. "A Comparative Analysis of 'Othello' and 'The Moor's Pavane': An Aristotelian Approach to Dances Based on Dramatic Literature." Ph.D. diss., Florida State University, 1977.

Gibbons, Ruth Elizabeth Goodling. "A Prismatic Approach to the Analysis of Style in Dance." Ph.D. diss., Texas Women's University, 1989.

Kress, Penny Pruitt. "The Legacy of José Limón." M.A. thesis, American University, 1982.

Wynne, Kathleen Mary. "The Life and Contribution of José Limón." M.S. thesis, Smith College, 1965.

Photographs

The José Limón Dance Foundation maintains an extensive collection of photographs dating from the inception of the Limón company to the present day. Included are approximately ten boxes of 8 x 10 prints and five boxes of oversized prints by various photographers. Filed according to dance titles, the photographs document the entire repertory of the company, including works by choreographers other than Limón. Access to the collection is by appointment only.

In addition to the very extensive holdings detailed below at the Dance Collection, the New York Public Library's Billy Rose Theatre Collection houses many items relating to Limón's Broadway career.

Antígona. Photographs by Walter Reuter and others. Limón Choreography: Photographs, v. 1, nos. 1.1–1.11. DC-NYPL.

Barren Sceptre. Limón Choreography: Photographs, v. 1, nos. 3.1–3.3. DC-NYPL.

Chaconne. Photographs by Marcus Blechman, Barbara Morgan, Gerda Peterich, and Walter Strate. Limón Choreography: Oversize Photographs, v. 1, nos. 1–5; Limón Choreography: Photographs, v. 1, nos 4.1–4.7. DC-NYPL.

A Choreographic Offering. Photographs by Philip A. Biscuti, Daniel Lewis, Fannie Helen Melcer, and Jack Mitchell. Limón Choreography: Photographs, v. 1, nos. 5.1–5.16. DC-NYPL.

Concerto Grosso. Photographs by John Lindquist, Fannie Helen Melcer, Gjon Mili, Gerda Peterich, and Walter Strate. Limón Choreography: Oversize Photographs, v. 1, nos. 15–18; Limón Choreography: Photographs, v. 2. DC-NYPL.

Danzas Mexicanas. Photographs by Don Forbes, John Lindquist, Barbara Morgan, and others. Limón Choreography: Photographs, v. 4, nos. 9.1–9.23. DC-NYPL.

Day on Earth. Photographs by Gjon Mili and others. Humphrey Choreography: Oversize Photographs, nos. 2–6. DC-NYPL.

Deliver the Goods. Photographs by the U.S. Army Camp Special Services Office, Camp Lee, Virginia, 1944. Limón Choreography: Photographs, v. 4, nos. 10.1–10.18. DC-NYPL.

The Demon. Limón Choreography: Photographs, v. 4, nos. 11.1–11.8. DC-NYPL.

Dialogues. Photographs by John Lindquist and Jacqueline Paul Roberts. Limón Choreography: Limón Choreography: Photographs, v. 4, nos. 12.1–12.20. DC-NYPL.

El Salón México. Photographs by Marcus Blechman. Humphrey Choreography: Oversize Photographs, nos. 53–57. DC-NYPL.

The Emperor Jones. Photographs by Radford Bascome, Gjon Mili, Harold G. Swahn, and others. Limón Choreography: Oversize Photographs, v. 1, nos. 25–26; Limón Choreography: Photographs, v. 5. DC-NYPL.

The Exiles. Photographs by Peter Basch, Philip A. Biscuti, John Lindquist, Robert I. Perry, W. H. Stephan, Walter Strate, and others. Limón Choreography: Oversize Photographs, v. 1, nos. 27–32; Limón Choreography: Photographs, v. 6, nos. 15.1–15.16. DC-NYPL.

Gray, Harriette Ann. Photographs. Includes photos of Limón. DC-NYPL.

Humphrey Choreography: Oversize Photographs. 57 black-and-white photographs of dance works choreographed by Doris Humphrey. Arranged alphabetically by title of dance. DC-NYPL.

Humphrey and Weidman Choreography: Photographs, ca. 1930–1970. 592 items in 8 volumes. Black-and-white photographs and a few color snapshots of forty dances choreographed by either Doris Humphrey or Charles Weidman. Arranged alphabetically by title of dance. DC-NYPL.

Humphrey-Weidman Group. Many photographs of Limón by Marcus Blechman, Thomas Bouchard, Alfred A. Cohn, Helen Hewett, Edward Moeller, Barbara Morgan, Maurice Seymour, and others, 1930–1943. DC-NYPL.

José Limón and Pauline Lawrence Limón Photograph Files, ca. 1910–1972. 1,342 black-and-white photographs. Includes childhood and family pictures as well as publicity shots of the company during its foreign tours. DC-NYPL.

La Malinche. Photographs by Marcus Blechman, Walter Strate, and Matthew Wysocki. Limón Choreography: Oversize Photographs, v. 1, nos. 33a–35; Limón Choreography: Photographs, v. 6, nos. 21.1–21.21. DC-NYPL.

Lament for Ignacio Sánchez Mejías. Photographs by John Lindquist, Jack Mitchell, Carmen Schiavone, Walter Strate, and Martha Swope. Humphrey Choreography: Oversize Photographs, nos. 16–37. DC-NYPL.

Limón Choreography: Oversize Photographs. 105 items in 2 volumes. Black-and-white photographs of dance works choreographed by José Limón. Arranged alphabetically by title of dance. DC-NYPL.

Limón Choreography: Photographs. 815 items in 14 volumes. Mostly black-and-white photographs of dance works choreographed by José Limón, ca. 1936–1972. Arranged alphabetically by title of dance. DC-NYPL.

Limón, José. Photographs. American Dance Festival Archives, Duke University.

Lindquist, John. Photographs. Pictures of Limón taken at Jacob's Pillow. Harvard Theatre Collection.

Los Cuatro Soles. Photographs by Walter Reuter and others. Limón Choreography: Photographs, v. 3. DC-NYPL.

Missa Brevis. Photographs by Warren Ballard, Philip A. Biscuti, Fannie Helen Melcer, Jack Mitchell, Marcia Roltner, and Dora Cargille Sanders. Limón Choreography: Photographs, v. 7. DC-NYPL.

The Moor's Pavane. Over 100 photographs by Arnold Eagle, Daniel Lewis, John Lindquist, Fannie Helen Melcer, Jack Mitchell, Gerda Peterich, Walter Reuter, Arks Smith, Alex Smoot, Walter Strate, and others. Limón Choreography: Photographs, v. 8; Limón Choreography: Oversize Photographs, v. 1, nos. 37–39, 41–43. DC-NYPL.

Museum of Modern Art. Photographs Expressional. Includes photographs of Limón by Romaine, Soichi Sunami, and others, 1930s–1940s. DC-NYPL.

My Son, My Enemy. Photographs by Farrell Grehan and Martha Swope, 1965. Limón Choreography: Oversize Photographs, v. 2, nos. 44–59; Limón Choreography: Photographs, v. 9, nos. 25.1–25.19. DC-NYPL.

New Dance. Photographs by Gjon Mili. Humphrey Choreography: Oversize Photographs, nos. 39–41. DC-NYPL.

Night Spell. Photograph by Walter Strate. Humphrey Choreography: Oversize Photographs, no. 42. DC-NYPL.

Ode to the Dance. Photographs by Arnold Eagle. Limón Choreography: Photographs, v. 9, nos. 26.1–26.42. DC-NYPL.

Ritmo Jondo. Humphrey Choreography: Oversize Photographs; Humphrey and Weidman Choreography: Photographs, v. 5. DC-NYPL.

Ruins and Visions. Photographs by Peter Basch. Humphrey Choreography: Oversize Photographs, nos. 45–52. DC-NYPL.

Sonata for Two Cellos. Limón Choreography: Photographs, v. 10, nos. 30.1–30.3. DC-NYPL.

The Story of Mankind. Humphrey and Weidman Choreography: Photographs, vols. 7 and 8. DC-NYPL.

Symphony for Strings. Photographs by Matthew Wysocki. Limón Choreography: Photographs, v. 10, nos. 32.1–32.5. DC-NYPL.

There is a Time. Photographs by Daniel Lewis, Fannie Helen Melcer, Gjon Mili, W. H. Stephan, and Matthew Wysocki. Limón Choreography: Oversize Photographs, v. 2, nos. 85–94; Limón Choreography: Photographs, v. 11 (55 items). DC-NYPL.

This Story is Legend. Photographs by Barbara Morgan and Romaine. Limón Choreography: Photographs, v. 12, nos. 35.1–35.5. DC-NYPL.

As Thousands Cheer. Photographs by Edward Moeller, Maurice Seymour, and Vandamm Studio. Humphrey-Weidman Group: Photographs, no. 173–178. Additional photographs in Musical Comedies: As Thousands Cheer (Photographs).

Three Inventories on Casey Jones. Photographs by Romaine. Limón Choreography: Photographs, v. 12, nos. 36.1–36.2. DC-NYPL.

Tonantzintla. Photographs by John Lindquist, Jack Mitchell, Robert I. Perry, and Walter Reuter. Limón Choreography: Oversize Photographs, v. 2, no. 95–96; Limón Choreography: Photographs, v. 12, nos. 37.1–37.31. DC-NYPL.

The Traitor. Photographs by Sandor Acs, Fannie Helen Melcer, Arks Smith, W. H. Stephan, Walter Strate, and Matthew Wysocki. Limón Choreography: Oversize Photographs, v. 2, nos. 98–100; Limón Choreography: Photographs, v. 13. DC-NYPL.

War Lyrics. Limón Choreography: Photographs, v. 14, nos. 43.1–43.8. DC-NYPL.

Western Folk Suite. Photographs by Marcus Blechman and Barbara Morgan. Limón Choreography: Oversize Photographs, v. 2, no. 103; Limón Choreography: Photographs, v. 14, nos. 44.1–44.5. DC-NYPL.

Wood, Roger. Dance photographs, 1944–1961. Chiefly 35 mm. negatives. Includes images of Limón. DC-NYPL.

Films and Videorecordings

There are more than 300 films and videotapes of Limón dances in the José Limón Dance Foundation Archives. The collection is open to qualified researchers by appointment but is mainly utilized by the Limón Dance Company to aid in mounting revivals. Many of the older recordings are duplicated in the Dance Collection, New York Public Library for the Performing Arts, where they are readily available to the public. Most of the Limón Foundation's videotapes were recorded in performance during the 1980s and 1990s.

All films in the Juilliard School Archives are also at the Dance Collection.

40 Years of Dance on BBC Television: From Karsavina to Mukhamedov; from "The Moor's Pavane" to "Strange Fish". 93 min., sd., b/w and color. Videocassette. [Second in a series of three screenings of BBC television programs on dance presented by the Dance Collection in conjunction with the BBC. Includes *The Moor's Pavane*, directed by Margaret Dale, 1957, with José Limón, Lucas Hoving, Pauline Koner, and Betty Jones.] DC-NYPL.

American Dance Festival Gala. Videotaped in performance by Dennis Diamond, Duke University, 17 June 1978. 95 min., sd., b/w. Videocassette. [Cassette 2 includes an interview with José Limón (excerpt from *Festival of the Dance*), an introduction to *The Moor's Pavane* with Lucas Hoving, Betty Jones, and Pauline Koner, and a performance of *The Moor's Pavane*.] DC-NYPL.

Black Choreographers' Social Comment in Their Work. "Eye on Dance," no. 119. Aired on WNYC-TV, 7 May 1984. 29 min., sd., color with b/w sequence. Videocassette. [In "Esoterica Balletica," Daniel Lewis discusses two works by José Limón, *The Unsung* and *The Winged*.] DC-NYPL.

Body Mechanics and Fundamental Movement. Filmed by Portia Mansfield, n.d. 16 mm., 30 1/2 min., si., color with b/w sequences. [Reel 2 contains footage of José Limón teaching dance to children.] DC-NYPL.

A Charles Weidman Celebration. Produced by the Charles Weidman School of Modern Dance, assisted by the Dance Collection, 30 Apr. 1989. 156 min., sd., color. [Cassettes 1 and 2 contain a panel discussion on the influence of Charles Weidman.] DC-NYPL.

Charles Weidman and Doris Humphrey. Filmed by Helen Knight, 1935–1939. 16 mm., 6 min., si., b/w. [Includes excerpts from José Limón's *Danzas Mexicanas* and Humphrey's *New Dance*.] DC-NYPL.

Contemporary Dance. Filmed by Portia Mansfield, 1946. 16 mm., 30 1/2 min., si., color. [Reel 1 includes José Limón in excerpts from *Danzas Mexicanas*.] DC-NYPL.

Creative Leisure. Produced by Herbert Kerkow, U.S. Department of the Army, 1951. 16 mm., 5 min., sd., b/w. [Scenes at Connecticut College School of Dance, including brief shots of José Limón and Doris Humphrey's *Invention*, performed by Limón, Betty Jones, and Ruth Currier.] DC-NYPL.

Creative Process: Graham, Humphrey and Limón. "Eye on Dance," no. 257. Aired on WNYC-TV, 25 Apr. 1988. 29 min., sd., color with b/w sequence. Videocassette. [Ruth Currier looks back on her past work as a dancer with the Limón company.] DC-NYPL.

Dance of the Century: From Modernism To Post-Modernism: American Dance. "Dance of the Century," no. 4. English version produced by Landseer Films of the series Danse du Siècle, coproduced by La Sept, Pathé Télévision, Duran, Ostankino, Sovtelexport, and Gédéon, in association with RAI 3, 1992. 53 min., sd., b/w and color. Videocassette. [Discussion of the technical and choreographic innovations of Doris Humphrey and her successor José Limón.

Includes excerpts from Humphrey's *Lament for Ignacio Sánchez Mejías* and Limón's *The Moor's Pavane*.] DC-NYPL.

Dance Companies: New York City Ballet vs. American Ballet Theatre. "Eye on Dance," no. 244. Aired on WNYC-TV, 7 Dec. 1987. 29 min., sd., color with b/w sequence. Videocassette. [Betty Jones reminisces about working with José Limón and Doris Humphrey. Includes a b/w excerpt from *The Moor's Pavane* with Limón, Lucas Hoving, and Pauline Koner.] DC-NYPL.

A Dance is Never Finished. Filmed in rehearsal at the Washington Cathedral in Washington, D.C. Aired on WETA-TV, 1968. 16 mm., 30 1/2 min., sd., b/w. [José Limón directs a rehearsal of *The Winged*. Performed by Louis Falco, Sarah Stackhouse, and Betty Jones (guest artist) with Jennifer Muller, Lenore Latimer, Jennifer Scanlon, Laura Glenn, Carla Maxwell, Tamara Woshakiwsky, Diane Mohrmann, Alice Condodina, Daniel Lewis, Fritz Ludin, Clyde Morgan, Avner Vered, Edward DeSoto, and Louis Solino.] DC-NYPL.

Dancers at Bennington School and Mills College. Filmed by Betty Lynd Thompson, 1938–1939. 16 mm., 14 1/2 min., si., color. [José Limón in an excerpt from *Danzas Mexicanas*.] DC-NYPL.

Dancers' Bodies: Preventing Dance Injuries. "Eye on Dance," no. 123. Aired on WNYC-TV, 21 May 1984. 28 min., sd., color. Videocassette. [In "Esoterica Balletica," Daniel Lewis discusses José Limón's *The Moor's Pavane*.] DC-NYPL.

A Dancer's Regime: The Daily Technique Class. "Eye on Dance," no. 233. Aired on WNYC-TV, 18 May 1987. 28 min., sd., color. Videocassette. [Betty Jones discusses Doris Humphrey's concept of fall and rebound, and José Limón's use of isolations and orchestrated movement.] DC-NYPL.

A Divine Madness. Directed by Leonard Aitken, 1979. 16 mm., 30 min., sd., color. [Documentary on the lives of Portia Mansfield and Charlotte Perry and the evolution of the Perry-Mansfield School of the Theatre and Dance. Includes dance excerpts performed by José Limón.] DC-NYPL.

Doris Humphrey. Filmed ca. 1935. 16 mm., 21 min., si., b/w. [Excerpts from Doris Humphrey's "Variations and Conclusion" from *New Dance* and Limón's *Danzas Mexicanas*.] DC-NYPL.

The Early Years: Aspects of Humphrey-Weidman. Videotaped by Ed Emshwiller at the State University of New York at Purchase, 10 Apr. 1981. 76 min., sd., color. [Video documentation of the festival "The Early Years: American Modern Dance from 1900 Through the 1930s." Includes lecture by Marcia Siegel, and panel discussion moderated by Siegel, with Eleanor King, Ernestine Stodelle, Letitia Ide, and Kenneth Bostock.] DC-NYPL.

The Early Years: Modern Dance on Film, 1900–1940. 1981. 21 min., sd., color. Videocassette. [Reflections on Bennington by José Limón and Charles Weidman; examples of Humphrey-Weidman technique, mid-1930s; Doris Humphrey's *Air for the G String*.] DC-NYPL.

Festival of the Dance: Glimpses Through Time of America's Own Art Form. Written and directed by Ted Steeg for the New Hampshire Network, 1973. 60 min., sd., b/w. Videocassette. [Includes interviews with Charles Weidman and José Limón, and excerpts from Doris Humphrey's *New Dance* and Limón's *The Emperor Jones*, performed by Clay Taliaferro and Edward DeSoto.] DC-NYPL.

Hoving, Lucas. *Lucas Hoving, a Life in Dance.* Directed by Thron Yeager.

Videotaped at the Theater Artaud, San Francisco, 3 Sept. 1991. 113 min., sd., color. DC-NYPL.

————. *Speaking of Dance: Lucas Hoving.* 1992. 55 min., sd., color. Videocassette. [An interview with Lucas Hoving.] DC-NYPL.

Humphrey, Doris. *Dance Overture.* Filmed by Helen Priest Rogers at Connecticut College, 1957. 16 mm., 10 1/2 min., si., b/w. DC-NYPL.

————. *Day on Earth.* Filmed by Helen Priest Rogers at Connecticut College, Film Notation Project, 1959. 19 1/2 min., sd., b/w. Videocassette. [Performed by José Limón, Letitia Ide, Ruth Currier, and Abigail English.] DC-NYPL.

————. *Day on Earth.* Filmed by Dwight Godwin, under the supervision of Martha Hill, at the Juilliard School, New York City, May 1972. 16 mm., 21 min., sd., color. [Directed by José Limón, with Letitia Ide, assisted by Billie Mahoney. Performed by Peter Sparling, Janet Eilber, Ann de Gange, Elizabeth Haight.] DC-NYPL.

————. *Fantasy and Fugue.* Excerpts. Filmed by Carol Lynn at Jacob's Pillow, Lee, Mass., 1953. 16 mm., 8 1/2 min., si., b/w. ["Fantasy" is performed by Betty Jones, José Limón, Lavina Nielsen, and Lucas Hoving; "Fugue in C Minor" by Betty Jones, José Limón, Lavina Nielsen, Lucas Hoving, Pauline Koner, and Ruth Currier.] DC-NYPL.

————. *Invention.* Filmed by Carol Lynn at Jacob's Pillow, 1951. 16 mm., 12 1/2 min., si., b/w. [Performed by José Limón, Betty Jones, and Ruth Currier.] DC-NYPL.

————. *Lament for Ignacio Sánchez Mejías.* Filmed by Helen Priest Rogers at Juilliard School, 1959. 16 mm., 19 1/2 min., si., b/w. [Performed by José Limón, Letitia Ide, Meg Mundy, and members of the Limón company.] DC-NYPL.

————. *Lament for Ignacio Sánchez Mejías.* Filmed by Dwight Godwin at the Juilliard School, under the supervision of Martha Hill, May 1972. 16 mm., 20 1/2 min., sd., color. [Directed by José Limón, assisted by Letitia Ide. Performed by members of the Juilliard Dance Ensemble.] DC-NYPL.

————. *Night Spell.* Filmed by Carol Lynn at Jacob's Pillow, 1952. 16 mm., 10 min., si., b/w. [Performed by José Limón, Lucas Hoving, Betty Jones, and Ruth Currier.] DC-NYPL.

————. *Night Spell.* Produced and directed by Dwight Godwin at Connecticut College, July 1960. 16 mm., 17 min., sd., b/w. [Performed by José Limón, Betty Jones, Ruth Currier, and Lucas Hoving.] DC-NYPL.

————. *Ritmo Jondo.* Excerpts. Filmed by Dwight Godwin, under the supervision of Martha Hill, at the Juilliard School, Feb. 1965. 16 mm., 12 1/2 min., sd., b/w. [Onstage rehearsal, directed by José Limón, assisted by Betty Jones. Performed by members of the Juilliard Dance Ensemble.] DC-NYPL.

————. *Ruins and Visions.* Excerpts. Filmed by Helen Priest Rogers at Connecticut College, 1957. 16 mm., 47 min., si., b/w. [Performed by Limón company.] DC-NYPL.

————. *Ruins and Visions.* Excerpts. Filmed by Helen Priest Rogers at Connecticut College, 1959. 16 mm., 11 min., si., b/w. [Performed by Limón company.] DC-NYPL.

————. *Ruins and Visions.* Excerpt. Filmed by Dwight Godwin, under the supervision of Martha Hill, at the Juilliard School, Apr. 1964. 16 mm., 8 min., sd., b/w. [Onstage rehearsal with members of the Juilliard Dance Ensemble.] DC-NYPL.

Humphrey-Weidman Company. Filmed by Ann Barzel at the Auditorium Theater, Chicago, 1938. 16 mm., 6 1/2 min., si., b/w. [Performance film featuring Doris Humphrey, Charles Weidman, José Limón, Bill Matons, Katherine Litz, Katherine Manning, and Sybil Shearer.] DC-NYPL.

Ide, Letitia. *Dance On: Letitia Ide*. Interview by Billie Mahoney. Directed by Sheri Carsello. Produced by Billie Mahoney in association with the Jazz Dance World Congress, Dance Films Association, and the International Dance Association, Aug. 1992. 29 min., sd., color. Videocassette. DC-NYPL.

José Limón. Filmed by Carol Lynn at Jacob's Pillow, 1948. 16 mm., 19 1/2 min., si., b/w. [Includes Limón's *Chaconne*, performed in practice clothes; *Sonata No. 4*, performed by José Limón and Miriam Pandor; an excerpt from *Concerto Grosso*, performed by José Limón, Miriam Pandor, and Betty Jones; and excerpts from Doris Humphrey's *Lament for Ignacio Sánchez Mejías*, performed by Limón and others.] DC-NYPL.

José Limón Technique, Volume 1. Taught by Daniel Lewis. Produced by Dennis Diamond, Video D Studios, 1987. 55 min., sd., color. DC-NYPL.

José Limón's Legacy: Humanity and Moral Dignity. "Eye on Dance," no. 310. Aired on WNYC-TV, 11 Feb. 1991. 29 min., sd., color with b/w sequences. [Includes excerpts from *The Moor's Pavane*, performed by Limón, Lucas Hoving, Betty Jones, and Pauline Koner, and *Missa Brevis*, performed by Carla Maxwell, Carlos Orta, Nina Watt, and others, as well as excerpts from a 1958 recording of the same work, performed by Limón and others.] DC-NYPL.

Koner, Pauline. *Dance On: Pauline Koner*. Interview by Billie Mahoney. Directed by William Hohauser, produced by Billie Mahoney, 8 Jan. 1984. 28 min., sd., b/w. DC-NYPL.

The Language of Dance. "A Time to Dance," no. 5. Conceived and written by Martha Myers, directed by Greg Harney, produced by Jac Venza, WGBH-TV, for National Educational Television, 1959. 16 mm., 29 min., sd., b/w. [Includes excerpts from *There is a Time*, performed by José Limón, Pauline Koner, with Lucas Hoving, Betty Jones, Lucy Venable, Lola Huth, Harlan McCallum, Chester Wolenski, and Robert Powell.] DC-NYPL.

Let's Take a Trip. Directed by Tim Kiley, written by Roger Englander, and produced by Stephen Fleischman for NBC-TV children's series "Let's Take a Trip," 1957. 16 mm., 28 min., sd., b/w. [A visit to the Dance Department of the Juilliard School. Includes footage of José Limón teaching a modern dance technique class and explaining what modern dance is all about. Excerpts from Humphrey's *Ritmo Jondo* featuring José Limón and Pauline Koner.] DC-NYPL.

Lewis, Daniel. *Dance On: Daniel Lewis*. Interview by Billie Mahoney. Directed by Lisa Green, produced by Video Workshop for Dance and Theatre, 14 Nov. 1982. 30 min., sd., b/w. DC-NYPL.

Limón, José. *The Apostate*. Excerpts filmed by Helen Priest Rogers at Connecticut College, 14 Aug. 1959. 13 min., si., b/w. [Performed by José Limón, Lucas Hoving, and Betty Jones.] DC-NYPL.

———. *The Apostate*. Produced and directed by Dwight Godwin at Connecticut College, July 1960. 16 mm., 22 min., sd., b/w. [Spoken introduction by José Limón. Performed by José Limón, Betty Jones, and Lucas Hoving.] DC-NYPL.

———. *Carlota*. Videotaped in rehearsal on 24 May 1976. 23 min., sd., b/w. [Performed by members of the Limón company without musical accompaniment.] DC-NYPL.

———. *Carlota*. Videotaped in performance at Duke University as part of the American Dance Festival Video Archival Project, July 1979. Directed by Dennis Diamond. 24 min., sd., b/w. [Performed by Carla Maxwell, Louis Solino, Robert Swinston, Sue Bernhard, Ginga Carmany, Nina Watt, Bill Cratty, Russell Lome, Jim May, and Douglas Varone.] DC-NYPL.

———. *Chaconne*. Filmed by Helen Priest Rogers at Connecticut College, 1954. 16 mm., 11 min., si., b/w. [Performed by José Limón.] DC-NYPL.

———. *Chaconne* (group version). Filmed by Helen Priest Rogers at Connecticut College, 17 Aug. 1962. 16 mm., 10 1/2 min., si., b/w. [Performed by members of Limón's 1962 repertory class during their final workshop.] DC-NYPL.

———. *A Choreographic Offering*. Filmed by Dwight Godwin at Connecticut College, 1964. 16 mm., 58 min., sd., b/w. [Performed by Betty Jones, Sarah Stackhouse, Louis Falco, members of the Limón company, and ensemble from Limón's advanced class. Unable to perform due to an injury, Limón rechoreographed his solo parts for Betty Jones.] DC-NYPL.

———. *Comedy*. Filmed in performance by Gardner Compton at Connecticut College, 10 Aug. 1968. 16 mm., 40 1/2 min., sd., b/w. [Performed by Jennifer Muller, Sarah Stackhouse, and Louis Falco, with Alice Condodina, Laura Glenn, Lenore Latimer, Carla Maxwell, Diane Mohrmann, Jennifer Scanlon, Tamara Woshakiwska, Edward DeSoto, Charles Hayward, Daniel Lewis, Clyde Morgan, Louis Solino, and Avner Vered.] DC-NYPL.

———. *Concerto Grosso*. Filmed by Carol Lynn at Jacob's Pillow, 1948–1952. 16 mm., 16 min., si., b/w. [Performed by José Limón, Miriam Pandor, and Betty Jones.] DC-NYPL.

———. *Concerto in D Minor After Vivaldi*. Filmed by Dwight Godwin at the Juilliard School, May 1963, under the supervision of Martha Hill. 16 mm., 12 1/2 min., sd., b/w. [Onstage rehearsal performed by members of the Juilliard Dance Ensemble.] DC-NYPL.

———. *Dances for Isadora*. Filmed by Dwight Godwin at Connecticut College, July 1972. 16 mm., 28 min., sd., b/w. [Performed by Ann Vachon, Carla Maxwell, Jennifer Scanlon, and Laura Glenn.] DC-NYPL.

———. *Dances: In Honor of Wraclaw, Warzawa, Poznan, and Katowice*. Filmed by Helen Priest Rogers at Connecticut College on 9 Aug. 1958. 16 mm., 32 min., si., b/w. [Performed by Ruth Currier, Lola Huth, Betty Jones, Lucy Venable, Michael Hollander, Harlan McCallum, and Chester Wolenski.] DC-NYPL.

———. *Dialogues*. Filmed by Carol Lynn at Jacob's Pillow, 1951. 16 mm., 15 1/2 min., si., b/w. [Performed by José Limón and Lucas Hoving.] DC-NYPL.

———. *The Emperor Jones*. Condensed version. Filmed by Helen Priest Rogers at Connecticut College, 17 Aug. 1957. 16 mm., 15 min., si., b/w. [Performed by José Limón, Lucas Hoving, Michael Hollander, Harlan McCallum, Chester Wolenski, Ronald Chase, Kenneth Bartmess, and Vol Quitzow.] DC-NYPL.

———. *The Emperor Jones*. Filmed in the 1950s. 16 mm., 23 min., sd., b/w. [Performed by José Limón, Lucas Hoving, and members of the Limón company.] DC-NYPL.

———. *The Emperor Jones*. Rehearsal film by Ted Steeg Productions at Connecticut College, 30 June 1972. 16 mm., 24 1/2 min., sd., color. [Staged by Daniel Lewis. Performed by Clay Taliaferro, Edward DeSoto, Raymond Johnson, Ryland Jordan, Rael Lamb, Marc Stevens, Ted Striggles, and Peter Woodin.] DC-NYPL.

———. *The Emperor Jones*. Filmed in performance by Ted Steeg Productions at Connecticut College, 28 July 1972. 16 mm., 24 1/2 min., sd., color. [Staged by Daniel Lewis. Performed by Clay Taliaferro, Edward DeSoto, Raymond Johnson, Ryland Jordan, Rael Lamb, Marc Stevens, Ted Striggles, and Peter Woodin.] DC-NYPL.

———. *The Emperor Jones*. Videotaped in performance at Connecticut College, 30 July 1972. 24 min., sd., b/w. [Staged by Daniel Lewis. Performed by Clay Taliaferro, Edward DeSoto, Raymond Johnson, Ryland Jordan, Rael Lamb, Marc Stevens, Ted Striggles, and Peter Woodin.] DC-NYPL.

———. *The Exiles*. Filmed by Helen Priest Rogers at Connecticut College, Aug. 1956. 17 min., si., b/w. Videocassette. [Onstage rehearsal in costume. Performed by José Limón and Ruth Currier.] DC-NYPL.

———. *The Exiles*. Filmed by Daniel Lewis at the 92nd Street YM-YWHA, 3 June 1969. 16 mm., 18 min., sd., b/w. [Performed by Sarah Stackhouse and Louis Falco.] DC-NYPL.

———. *MacAber's Dance*. Filmed by Dwight Godwin, under the supervision of Martha Hill, at the Juilliard School, May 1967. 16 mm., 21 min., sd., b/w. [Performed by members of the Juilliard Dance Ensemble.] DC-NYPL.

———. *La Malinche*. Filmed by Helen Priest Rogers at Connecticut College, 1962. 16 mm., 17 min., si., b/w. [Performed by José Limón, Lola Huth, and Harlan McCallum.] DC-NYPL.

———. *La Malinche*. Filmed by Dwight Godwin at the Juilliard School, Mar. 1968. 16 mm., 17 1/2 min., sd., b/w. [Rehearsal, in costume, directed by José Limón. Performed by members of the Juilliard Dance Ensemble.] DC-NYPL.

———. *La Malinche*. Filmed ca. 1969. 16 mm., 18 min., sd., b/w. [Performed by Daniel Lewis, Laura Glenn, and Edward DeSoto.] DC-NYPL.

———. *La Malinche*. Filmed by Bill Hannah for University of North Carolina Educational Television, Winston-Salem, 1971. 16 mm., 17 1/2 min., sd., color. [Performed by Pauline Koner, Gyula Pandi, and Edward DeSoto.] DC-NYPL.

———. *Mexican Suite*. Filmed in 1951. 16 mm., 2 1/2 min., si., b/w. [Excerpts from the "Peón" and "Revolucionario" sections of *Danzas Mexicanas*.] DC-NYPL.

———. *Missa Brevis*. Filmed by Helen Priest Rogers at the Juilliard School, 1958 or 1959. 16 mm., 30 1/2 min., si., b/w. [Performed by José Limón, Ruth Currier, Betty Jones, Lucy Venable, members of the José Limón Dance Company, and the Juilliard Dance Theatre.] DC-NYPL.

———. *Missa Brevis*. Filmed by Dwight Godwin at Connecticut College, Aug. 1963. 16 mm., 34 min., sd., b/w. [Performed by José Limón, Betty Jones, and members of the Limón company.] DC-NYPL.

———. *The Moor's Pavane*. Condensed version, directed and photographed by Walter Strate. 16 mm., 16 min., sd., color, 1950. [Performed by José Limón, Betty Jones, Lucas Hoving, and Ruth Currier.] DC-NYPL.

———. *The Moor's Pavane*. Filmed by Carol Lynn at Jacob's Pillow, 1951. 16 mm., 20 1/2 min., si., b/w. [Performed by José Limón, Lucas Hoving, Pauline Koner, and Betty Jones.] DC-NYPL.

———. *The Moor's Pavane*. Produced by Robert Saudek Associates. Aired on WCBS-TV in the "Omnibus" series, 15 Nov. 1953. 16 mm., 17 min., sd., b/w. [Performed by José Limón, Lucas Hoving, Pauline Koner, and Betty Jones.] DC-NYPL.

———. *The Moor's Pavane*. Filmed by Helen Priest Rogers at Connecticut College, 18 Aug. 1957. 16 mm., 18 1/2 min., si., b/w. [Performed by José Limón, Lucas Hoving, Pauline Koner, Betty Jones.] DC-NYPL.

——. *The Moor's Pavane*. Kinescope of an unidentified telecast, 1950s. 20 min., sd., b/w. [Performed by José Limón, Lucas Hoving, Pauline Koner, and Betty Jones.] DC-NYPL.

——. *The Moor's Pavane*. Filmed by Dwight Godwin at Connecticut College, July 1972. 16 mm., 22 min., sd., b/w. [Performed by Edward DeSoto, Daniel Lewis, Carla Maxwell, and Jennifer Scanlon.] DC-NYPL.

——. *The Moor's Pavane*. Videotaped in performance by Judith Mann at the 92nd Street YM-YWHA, 7 May 1974. 22 min., sd., color. [Performed by Clay Taliaferro, Louis Solino, Carla Maxwell, and Jennifer Scanlon.] DC-NYPL.

——. *The Moirai*. Filmed by Helen Priest Rogers at Connecticut College, 19 Aug. 1961. 16 mm., 27 1/2 min., si. at sd. speed, b/w. [Performed by Betty Jones, Lola Huth, Ruth Currier, and Chester Wolenski.] DC-NYPL.

——. *Orfeo*. Videotaped on 24 May 1976. 19 min., sd., b/w. [Dress rehearsal with members of the Limón company.] DC-NYPL.

——. *Performance*. Filmed by Dwight Godwin, under the supervision of Martha Hill, at the Juilliard School, Apr. 1961. 16 mm., 43 min., sd., b/w. [Performed by members of the Juilliard Dance Ensemble.] DC-NYPL.

——. *La Piñata*. Filmed by Dwight Godwin, under the supervision of Martha Hill, at the Juilliard School, Mar. 1969. 16 mm., 27 min., sd., color. [Onstage rehearsal with members of the Juilliard Dance Ensemble.] DC-NYPL.

——. *Psalm*. Filmed by Gardner Compton at Connecticut College, 1967. 16 mm., 40 min., sd., b/w. [Studio rehearsal by students of Connecticut College School of Dance.] DC-NYPL.

——. *Psalm*. Filmed by Dwight Godwin at Connecticut College, 1967. 16 mm., 40 min., sd., b/w. [Studio rehearsal in costume with Louis Falco, Sarah Stackhouse, Jennifer Muller, and ensemble.] DC-NYPL.

——. *Revel*. Filmed by Dwight Godwin, under the supervision of Martha Hill, at the Juilliard School, May 1971. 16 mm., 22 min., sd., color. [Stage rehearsal, performed by members of the Juilliard Dance Ensemble.] DC-NYPL.

——. *Scherzo*. Filmed at Connecticut College, ca. 1955. 16 mm., 11 min., si, b/w. [Performed by José Limón and three male dancers.] DC-NYPL.

——. *Serenata*. Filmed by Helen Priest Rogers at Connecticut College, 9 Aug. 1958. 16 mm., 15 1/2 min., si., b/w. [Performed by José Limón, Pauline Koner, Betty Jones, and Chester Wolenski.] DC-NYPL.

——. *Sonata for Two Cellos*. Filmed by Helen Priest Rogers at Connecticut College, 13 Aug. 1961. 16 mm., 12 min., si., b/w. [Performed by José Limón.] DC-NYPL.

——. *Symphony for Strings*. Excerpts. Filmed by Helen Priest Rogers at Connecticut College, Aug. 1955. 16 mm., 10 min., si., b/w. [Performed by José Limón, Pauline Koner, Lucas Hoving, Betty Jones, Ruth Currier, and Lavina Nielsen.] DC-NYPL.

——. *Symphony for Strings*. Filmed by Helen Priest Rogers at Connecticut College, Aug. 1955. 16 mm., 18 min., si., b/w. [Onstage rehearsal, in practice clothes. Performed by José Limón, Ruth Currier, Betty Jones, Pauline Koner, Lavina Nielsen, and Lucas Hoving.] DC-NYPL.

——. *Tenebrae 1914*. Filmed by Helen Priest Rogers at Connecticut College, 13 Aug. 1959. 16 mm., 26 1/2 min., si., b/w. [Performed by Ruth Currier, Harlan

McCallum, Chester Wolenski, Robert Powell, James Payton, and Stephen Paxton.] DC-NYPL.

———. *There is a Time*. Excerpts. Filmed by Helen Priest Rogers at Connecticut College, Aug. 1956. 16 mm., 38 1/2 min., si., b/w. [Performed by José Limón and members of his company.] DC-NYPL.

———. *There is a Time*. Filmed by Dwight Godwin at the Juilliard School, under the supervision of Martha Hill, May 1966. 16 mm., 39 min., sd., b/w. [Onstage rehearsal with members of the Juilliard Dance Ensemble.] DC-NYPL.

———. *There is a Time*. Filmed by Dwight Godwin at Connecticut College, July 1972. 16 mm., 38 1/2 min., sd., b/w. [Performed by Daniel Lewis, Edward De Soto, Ann Vachon, Clay Taliaferro, Laura Glenn, Louis Solino, and Jennifer Scanlon, with Nina Watt, Peter Sparling, Robyn Cutler, Ryland Jordan, Risa Steinberg, Carla Maxwell, Marc Stevens, and Aaron Osborne.] DC-NYPL.

———. *Tonantzintla*. Filmed by Dwight Godwin at the Juilliard School, Mar. 1968. 16 mm., 10 1/2 min., sd., color. [Rehearsal with sets and costumes. Performed by members of the Juilliard Dance Ensemble.] DC-NYPL.

———. *The Traitor*. Filmed by Helen Priest Rogers at Connecticut College, Aug. 1955. 16 mm., 20 min., si., b/w. [Performed by José Limón, Lucas Hoving, and members of the Limón company.] DC-NYPL.

———. *Two Essays for Large Ensemble*. Filmed by Dwight Godwin, under the supervision of Martha Hill, at the Juilliard School, Apr. 1964. 16 mm., 15 1/2 min., sd., b/w. [Onstage rehearsal with members of the Juilliard Dance Ensemble.] DC-NYPL.

———. *The Unsung*. Filmed by Dwight Godwin, under the supervision of Martha Hill, at the Juilliard School, 23 May 1970. 16 mm., 33 min., sd., b/w. [Onstage rehearsal with members of the Juilliard Dance Ensemble.] DC-NYPL.

———. *The Unsung*. Filmed by Dwight Godwin at Connecticut College, July 1972. 16 mm., 28 1/2 min., sd., b/w. [Performed by Edward DeSoto, Daniel Lewis, Aaron Osborne, Louis Solino, Peter Sparling, Ryland Jordan, and Marc Stevens.] DC-NYPL.

———. *Variations on a Theme of Paganini*. Filmed by Dwight Godwin, under the supervision of Martha Hill, at the Juilliard School, Feb. 1965. 16 mm., 14 1/2 min., sd., b/w. [Onstage rehearsal with members of the Juilliard Dance Ensemble.] DC-NYPL.

———. *The Winged*. Filmed by Dwight Godwin, under the supervision of Martha Hill, at the Juilliard School, May 1972. 16 mm., 40 1/2 min., sd., color. [Performed by members of the Juilliard Dance Ensemble.] DC-NYPL.

———. *The Winged*. Filmed by Dwight Godwin at Connecticut College, July 1972. 48 min., sd., b/w. Videocassette. [Performed by the Limón company.] DC-NYPL.

Limón, José, and Pauline Koner. *Barren Sceptre*. Filmed by Dwight Godwin at Connecticut College, July 1960. 16 mm., 26 1/2 min., sd., b/w. [Performed by José Limón and Pauline Koner. Includes a short discussion of the work by Limón and Koner.] DC-NYPL.

Limón, José, and May O'Donnell. *Curtain Raiser*. Filmed under the supervision of Betty Lynd Thompson as part of the series "Dances on American Themes," ca. 1941. 6 min., sd., color. Videocassette. [Performed by José Limón and May O'Donnell.] DC-NYPL.

Making Dance American. Directed by Lisa Jackson. Produced by Robert Kanter, Joseph Krakora, and the Eugene O'Neill Theater Center, in association with Robert Kanter Productions. Aired on Connecticut Public Television, 1986. 57 min., sd., color with b/w sequences. Videocassette. [May O'Donnell discusses her partnership with José Limón. Dance excerpts include *Curtain Raiser* and *Three Inventories on Casey Jones*, choreography and performance by O'Donnell and Limón.] DC-NYPL.

Martha Hill Video Project. Videotaped at the Hong Kong Academy for the Performing Arts during the Fifth Hong Kong International Dance Conference, July 1990. 342 min., sd., color. [Includes interview of Martha Hill by Daniel Lewis.] DC-NYPL.

May, Jim. *Dance On: Jim May*. Interview by Billie Mahoney. Produced by Billie Mahoney in association with Dance Films Association, July 1990. 30 min., sd., color. Videocassette. DC-NYPL.

Meeting the Challenge: The Bennington Years. "Eye on Dance," no. 223. Aired on WNYC-TV, 30 Mar. 1987. 29 min., sd., color with b/w sequences. Videocassette. [Daniel Lewis recalls working with José Limón on the creation of *The Unsung*. Includes excerpts from *Three Inventories on Casey Jones*, choreographed and performed by May O'Donnell and Limón, and Humphrey's *Invention*, performed by Limón, Betty Jones, and Ruth Currier.] DC-NYPL.

Modern Dance Selections. Filmed in performance by Ann Barzel, 1938–1970. 16 mm., 45 min., si., b/w and color. [Includes *La Malinche* and *The Story of Mankind*, filmed ca. 1949, and *La Malinche, There is a Time*, and *The Moor's Pavane*, filmed in 1970.] DC-NYPL.

Mythology and the Arts, Part 2: Artist as Hero. "Eye on Dance," no. 175. Aired on WNYC-TV, 12 Dec. 1985. 29 min., sd., color, Videocassette. [In "Esoterica Balletica," Daniel Lewis talks about his book, *The Illustrated Dance Technique of José Limón*. Jane Carrington demonstrates some of Limón's movement ideas.] DC-NYPL.

On Your Own: Jennifer Muller and Marjorie Mussman. "Eye on Dance," no. 8. Aired on WNYC-TV, 19 Feb. 1981. 29 min., sd., b/w. Videocassette. [Jennifer Muller and Marjorie Mussman recall their experiences as members of the Limón company.] DC-NYPL.

On Your Own: Peter Sparling and Nina Wiener. "Eye on Dance," no. 7. Aired on WNYC-TV, 12 Feb. 1981. 28 min., sd. b/w. Videocassette. [Peter Sparling talks about studying with José Limón at the Juilliard School and his subsequent entry into the Limón company.] DC-NYPL.

Passing on Dance: After the Founding Choreographer. "Eye on Dance," no. 63. Aired on WNYC-TV, 25 Oct. 1982. 28 min., sd., color. Videocassette. [Carla Maxwell, Daniel Lewis, and Milton Myers discuss the difficult process of continuing a dance company after the death of its founding choreographer. An excerpt from *There is a Time* is performed by the Limón company.] DC-NYPL.

Pauline Koner. Probably filmed at the North Carolina School of the Arts, ca. Feb. 1971. 16 mm., 31 min., sd., color. [Outtakes from a film or films featuring Pauline Koner. Includes a discussion of the creation of *La Malinche* as well as excerpts performed by Koner.] DC-NYPL.

Perry-Mansfield Celebrities. Filmed by Portia Mansfield, 1930–1950. 16 mm., 48 min., si., color. [Includes shots of Doris Humphrey, José Limón, and Charles Weidman.] DC-NYPL.

Political and Social Comment in Dance. "Eye on Dance," no. 116. Aired on WNYC-TV, 16 Apr. 1984. 29 min., sd., color. Videocassette. [In "Esoterica Balletica," Daniel Lewis talks about Limón's inspiration and choreography for *Missa Brevis*.] DC-NYPL.

Scanlon, Jennifer. *Dance On: Jennifer Scanlon*. Interview by Billie Mahoney. Directed by William Hohauser, produced by Video Workshop for Dance and Theatre, 25 Nov. 1984. 27 min., sd., color. Videocassette. DC-NYPL.

Students and Teachers at Bennington. Filmed by Ann Hutchinson Guest, 1939 and 1940s. 16 mm., 12 1/2 min., si., color. [Includes brief clips of Charles Weidman and Doris Humphrey as well as footage demonstrating elements of Humphrey technique.] DC-NYPL.

Taliaferro, Clay. *Dance On: Clay Taliaferro*. Interview by Billie Mahoney. Directed by Russell Aaronson, produced by Billie Mahoney, 8 Feb. 1981. 28 min., sd., b/w. Videocassette. DC-NYPL.

Teresita, Eleanor King, José Limón. Filmed by G. Mortimer Lichtenauer, 1931. 6 1/2 min., si., b/w. Videocassette. [Excerpts from *Mazurka* and *B Minor Suite*, choreographed and performed by Eleanor King and José Limón, and Limón's *Two Preludes*. Informal shots of Eleanor King, José Limón, and Charles Weidman.] DC-NYPL.

Terpsichorean Tales: German/American Modern Dance. "Eye on Dance," no. 165. Aired on WNYC-TV, 18 Oct. 1985. 28 min., sd., color. Videocassette. [Interview with Selma Jeanne Cohen, Letitia Ide, and Lutz Förster. Includes excerpts from Humphrey's *Day on Earth*, performed by the Daniel Lewis Dance Repertory Company, Limón's *The Moor's Pavane*, performed by the Limón company with Förster as Iago, and *There is a Time*, performed by the Limón company.] DC-NYPL.

Voices of Dance: Choreographers from the 50s and 60s. "Eye on Dance," no. 164. Produced by ARC Videodance. Aired on WNYC-TV, 24 June 1985. 29 min., sd., color. Videocassette. [Interview with Risa Steinberg, Jim May, and Toby Armour.] DC-NYPL.

Woodford, Charles Humphrey. *Dance On: Charles Humphrey Woodford*. Interview by Billie Mahoney, Aug. 1992. 30 min., sd., color. Videocassette. DC-NYPL.

Audiorecordings

Bales, William. Interview by Selma Jeanne Cohen, 16 Apr. 1971. [Reel 9 includes discussion of a cross-country tour with the Humphrey-Weidman Company in the late 1930s; Reel 10 of Doris Humphrey's work for and with José Limón after her retirement from dancing.] DC-NYPL.

Bales, William. Interview by Tobi Tobias, 23 Feb., 5 and 25 Mar., 18 Apr. 1977. Typescript available. [Reel 1 includes discussion of José Limón's classes; Reel 2 of Doris Humphrey, Charles Weidman, Pauline Lawrence, Limón, the use of weight in early modern dance, Humphrey-Weidman technique, and the company's cross-country tour, ca. 1938.] DC-NYPL.

Bernstein, Joan Levy. Interview by Linda Small, 1 May 1978. Typescript available. [Includes discussion of Doris Humphrey, modern dance at Bennington College, and José Limón.] DC-NYPL.

Currier, Ruth. Interview by John Gruen. *The Sound of Dance*, WNCN-FM, 29 Mar. 1976. [Includes discussion of the activities of the Limón company after the choreographer's death, his working methods, and various productions of *The Moor's Pavane*.] DC-NYPL.

Falco, Louis. Interview by John Gruen. *The Sound of Dance*, WNCN-FM, 3 May 1976. [Includes discussion of *The Moor's Pavane* and working with Jose Limón.] DC-NYPL.

Fonaroff, Nina. Interview by Elizabeth Kendall, 27 and 28 Apr. 1976. Typescript available. [Reel 2 includes discussion of Doris Humphrey and José Limón.] DC-NYPL.

Gray, Harriette Ann. Interview by Jeanne Selma Cohen, 21 Oct. 1970. [Reel 13 includes discussion of José Limón, Pauline Lawrence, Charles Weidman, and the Eighteenth Street Studio.] DC-NYPL.

Herbert, Verna. Interview by Lesley Farlow, 14 Oct. 1989. [Verna Herbert, a pianist and music teacher, talks about meeting José Limón in 1929 and her friendship with him.] DC-NYPL.

Jones, Betty. Interview by Norton Owen, 20 May 1996. Typescript available. [Cassette 1 includes discussion of Jones's first experiences with the Limón company, the relationship between Doris Humphrey and José Limón, the Humphrey and Limón techniques, Limón's attitude toward religion, *Missa Brevis*, and the creation of *A Choreographic Offering*. Cassette 2 continues the discussion of *A Choreographic Offering*.] DC-NYPL.

Koner, Pauline. Interview by David Raher, 13 Oct. 1973. [Koner discusses working with José Limón on *The Moor's Pavane* and *Emperor Jones*, various versions of *The Moor's Pavane*, and *Barren Sceptre*.] DC-NYPL.

Koner, Pauline. Interview by Peter Conway, Mar. and June 1975. Typescript available. [Reel 1 includes discussion of *The Moor's, Pavane*; Reel 2 of *La Malinche* and Lucas Hoving, as well as *The Moor's Pavane*.] DC-NYPL.

Koner, Pauline. Telephone interview with Charles Humphrey Woodford, ca. 1984–1985. [Woodford discusses his childhood memories of José Limón, Pauline Lawrence, Limón's later years, and Limón's family.] DC-NYPL.

Koner, Pauline. Telephone interview with Letitia Ide, ca. 1984–1985. [Ide discusses José Limón.] DC-NYPL.

Limón, José. Interview excerpts. Dubbed from the audio portion of the outtakes from the film *Festival of the Dance*, 1972–1973. Interviewers are unidentified. [In the fourth excerpt, José Limón briefly discusses *Emperor Jones*, in the sixth, *Emperor Jones*.] DC-NYPL.

———. Interview by Marian Horosko. *World of Dance*, WNYC, 1964. DC-NYPL.

———. Speech at the Juilliard School, 5 Oct. 1966. [Limón discusses the relationship of music and dance.] DC-NYPL.

Lloyd, Norman and Ruth. Interview by Selma Jeanne Cohen, 20 Jan. 1971. [Reel 20 includes discussion of Humphrey's influence on Limón; Reel 21 of various Limón works and the score for *La Malinche*.] DC-NYPL.

Mansfield, Portia. Spontaneous commentary recorded ca. 1950 by Mansfield while watching the film *Perry-Mansfield Celebrities*. [Included are comments about Doris Humphrey, José Limón, Charles Weidman, and Eleanor King.] DC-NYPL.

Maxwell, Carla. Interview by John Gruen. *The Sound of Dance*, WNCN-FM, 10 Apr. 1977. Typescript available. [Maxwell discusses her appointment as director of the José Limón Dance Company.] DC-NYPL.

———. Interview by Robert Johnson, 28 May 1996. Typescript available. [Includes discussion of the relationship between Doris Humphrey and José Limón, Humphrey's *Day on Earth* and *Ritmo Jondo*, issues in the reconstruction and performance of Humphrey's and Limón's works, and the Humphrey and Limón techniques.] DC-NYPL.

Morgan, Barbara. Interview by Lesley Farlow, 20 Nov. 1985. Typescript available. [Includes discussion of photographing dance, particularly the works of José Limón and Martha Graham.] DC-NYPL.

O'Donnell, May. Interview by Agnes de Mille, 16 Jan. 1984. [Side 2 includes discussion of Charles Weidman and José Limón.] DC-NYPL.

Robinson, Helen Mary. Interviewed by Selma Jeanne Cohen, 25 and 26 Oct. 1970. [Reel 26 includes discussion of the apartment on Tenth Street shared by José Limón, Charles Weidman, Doris Humphrey, and Pauline Lawrence, and Weidman's farm; Reel 27 of the Humphrey-Weidman company tours, Pauline Lawrence, and Limón; Reel 28 of Charles Humphrey Woodford, the dancers' poverty, Humphrey-Weidman company members, films of the Humphrey-Weidman company, and Pauline Lawrence.] DC-NYPL.

Scanlon, Jennifer. Interview by John Gruen. *The Sound of Dance*, WNCN-FM, 17 Dec. 1978. [Scanlon discusses working with José Limón.] DC-NYPL.

Seckler, Beatrice. Interview by Susan Kraft, 6 and 20 Oct. 1993. Typescript available. [Cassette 1 includes discussion of the trio formed by Seckler, José Limón, and Dorothy Bird. Cassette 2 includes discussion of Bennington and Humphrey-Weidman choreography.] DC-NYPL.

Sherman, Jane. Interview by Lesley Farlow, 10 Feb. 1996. [Sherman discusses Doris Humphrey's role in the Denishawn company, working with Humphrey on the Butterfly étude, the amateur technical level of the Denishawn company, Humphrey's first independent concert with Charles Weidman, her reasons for leaving Denishawn and Sherman's for joining her, Humphrey's *Color Harmony*, Sherman's decision to leave Humphrey's company and, eventually, dance.] DC-NYPL.

Sokolow, Anna. Interview by Marian Horosko. *Profiles*, WNCN-FM, 5 Mar. 1967. [Sokolow discusses the formation of the first modern dance repertory company, the American Dance Theater, with José Limón, Donald McKayle, and herself as choreographers.] DC-NYPL.

Stodelle, Ernestine. Interview by Lesley Farlow, 29 April 1996. [Stodelle discusses her teaching and reconstruction of Doris Humphrey's choreography; general theoretical issues in relation to Humphrey's work, *Water Study* and *Dionysiaques* in particular; Stodelle's early years as a dancer during the Depression; the difficulty of teaching contemporary dancers Humphrey's work; the importance of letting the choreography speak for itself; various reconstructions, including *The Call*; and Charles Weidman.] DC-NYPL.

Surinach, Carlos. Interview by Katy Matheson, 27 Feb. 1979. Typescript. [Surinach discusses *Ritmo Jondo* and working with Doris Humphrey and José Limón.] DC-NYPL.

Taliaferro, Clay. Interview by Lucile Brahms Nathanson. *Making the Dance Scene*, WHPC-FM, Nassau Community College, 1970s. [Includes discussion of José Limón.] DC-NYPL.

Weidman, Charles. Interview by Marian Horosko and Genevieve Oswald, 8 Dec. 1966. [Reel 5 includes a discussion of José Limón as a performer.] DC-NYPL.

———. Interview by Marian Horosko, 7 Aug. 1967. [Reel 17 includes a discussion of José Limón's first concert and Weidman's separation from Doris Humphrey.] DC-NYPL.

———. Interview by Marian Horosko, 1960s. [Reel 16 includes a discussion of José Limón's early choreographic ventures.] DC-NYPL.

MELINDA COPEL is completing her doctorate in dance at Temple University. Her current research is about the Limón company tours sponsored by the U.S. State Department during the Cold War.

LYNN GARAFOLA is the author of *Diaghilev's Ballets Russes* and editor of several books, most recently *Rethinking the Sylph: New Perspectives on the Romantic Ballet*. A senior editor of *Dance Magazine* and contributor to numerous journals, she is co-curator of the exhibition *Dance for a City: Fifty Years of New York City Ballet*.

DEBORAH JOWITT is the principal dance critic of *The Village Voice* and teaches dance history courses at New York University's Tisch School of the Arts. Her *Time and the Dancing Image* won the de la Torre Bueno Prize for 1988.

CARLA MAXWELL joined the Limón Dance Company in 1965 and since 1978 has served as its Artistic Director. An authority on Limón style and technique, she has taught internationally and staged the choreographer's works for numerous companies. She is the recipient of the 1995 Dance Magazine Award.

NORTON OWEN is Institute Director of the José Limón Dance Foundation and Director of Preservation for the Jacob's Pillow Dance Festival. He is the author of *A Certain Place: The Jacob's Pillow Story* and numerous articles for *Dance Magazine*, *Performing Arts Resources*, and other publications. He has served as curator for many exhibitions at the National Museum of Dance in Saratoga Springs, New York.

Throughout this index, references to endnotes are designated by the page number followed by "*n*" and the note number.

Cornish School of Fine and Applied
Arts, 164*n*90
Covarrubias, Miguel, xviii, 120,
125–32
Covarrubias, Rose, 125, 128
Crane, Hart, 92
Crystal, Rose, 28, 156*n*37
Cunningham, Merce, 166*n*98, 167*n*109
Works: (with Jean Erdman) *Seeds of
Brightness*, 166*n*98
Currier, Ruth, xvi

Dance: absolute, 120; American, 18, 28,
53, 60, 61, 73; commercialization,
49–50, 73; designs, 22; modern, xi,
xiii, 18, 21, 48, 117; movements, 22,
27, 29; patterns, 22; "pure," 22, 28,
51; technique, 37, 75
Dance Center, 47, 48, 153*n*9, 154*n*13,
160*n*69
Dance Collection (New York Public
Library), xix, 117
Dance Players, 162*n*81
Dance Repertory Theatre, 30, 31, 32
Danilova, Alexandra, 110, 171*n*134
Daunt, Yvonne, 169*n*116
Davenport, Molly, 113, 171*n*139
Davies, Evelyn, 63, 88
de Mille, Agnes, xvi, 30, 39, 161*n*77,
161*n*78
Works: *Carousel*, 161*n*77; *Fall River
Legend*, xvi; *Oklahoma!*, 50,
161*n*77; *Rodeo*, 171*n*134
Denishawn, xi, xiv, 18, 21, 23,25, 45,
61, 85, 160*n*64, 171*n*130
Desca, Eva, 51, 161*n*75
Díaz, Porfirio, 152*n*2, 152*n*5
Dooley, Betts, 119
Dowling, Edward Duryea, 170*n*125
Dubin, Al, 170*n*125
Dudley, Jane, 155*n*25, 167*n*107
Works: with Maslow, Bales, and Hill:
People, Yes!, The, 167*n*107
Dudley-Maslow-Bales Trio, 164*n*92,
167*n*107, 167*n*107
Duke of Sacramento (Loring), 162*n*81
Duncan, Isadora, xi, xiv, 1, 4, 16, 18,
22, 34, 44, 53, 95, 100, 102, 117, 123;
childhood house of, 100–1

Dunham, Katherine, 169*n*119
Works: *Carib Song*, 169*n*119
Durante, Jimmy, 92, 93
Dybbuk, The, 154*n*11, 157*n*43

Eisenstein, Sergei, 70
Elizabeth Sprague Coolidge
Foundation, 158*n*50
Empire State Music Festival, 121
Enters, Angna, 153*n*10
Erdman, Jean, 166*n*98, 167*n*107,
169*n*116
Works: *Changingwoman*, 169*n*116;
Four-Four Time, 167*n*107; (with
Merce Cunningham) *Seeds of
Brightness*, 166*n*98

Falco, Louis, xvii
Falkenstein, Clare, 98, 99–100, 104
Federal Dance Project, 158*n*56
Federal Dance Theatre, 152*n*8, 153*n*9
Fergusson, Francis, 79, 92, 166–67*n*106
Findlay, Elsa, 18, 154*n*12
Works: *Men and Machines*, 169*n*116
Findlay, Joseph John, 154*n*12
Flade, Tina, 158*n*46
Works: *Paeans*, 158*n*46
Flemming, Jessica, 161*n*75
Fokine, Michel, 44, 53, 60, 95, 152*n*8,
153*n*9, 158*n*57
Works: *Spectre de la Rose, Le*, 95;
Sylphides, Les, 74; *Thunderbird*,
153*n*9
Ford, Byngton, 108
Frampton, Eleanor, 45, 89, 160*n*64
Franco, Francisco, 77, 78
Frankenstein, Alfred, 96, 170*n*128
Franklin, Frederic, 110
Furness, Robert Allason, 20

Galpern, Lasar, 152*n*8
García, Gloria, 113, 171*n*138
García Lorca, Federico, xv, 77, 151*n*9
Garden, Mary, 46–47, 60
Geddes, Norman Bel, xiii, 20, 44, 52,
69, 155*n*15, 162*n*79
Productions: *Dead End*, 155*n*15;

UNIVERSITY PRESS OF NEW ENGLAND
publishes books under its own imprint and is the publisher for
Brandeis University Press, Dartmouth College, Middlebury College Press,
University of New Hampshire, Tufts University, and Wesleyan University Press.

Library of Congress Cataloging-in-Publication Data

José Limón
    José Limón : an unfinished memoir /edited by Lynn Garafola ;
    introduction by Deborah Jowitt ; afterword by Norton Owen ; foreword
    by Carla Maxwell.
        p. cm.—(A studies in dance history book)
    Includes bibliographical references (p.) and index.
    ISBN 0–8195–6374–9
    1. Limón, José. 2. Dancers—United States—Biography.
    3. Choreographers—United States—Biography. I. Garafola, Lynn.
    II. Title. III. Series: Studies in dance history (unnumbered)
    GV1785.L515A3 1999
    792.8'028'092—dc21
    [b]   98–30941